WOMEN AND THE NATIONAL EXPERIENCE

Third Edition

WOMEN AND THE NATIONAL EXPERIENCE

SOURCES IN WOMEN'S HISTORY

VOLUME 1 TO 1877

Ellen Skinner

Professor Emerita, Pace University

Prentice Hall

Boston   Columbus   Indianapolis   New York   San Francisco   Upper Saddle River
Amsterdam   Cape Town   Dubai   London   Madrid   Milan   Munich   Paris   Montréal   Toronto
Delhi   Mexico City   São Paulo   Sydney   Hong Kong   Seoul   Singapore   Taipei   Tokyo

Editorial Director: Craig Campanella
Publisher: Charlyce Jones Owen
Editorial Assistant: Maureen Diana
Director of Marketing: Brandy Dawson
Senior Marketing Manager: Maureen E. Prado Roberts
Marketing Assistant: Marissa O'Brien
Senior Managing Editor: Ann Marie McCarthy
Project Manager: Debra A. Wechsler
Operations Specialist: Christina Amato
Cover Designer: Bruce Kenselaar
Manager, Visual Research: Beth Brenzel

Photo Researcher: Billy Ray
Manager, Cover Visual Research & Permissions: Rita Wenning
Cover Art: Frances Ellen Watkins Harper: Library of Congress.
Full-Service Project Management: Shiny Rajesh, Integra
Composition: Integra

Text Font: 10/12 Garamond

Credits and acknowledgments borrowed from other sources and reproduced, with permission, in this textbook appear on appropriate page within text.

Library of Congress Cataloging-in-Publication Data

Women and the national experience: sources in women's history/
[edited by] Ellen Skinner.—3rd ed.
    p. cm.
ISBN-13: 978-0-205-74315-5 (alk. paper)
ISBN-10: 0-205-74315-3 (alk. paper)
    1. Women—United States—History—Sources.   2. Women's rights—United States—History—Sources.   I. Skinner, Ellen.
HQ1410.W644 2011
305.40973—dc22

                                                    2010033712

4 2020

Prentice Hall
is an imprint of

www.pearsonhighered.com

Combined Volume
ISBN 10:   0-205-74315-3
ISBN 13: 978-0-205-74315-5
Volume 1
ISBN 10:   0-205-80935-9
ISBN 13: 978-0-205-80935-6
Volume 2
ISBN 10:   0-205-80934-0
ISBN 13: 978-0-205-80934-9

CONTENTS

Chapter 8   WESTERN EXPANSION: DIFFERENT VIEWPOINTS, DIVERSE STORIES   138

Chapter 9   THE CIVIL WAR, RECONSTRUCTION: GENDER AND RACIAL ISSUES   161

PREFACE

The expansion of the third edition of **Women and the National Experience** from one to two volumes has made possible a more inclusive range of women's voices, an increased number of topics, and a geographic lens with significant focus on the American West. The new two-volume edition also permits greater documentary coverage of little-known women who, along with those who are more familiar and famous, demonstrate the dynamic interaction between diverse women and the national experience. Primary documents include private letters, diary entries, cartoons, photographs, newspaper accounts, songs, public speeches, records from Supreme Court decisions, and excerpts from memoirs and autobiographies. Chapter introductions and document headnotes provide historical context and biographical information. Although the chapters are arranged chronologically, each chapter focuses on a particular topic of significance within the field of women's history but also relates to major national developments. Chapter introductions incorporate current scholarship and historiography. The intersection of gender, race, class, religion, and sexual identity illuminates the complexities of identity, but as the voices of women past and present testify, individual experience and achievement express more than composite identity. As in previous editions, all documents demonstrate the centrality of women's history to the national experience. New documents expand the earlier emphasis on the multiplicity of women's voices. A wide range of documents focus on women who crossed gender barriers and widened women's roles. Sources also include the views of women who resisted change and upheld prescribed norms. Also included are the voices of women such as Catharine Beecher and Sarah Josepha Hale, editor of the popular *Godey's Lady's Book* who struggled to preserve domestic norms for women but still facilitated increased opportunity.

Fortunately, more primary sources are now available than when the earlier editions of *Women and the National Experience* were published, including translations of Spanish and Mexican women's voices. The inclusion of primary sources from New Spain allows students to compare the nun Sor Juana's experience of convent life in Mexico to that of Anne Hutchinson, a Puritan dissident, wife, and mother from the Massachusetts Bay Colony. The differences between the two women spanned geography, culture, language, status, and religion, yet both encountered persecution because of their subversion of gender roles and refusal to accept intellectual subordination. Cross-cultural comparisons of documents also illuminate the dysfunctional marriage of a Spanish woman, Eulalia Callis, who married Pedro Fages, the military governor of California and the marital misery of Puritan New Englander, Abigail Abbott Bailey, whose decades of wifely endurance ended in divorce only after she found that her husband had committed incest with their daughter.

Mohawk Indian Molly Brant's partnership with British imperial official Sir William Johnson, superintendent of Indian affairs, fostered coexistence of American Indians and the British imperial administration prior to and during the American Revolution. Brant's letters to British officials as well as the documents of Indian women, including Nancy Ward (Cherokee) and Sarah Winnemucca (Piute) provide further evidence of the role of American Indian women as negotiators and mediators in cross-cultural encounters. Although documents focus on women's agency, primary sources also reveal the grim consequences of oppression. A labor contract illustrates the coercive terms dictated to Chinese immigrant women, many of whom were brought to California as prostitutes. Autobiographical accounts and interviews of enslaved women demonstrate successful acts of defiance, but also the impact of abusive power. Generations of diverse American Indian women used a variety of strategies in pursuit if their own and tribal interest, yet others fell victim to rape, sexual exploitation, and disease.

Documents also highlight little-known women such as African American Elizabeth Jennings Graham, who put her safety at risk when she refused to leave a New York City racially segregated horse-drawn omnibus in 1854, a century before Rosa Parks's well-publicized resistance to segregation. Pioneers for racial equality also included white schoolmistress Prudence Crandall, who was imprisoned and put on trial for disobeying a town law and admitting black students to her newly opened school for girls in 1834. Far removed from Crandall's small Connecticut town of Canterbury, Chinese immigrants Mary Tape and her husband sued the San Francisco Board of Education for its refusal to allow their daughter to attend their all-white neighborhood school. Writing in 1885 to the school board, Mary Tape defended integration and spared no words condemning the racist objectives of the white school board.

WHAT'S NEW TO THIS EDITION

The third edition has been expanded with more than one hundred new documents and seven new chapters into a two-volume collection of primary sources in American women's history. Approximately one hundred new documents accompany the new chapters and are supplemented by biographical information and questions that focus student attention on key aspects of the sources. Extensive revisions, updated research, and approximately thirty-five additional documents enrich the chapters that bridge the second and third editions. Photographs, cartoons and illustrations add visual source material.

HIGHLIGHTS OF THE NEW EDITION

- Two new chapters on the multicultural West cover the entire sweep of nineteenth-century American settlement; expand the geographic reach of previous editions and the range of diverse voices.
- A new thematic chapter provides an overview of the intersection of environmental and women's history, a field that until recently has received limited attention.
- Reaching beyond national borders to the wider context of an interrelated global world, a new chapter focuses on the campaign for women's rights on a national and global stage.
- A wide range of documents and a new chapter examine the personal side of women's experience as well as the overlap between personal lives and public policy, particularly with reference to reproductive issues. Documents in different chapters address changing sexual standards, and the social construction of heterosexual and lesbian identity. Lesbian voices include pioneer blues singer Ma Rainey, Audre Lorde, and Mab Segrest.
- New documents illuminate the diverse ways women from the colonial period to the present have struggled for empowerment in marriage, the workplace, recreation and education.
- Two new chapters on enslavement and abolitionism highlight the voices of enslaved women such as Harriet Jacobs, Elizabeth Keckley, and Bethany Veney as well as the dual objective of African American women (Sarah Mapps Douglas, Sarah Remond, and Frances Ellen Watkins Harper) to achieve abolition and racial equality. White counterparts in the struggle include the iconic Angelina Grimké and the less well-known Prudence Crandall and Lydia Maria Child.
- Greater inclusion of the voices of young women include teenaged Lowell Mills factory worker Barilla Taylor and 1920's "flapper" Ellen Welles Page as well as the wartime gender role-crossing of Revolutionary war soldier Deborah Sampson and World War II air force transport pilot, Ann Baumgartner Carl.
- New documents illuminate the less well-known voices of women from diverse religious groups such as Mormon women Fanny Stenhouse and Emmeline Wells, whose outspoken voices present contradictory views on polygamy. New documents also depict the activist resistance of Catholic nuns to the patriarchal suppression of gender equality.

NEW CHAPTERS:

Chapter 4 From Moral Reform to Free Love and Voluntary Motherhood: Issues of Vulnerability and Sexual Agency (8 new documents)

A new chapter discusses female empowerment from a variety of perspectives including moral reform, voluntary motherhood, and free love. This chapter focuses on the struggle of women to limit male sexual entitlement to the female body. The growing exercise of female agency embedded in the language of nineteenth-century moral reform ranged from the chastisement of men who had sex outside of marriage to increasing efforts to suppress prostitution. Over time women also began to support the right of married women to exercise reproductive choice. Primary sources include Paulina Wright Davis and Harriot Stanton Blatch's advocacy of voluntary motherhood, as well as Victoria Woodhull's bold assertion of a woman's right to freely choose her sexual partners.

Chapter 5 Enslaved Women: Race, Gender, and the Plantation Patriarchy (6 new documents)

Narratives of former slaves Harriet Jacobs and Elizabeth Keckley, as well as little-known Bethany Veney, testify to the multiple examples of enslaved women's agency but also depict their gender-specific vulnerability. In addition to the evidence from slave narratives, the journal of plantation mistress Ella Gertrude Clanton Thomas provides evidence of sexual exploitation of enslaved women. The firsthand observations of Fanny Kemble, an abolitionist married to a plantation owner, depicts the miserable conditions enslaved women confronted on a routine basis.

Chapter 6 Abolitionist Women and the Controversy over Racial Equality (8 new documents)

The chapter introduces students to little-known African American women whose focus on civil rights accompanied their antislavery struggle. Advocates such as African American Maria Stewart, Sarah Mapps Douglas, and Sarah Remond combined their crusade for abolition with a call for racial justice and equality. Elizabeth Jennings Graham was the unacknowledged Rosa Parks of her era. Primary sources also demonstrate that some white women such as the Grimké sisters, Prudence Crandall and Lydia Maria Child supported not just the abolition of slavery, but also racial equality.

Chapter 8 Western Expansion: Different Viewpoints, Diverse Stories (11 new documents)

The pre–Civil War West provides the historical context for a wide range of new documents emphasizing divergent perspectives and multicultural voices. Anglo-Americans migrating to the West joined a multiracial, multicultural population. Documents illuminate the voices of Mexican and American Indian women such as Eulalia Perez, a chief administrator of the San Gabriel mission during Spanish rule, as well as Isadora Filomena, a member of the Churucto tribe of California Indians. The experiences of Anglo-American settlers in California such as Luzena Wilson and Mary Ballou sharply contrasted with that of women such as Rosalia Vallejo Leese who, many years after the United States took control of California, expressed enduring hostility to American acculturation. Biddy Mason, brought to California as a slave successfully sued for her freedom, in contrast to Chinese immigrant women who arrived in San Francisco as prostitutes bound to indentured labor contracts. Servitude rather than opportunity molded their experience.

Chapter 11 Women's Roles: Americanization and the Multicultural West (10 new documents)

Homestead Act legislation promoted population growth and over the decades provided settlers including Mattie Oblinger and her family as well as the German-Jewish immigrant family of Sarah

Thal with the opportunity for land and home ownership. Government-supported Americanization or assimilation programs targeted American Indians. Pioneer anthropologist Alice Fletcher promoted Americanization programs ranging from instruction in appropriate gender norms to private landownership. For Johanna July, a black Seminole Indian and horse trainer, her lifestyle expressed her determination to forge an identity in defiance of appropriate middle-class gender norms. Chinese born. Mary Tape's crusade to end the segregation of Chinese students in California expresses the fierce determination of a mother who also was a pioneer advocate for equality of educational opportunity.

Chapter 17 From Municipal House Keeping to Environmental Justice (11 new documents)

The chapter provides students with an overview of the significance of women and gender assumptions in shaping the nation's environmental history from the nineteenth through the early twenty-first centuries. Long before the 1962 publication of Rachel Carson's *Silent Spring,* women environmentalists such as Ellen Swallow Richards and Alice Hamilton struggled against male-imposed barriers in pursuit of educational and career opportunity. Lois Gibbs became a politically involved activist who led her upstate New York, Love Canal community in a fight for justice against Hooker Chemical's toxic dumping. More recently, women of color, including African American Margie Eugene Richard, have assumed leadership roles in the fight the chemical contamination of communities of color.

Chapter 21 Women's Rights: National and Global Perspectives (10 new documents)

In recent years, American women's history has moved beyond national borders to consider transnational and global connections. This new field of inquiry reflects contemporary globalization as well as the greater overlap but contested construct of women's rights as human rights on a worldwide scale. From Hillary Clinton's Beijing speech in 1995 equating women's rights with human rights to the present, documents highlight the national and international effort and the role of American activists such as Robin Morgan and Eleanor Smeal to end multiple forms of violence against women, including trafficking and the Taliban violence in Afghanistan. Efforts to end gender-specific violence frequently collide with cultural norms as in the asylum case of Fauziya Kasinga who fled her country for America to prevent culturally prescribed genital cutting. A range of primary sources express the polarized policy positions of Presidents Bush and Obama on issues such as pay equity and reproductive rights and also demonstrate the dramatic divergence between women's rights activists and their conservative opponents.

ACKNOWLEDGMENTS

I would like to thank my friend and colleague Professor Marilyn Weigold for her invaluable suggestions. Her guidance rescued me more than once. My husband's computer skills also provided timely rescue and kept me on an even keel. Professor Bridget Crawford, Pace University Law School, provided insights and her manuscript with reference to third-wave feminism. Many thanks also to Steve Feyl and the Pace University Library Research and Information team for helping me locate the voices of colonial Spanish women and Mohawk Molly Brown and civil rights activist Elizabeth Jennings Graham.

Major thanks to Linda Benson, copy editor, for meticulous scrutiny and excellent suggestions. I would also like to acknowledge Lynn Hawley, San Joaquin Delta College; Sara Lee, American River College; and Paula Wheeler Carlo, Nassau Community College, who took the time to review the manuscript. Thanks also to Maureen Diana, editorial assistant for support and patience incorporating my revisions. Debra Wechsler's project supervision and guidance and Shiny Rajesh's assistance helped me navigate electronic hurdles. Thanks to Shiny's patience and expertise in dealing with my daily updates, I was able to reach the finish line on time. Above all, thanks to Charlyce Jones Owen, publisher, Prentice Hall, for providing the opportunity to develop this project. Your support, encouragement, and understanding made the third edition happen.

ABOUT THE AUTHOR

A graduate of Smith College, Ellen Skinner received a master of arts degree from Columbia University and a Ph.D. from New York University. She chaired the history department at Pace University's Westchester campus from 1987 to 2006. Her teaching career spanned four decades and in 2008 she was appointed professor emerita. In both her teaching and writing, she strives to make women's history accessible to students and relevant to their lives. Now in its third edition, **Women and the National Experience** was first published in 1996. Professor Skinner continues to teach women's history online and to search the archives for women's lost voices. Her current research focuses on women's human rights as well as the connections between women's history and the environment.

CHAPTER 1

Gender, Race, and Class in the Colonial Era

New research in women's history during the colonial period has retrieved the diverse voices and experiences of Spanish, Mexican, American Indian, and African American women. A shift in emphasis toward the acknowledgment of a multicultural past is widening the lens to include the agency of marginalized groups that previously were only a sidebar in the Anglo-American historical narrative.

In colonial America and in Europe, people commonly believed that women were the "weaker vessel"—morally and mentally deficient and physically inferior to men. As the weaker sex, women were subordinate to men and subject to male authority—first to their fathers and then to their husbands. Patriarchal norms prevailed; within the family and society, men were the "head," the "governing body." Women were expected to be wives and mothers and to lead quiet, unassuming private lives, like that of the exemplary Anne Bradstreet, whose literary gifts remained hidden within the confines of her family. Women who violated the gendered norms of domestic constraints and, like Anne Hutchinson, developed a public identity risked communal censure and punishment. Anne Hutchinson's religious teaching combined with her challenge to ministerial authority resulted in a court trial and her banishment from the Puritan colony. Cloistered life for Spanish Catholic nuns in colonial Mexico utilized gender and religious controls to instill discipline, including controlling women who asserted their intellect. Known for her brilliance and creative writing, Sister Juana argued on behalf of female intelligence. Her punishment resulted in coercive silencing and the destruction of her library.

At marriage, the legal identity of a colonial Anglo-American woman was erased and became subsumed under that of her husband, in a tradition referred to as *femme covert,* from the French, meaning "covered woman." This tradition ensured that married women could not own or control property, obtain guardianship over their children, or sue or be sued in court. Husbands had complete authority over their wives and children; however, they were expected to be benevolent patriarchs. Protestant minister Benjamin Wadsworth counseled husbands to rule their wives with love and kindness.

For most women, marriage, motherhood, frequent pregnancies, the care of large families, and responsibility for household production molded daily existence. Women were expected to bear many children. Pain, suffering, and even death in childbirth were considered part of female destiny. In a society characterized by frequent births, midwives played a critical role. Colonial women actively participated in the production of the food and goods on which family survival depended. Women sustained their families by spinning cloth, churning butter, making soap and candles, and tending chickens and cows. In addition to these gender-specific tasks, women were expected to have both the physical strength and multiple skills to participate in other household production activities. Wives also helped their husbands in shoe making, inn keeping, and flour production. Some widows and single women ran small businesses and taverns. Although their contribution to economic survival was vital, women's social status remained secondary and supplemental to that of men. Moreover, because women were believed to be destined at birth for maternal and domestic roles, education was perceived to be unnecessary. Although some colonial women were literate, an educational gender gap favored men.

Male control of religious institutions and instruction fortified the restrictions that constricted women's lives. Christian teachings stressed womanly virtue, humility, submission, modesty, and public silence. Although this perception would change, seventeenth-century women were still linked with Eve as bearing the primary responsibility for the expulsion from the Garden of Eden.

The Puritans considered the conversion experience possible for both men and women. Nonetheless, gendered assumptions about women facilitated the attribution of women as witches. Cotton Mather, the respected Puritan minister, recorded the Salem, Massachusetts, witchcraft trials. The majority of those executed, including Susannah Martin, were women. Puritan men also strictly enforced the ban on women speaking in public or assuming religious leadership. A rare expression of gender equity occurred within the Quaker religion. Women shared with men the right to speak at religious meetings.

A division of labor and authority by gender also prevailed among American Indians. Yet, in many significant ways, as Mary Jemison's narrative of her life among the Seneca reveals, Indian women's life experiences were different from those of European women. Indian women left no written testimony. The primary documents that survive are mainly observations of European explorers, missionaries, and male colonists. Because these writers lacked familiarity with indigenous people, much of their interpretations was biased and reflected European, rather than Indian, perspectives. Despite these limitations, the available evidence indicates that indigenous women possessed more power and authority than their colonial counterparts. Although earlier studies of cultural encounters between Europeans and Indian women portrayed a decline of power for these women, newer studies support cultural adaptation that reaffirmed female influence. Molly Brant's dual alliances with her native Mohawk tribe and British colonial officials exemplified her successful cross-cultural negotiations (see Chapter 2). But neither Indian women's nor men's authority could prevent the displacement, death, and tribal loss that accompanied colonial settlement.

Within colonial society, social relationships reflected a complex set of distinctions—the intertwining of race, class, and gender. Thus, although women were, in general, subordinate to men, elite white women shared with men certain privileges based on their race and class. Indentured servants and African American slaves were at the bottom of the social hierarchy, and their lives were limited by their oppression. Statutes in Virginia and Maryland outlawed interracial unions and penalized the children of unions of white men and slave women by keeping them enslaved. Unusually gifted, Phillis Wheatley was emancipated from bondage by her Massachusetts owner. But the great majority of colonial slaves were not so fortunate and lived out their lives in slavery. Both indentured servants and enslaved women were vulnerable to sexual exploitation and had little or no defense against unwanted sexual advances. Indentured servants who became pregnant were subject to extended terms of servitude. Elizabeth Sprigs's letter, begging her father for help, provides testimony to the deprivation that indentured servants encountered.

ANNE HUTCHINSON, *Trial* (1638)

Anne Hutchinson (1591–1643) arrived with her husband and children in the Puritan colony of Massachusetts Bay in 1634 and soon attracted a following of women and men to her informal religious meetings. She challenged both orthodox religious tenets and male authority. The following document is from her 1637 trial, at which she was found guilty of holding unacceptable religious beliefs and infecting others with her views. From the orthodox Puritan perspective, her particular theological offense was her emphasis on salvation as an inward covenant of Grace. This led her to question whether the Puritan "elect," including male religious leaders, who were outwardly pious were actually saved.

Declared guilty of heresy, she was banished from the colony and ultimately settled with her family in the Dutch colony of New Netherland (later known as New York). In 1643 she was killed in an Indian attack. Her trial and banishment reflected more than orthodox outrage at her non-conformist beliefs—it expressed disapproval of her transgression of prescribed gender roles. As a religious instructor, she violated the ban against women assuming religious authority as well as speaking in public, to mixed audiences of men and women. What evidence did the court offer that Hutchinson's behavior was inappropriate for a woman? What defense did Hutchinson provide. In what way would her audience of men as well as women further destabilize gender roles?*

One Mistris Hutchinson, the wife of Mr. William Hutchinson of Boston (a very honest and peaceable man of good estate) and the daughter of Mr. Marbury, sometimes a Preacher in Lincolnshire, after of London [was] a woman of haughty and fierce carriage, of a nimble wit and active spirit, and a very voluble tongue, more bold than a man, though in understanding and judgment, inferior to many women. This woman had learned her skill in England, and had discovered some of her opinions in the Ship, as she came over, which has caused some jealousie of her, which gave occasion of some delay of her admission, when she cunningly dissembled and coloured her opinions; as she soon got over that block, and was admitted into the Church, then she began to go to work, and became a woman very helpfull in the times of child-birth, and other occasions of bodily infirmities, and well furnished with means for those purposes, she easily insinuated her selfe into the affections of many. . . . But when she had thus prepared the way by such wholesome truths, then she begins to set forth her own stuffe, and taught that no sanctification was nay evidence of a good estate, except their justification were first cleared up to them by the immediate witnesse of the Spirit, and that to see any work of grace (either faith or repentance, &c.) before this immediate witnesse, was a Covenant of works: whereupon many good soules, that had been of long approved godlinesse, were brought to

---

* From John Winthrop, *The Short Story of the Rise, Reign and Ruin of the Antinomians of New England* (London, 1644).

renounce all the work of grace in them, and to wait for this immediate revelation. . . . Indeed it was a wonder upon what a sudden the whole Church of Boston (some few excepted) were become her new converts, and infected with her opinions, and many also out of the Church, and of other Churches also, yea, many profane persons became of her opinion, for it was a very easie, and acceptable way to heaven, to see nothing, to have nothing, but waite for Christ to do all; so that after she had thus prevailed, and had drawn some of eminent place and parts to her party (whereof some profited so well, as in a few months they outwent their teacher) then she kept open house for all comers, and set up two Lecture dayes in the week, when they usually met at her house, threescore or fourescore persons, the pretense was to repeate Sermons, but when that was done, she would comment upon the Doctrines, and interpret all passages at her pleasure. . . .

COURT: What say you to your weekly publick meetings? can you shew a warrant for them?

HUTCH: I will shew you how I took it up, there were such meetings in use before I came, and because I went to none of them, this was the speciall reason of my taking up this course, wee began it but with five or six, and though it grew to more in future time, yet being tolerated at the first, I knew not why it might not continue.

COURT: There were private meetings indeed, and arte still in many places, of some few neighbours, but not so publick and frequent as yours, and are of use for increase of love, and mutuall edification, but yours are of another nature, if they had been such as yours they had been evil, and therefore no good warrant to justifie yours; but answer by what authority, or rule, you uphold them.

HUTCH: By Tit. 2 where the elder women are to teach the younger.

COURT: So wee allow you to do, as the Apostle there meanes, privately, and upon occasion, but that gives no warrant of such set meetings for that purpose; and besides, you take upon you to teach many that are elder than your selfe, neither do you teach them that which the Apostle commands, *viz,* to keep at home.

HUTCH: Will you please to give mee a rule against it, and I will yield?

COURT: You must have a rule for it, or else you cannot do it in faith, yet you have a plaine rule against it; I permit not a woman to teach.

HUTCH: That is meant of teaching me.

COURT: If a man in distresse of conscience or other temptation, &c. should come and ask your counsell in private, might you not teach him?

HUTCH: Yes.

COURT: Then it is cleare, that it is not meant of teaching men, but of teaching in publick.

HUTCH: It is said, I will poure my Spirit upon your Daughters, and they shall prophesie, &c. If God give mee a gift of Prophecy, I may use it. . . .

COURT: Yes, you are the woman of most note, and of best abilities, and if some other take upon them the like, it is by your teaching and example, but you shew not in all this, by what authority you take upon you to bee such a publick instructor: (after shee had stood a short time, the Court gave her leave to sit downe, for her countenance discovered some bodily infirmity).

HUTCH: Here is my authority, Aquila and Priscilla, tooke upon them to instruct Apollo, more perfectly, yet he was a man of good parts, but they being better instructed might teach him.

COURT: See how your argument stands, Priscilla with her husband, tooke Apollo home and instruct him privately, therefore Mistris Hutchinson without her husband may teach sixty or eighty.

HUTCH: I call them not, but if they come to me, I may instruct them.

COURT: Yet you shew us not a rule.

HUTCH: I have given you two places of Scripture.

COURT: But neither of them will sute your practise.

HUTCH: Must I shew my name written therein?

COURT: You must shew that which must be equivalent, seeing your Ministry is publicke, you would have them receive your instruction, as coming from such an Ordinance.

HUTCH: They must not take it as it comes from me, but as it comes from the Lord Jesus Christ, and if I tooke upon me a publick Ministry, I should breake a rule, but not in exercising a gift of Prophecy, and I would see a rule to turne away them that come to me.

COURT: It is your exercise which drawes them, and by occasion thereof, many families are neglected, and much time lost, and a great damage comes to the Common-Wealth thereby, which wee that are be trusted with, as the Fathers of the Common-Wealth, are not to suffer. . . .

Forasmuch as you, Mrs. Huchison, have highly transgressed & offended, & forasmuch as yow have soe many ways troubled the Church with yor Errors & *have drawen away many a poor soule & have* upheld yor Revelations: *& forasmuch as* you have made a Lye, *&c. Therefore in the name of our Lord Je: Ch: & in the name of the Church I doe not only pronounce you worthy to be cast owt, but* I doe cast yow out *& in the name of Ch.* I doe deliver you up to Satan, *that yow may learne no more to blaspheme, to seduce & to lye, & I doe account yow from this time forth to be a Hethen & a Publican & soe to be held of all the Bretheren & Sisters, of this Congregation, & of others: therefor* I command yow *in the name of Ch: Je: & of this Church* as a Leper to withdraw yor selfe owt of the Congregation; *that as formerly yow have dispised & contemned the Holy Ordinances of God, & turned yor Backe on them, soe yow may now have no part in them nor benefit by them. . . .*

Then God himselfe was pleased to step in with his casting voice, and bring in his owne vote and suffrage from heaven, by testifying his displeasure against their opinions and practices, as clearly as if he had pointed with his finger, in causing the two fomenting women in the time of the height of the Opinions to produce out of their wombs, as before they had out of their braines, such monstrous births as no Chronicle (I thinke) hardly ever recorded the life. Mistris Dier brought forth her birth of a woman child, a fist, a beast, and a fowle, all woven together in one, and without an head. . . .

SOR (SISTER) JUANA INES DE LA CRUX, *Response to the Most Illustrious Poetess, Sor Filotea De La Cruz* (1691)

Sor (Sister) Juana Ines de la Crux (c. 1648–1694) subverted the gendered Spanish assumption of female intellectual inferiority. Her defiance occurred in a Mexican convent during the same time period that Anne Bradstreet modestly was combining poetry writing with wifely duties and motherhood. In contrast to a life of marriage and maternity, Sor Juana chose to live in a convent where unmarried women could reside in a protected environment. She lived an intense life of the mind, and her affirmation of intellectual and artistic creativity subverted male claims that demeaned female intelligence. She boldly defended the unequivocal right of women to acquire knowledge. Her poetry and playwriting as well as her prodigious acquisition of knowledge attracted the attention of church officials. In time, the bishops forced her to end her writing and dismantle her library. Although she used a different name, she addressed the following letter to the bishop who eventually succeeded in making Juana conform to standards of quiet contemplation and, at least outwardly, nonintellectual docility.

How did Sor Juana gain information from the pursuit of ordinary domestic chores such as cooking? What does this tell you about the quality of her intellect? What arguments does she advance on the right of women to use their intellectual potential?*

I began to study Latin grammar—in all, I believe, I had no more than twenty lessons—and so intense was my concern that though among women (especially a woman in the flower of her youth) the natural adornment of one's hair is held in such high esteem, I cut off mine to the breadth of some four to six fingers, measuring the place it had reached, and imposing upon myself the condition that if by the time it had again grown to that length I had not learned such and such a thing I had set for myself to learn while my hair was growing, I would again cut it off as punishment for being so slow-witted. And it did happen that my hair grew out and still I had not learned what I had set for myself—because my hair grew quickly and I learned slowly—and in fact I did cut it in punishment for such stupidity: for there seemed to me no cause for a head to be adorned with hair and naked of learning—which was the more desired embellishment. And so I entered the religious order, knowing that life there entailed certain conditions (I refer to superficial, and not fundamental, regards) most repugnant to my nature; but given the total antipathy I felt for marriage, I deemed convent life the least unsuitable and the most honorable I could elect if I were to insure my salvation. Working against that end, first (as, finally, the most important) was the matter of all the trivial aspects of my nature that nourished my pride, such as wishing to live alone, and wishing to have no obligatory occupation that would inhibit the freedom of my studies, nor the sounds of a community that would intrude upon the peaceful silence of my books. These desires caused me to falter some while in my decision, until certain learned persons

enlightened me, explaining that they were temptation, and, with divine favor, I overcame them, and took upon myself the state which now so unworthily I hold. I believed that I was fleeing from myself, but—wretch that I am!—I brought with me my worst enemy, my inclination, which I do not know whether to consider a gift or a punishment from Heaven, for once dimmed and encumbered by the many activities common to Religion, that inclination exploded in me like gunpowder, proving how *privation is the source of appetite. . . .*

And what shall I tell you, lady, of the natural secrets I have discovered while cooking? I see that an egg holds together and fries in butter or in oil, but, on the contrary in syrup shrivels into shreds; observe that to keep sugar in a liquid state one need only add a drop or two of water in which a quince or other bitter fruit has been soaked; observe that the yolk and the white of one egg are so dissimilar that each with sugar produces a result not obtainable with both together. I do not wish to weary you with such inconsequential matters, and make mention of them only to give you full notice of my nature, for I believe they will be occasion for laughter. But, lady, as women, what wisdom may be ours if not the philosophies of the kitchen? Lupercio Leonardo spoke well when he said: how well one may philosophize when preparing dinner. And I often say when observing these trivial details: had Aristotle prepared victuals, he would have written more. And pursuing the manner of my cogitations, I tell you that this process is so continuous in me that I have no need for books. And on one occasion, when because of a grave upset of the stomach the physicians forbade me

---

* Sor. Juana Inez de la Cruz, "Response to the Most Illustrious Poetess, 1691, trans. Margaret Sayers Peden, as seen in The Western Women's Reader by Schlissel and Lavender and published by HarperPerennial.

to study I passed thus some days, but then I proposed that it would be less harmful if they allowed me books, because so vigorous and vehement were my cogitations that my spirit was consumed more greatly in a quarter of an hour than in four days' studying books. And thus they were persuaded to allow me to read. And moreover, lady, not even have my dreams been excluded from this ceaseless agitation of my imagination; indeed, in dreams it is wont to work more freely and less encumbered, collating with greater clarity and calm the gleanings of the day, arguing and making verses, of which I could offer you an extended catalogue, as well as of some arguments and inventions that I have better achieved sleeping than awake. I relinquish this subject in order not to tire you, for the above is sufficient to allow your discretion and acuity to penetrate perfectly and perceive my nature, as well as the beginnings, the methods, and the present state of my studies.

Anne Bradstreet, *Before the Birth of One of Her Children* (c. 1650)

Although Anne Bradstreet (1612–1672) is now considered the seventeenth century's leading colonial poet, she did not write for publication. She wrote privately, for her family, in part because Puritan culture limited married women's roles to the home and family. In the following poem, Bradstreet addressed the possibility that she might die in childbirth. During the colonial era, death during childbirth was a significant threat. What did Bradstreet mean by the plea that her "babes" be protected from "stepdam's injury"? For whom is the poem written?*

> *All things within this fading world*
> *have end.*
> *Adversity doth still our joys attend;*
> *No ties so strong, no friends so dear and*
> *sweet,*
> *But with death's parting blow are sure*
> *to meet.*
> *The sentence passed is most*
> *irrevocable,*
> *A common thing, yet, oh, inevitable.*
> *How soon, my dear, death may my steps*
> *attend,*
> *How soon it may be thy lot to lose thy*
> *friend,*
> *We both are ignorant; yet love bids me*
> *These farewell lines to recommend to*
> *thee,*
> *That when that knot's untied that made*
> *us one*
> *I may seem thine who in effect am none.*
> *And if I see not half my days that are due,*
> *What nature would God grant to yours*
> *and you.*

> *The many faults that well you know I*
> *have*
> *Let be interred in my oblivion's grave;*
> *If any worth or virtue were in me,*
> *Let that live freshly in thy memory,*
> *And when thou feelest no grief, as I no*
> *harms,*
> *Yet love thy dead, who long lay in thine*
> *arms;*
> *And when thy loss shall be repaid with*
> *gains*
> *Look to my little babes, my dear*
> *remains,*
> *And if thou love thyself, or lovedst me,*
> *These oh protect from stepdam's injury.*
> *And if chance to thine eyes shall bring*
> *this verse,*
> *With some sad sighs honor my absent*
> *hearse;*
> *And kiss this paper for thy love's dear*
> *sake,*
> *Who with salt tears this last farewell did*
> *take.*

---

* From Anne Bradstreet, *The Poems of Mrs. Anne Bradstreet* (Boston, 1758).

ASSEMBLY OF VIRGINIA, STATUTE OUTLAWING INTERRACIAL UNIONS (1691)

This statute tells us as much about the definition of race as it does about the process of enslavement. Passed to end the development of an interracial free community, the legislation reflects the power whites assumed over people of color and the construction of permanent racial enslavement. In New Spain, a range of racial classifications developed and helped address the need for population growth while still preserving the privileged position of Spanish whites. The construction of polarized categories of white and black characterized Anglo-colonial America. Laws against interracial unions passed the status of an enslaved mother on to her children, thereby increasing the number of slaves. Some laws sought to guard the sexual purity of white women from interracial sexual relationships. In actuality, the greatest numbers of interracial sexual unions occurred between white men and women of color.

In the following statute, the lawmakers punished interracial children with thirty years of bondage. What objectives did the statute seek to accomplish? What do terms such as *abominable mixture* and *spurious issue* tell us about English colonists' construction of racial categories?*

[1691] . . . for prevention of that abominable mixture and spurious issue which hereafter may encrease in this dominion, as well as by negroes, mulattos, and Indians intermarrying with English, or other white women, as by their unlawfull accompanying with one another, *Be it enacted* . . . that . . . whatsoever English or other white man or woman being free, shall intermarry with a negro, mulatto or Indian man or woman bond or free shall within three months after such marriage be banished and removed from this dominion forever. . . .

And be it further enacted . . . That if any English woman being free shall have a bastard child by any negro or mulatto, she pay the sum of fifteen pounds sterling, within one month after such bastard child shall be born, to the Church wardens of the parish . . . and in default of such payment she shall be taken into the possession of the said Church wardens and disposed of for five yeares, and the said fine of fifteen pounds, or whatever the woman shall be disposed of for, shall be paid, one third part

to their majesties . . . and one other third part to the use of the parish . . . and the other third part to the informer, and that such bastard child be bound out as a servant by the said Church wardens until he or she shall attain the age of thirty yeares, and in case such English woman that shall have such bastard child be a servant, she shall be sold by the said church wardens (after her time is expired that she ought by law serve her master), for five yeares, and the money she shall be sold for divided as if before appointed, and the child to serve as aforesaid.

[1705] *And be it further enacted,* That no minister of the church of England, or other minister, or person whatsoever, within this colony and dominion, shall hereafter wittingly presume to marry a white man with a negro or mulatto woman; or to marry a white woman with a negro or mulatto man, upon paid of forfeiting or paying, for every such marriage the sum of ten thousand pounds of tobacco; one half to our sovereign lady the Queen . . . and the other half to the informer.

---

* From the Assembly of Virginia, Act XVI, April 1691, in William Waller Henning, *The Statutes at Large: Being a Collection of All the Laws of Virginia, from the First Session of the Legislature, in the Year 1619,* 13 vols. (New York: 1823), 3: 86–87; and Assembly of Virginia, chap. XLIX, sec. XX, October 1705, in Henning, 3: 453.

COTTON MATHER, *The Wonders of the Invisible World: Trial of Susanna Martin* (1692)

A series of witchcraft trials were held in Salem, Massachusetts, during 1692. The highly influential Puritan minister Cotton Mather (1663–1728) recorded the proceedings described in this document. As alleged witches and accusers, women played a major role in the trials. The allegation that women were morally weak and easily seduced by the devil had deep roots in European history, and the accusation of witchcraft frequently resulted in death. Why does Mather seem surprised by Susannah Martin's insistence of her innocence? What particular manifestations of "She-Devil" behavior did Mather believe Susannah Martin manifested?*

I. Susanna Martin, pleading Not Guilty to the Indictment of Witchcraft brought in against her, there were produced the evidences of many persons very sensibly and grievously Bewitched; who all complained of the prisoner at the Bar, as the person whom they Believed the cause of their Miseries. And now, as well as in the other Trials, there was an extraordinary endeavor by Witchcrafts, with Cruel and Frequent Fits, to hinder the poor sufferers from giving in their complaints; which the Court was forced with much patience to obtain, by much waiting and watching for it. . . .

IV. John Atkinson Testify'd, That he Exchanged a Cow with a Son of Susanna Martins's, whereat she muttered, and was unwilling he should have it. Going to Receive this Cow, tho' he Hamstring'd her, and Halter'd her, she of a Tame Creature grew so mad, that they could scarce get her along. She broke all the Ropes that were fastened unto her, and though she was Ty'd fast unto a Tree, yet she made her Escape, and gave them such further Trouble, as they could ascribe to no cause but Witchcraft.

V. Bernard testify'd, That being in Bed on a Lords-day Night, he heard a scrabbling at the Window, whereat he then saw Susanna Martin come in, and jump down upon the Floor. She took hold of this Deponents Feet, and drawing his Body up into a Heap, she lay upon him near Two Hours; in all which time he could neither speak nor stir. At length, when he could begin to move, he laid hold on her Hand, and pulling it up to his mouth, he bit three of the Fingers, as he judged unto the Bone. Whereupon she went from the Chamber, down the Stairs, out at the Door. This Deponent thereupon called unto the people of the House, to advise them of what passed; and he himself did follow her. The people saw her not; but there being a Bucket at the Left-hand of the Door, there was a drop of Blood found on it; and several more drops of Blood upon the Snow newly fallen abroad. There was likewise the print of her two feet just without the Threshold; but no more sign of any Footing further off. . . .

VI. Robert Downer testifyed, That this Prisoner being some years ago prosecuted at Court for a Witch, he then said unto her, He believed she was a Witch. Whereat she being dissatisfied, said, That some She-Devil would Shortly fetch him away! Which words were heard by others, as well as himself. The night following, as he lay in his Bed, there came in at the Window the likeness of a Cat, which Flew upon him, took fast hold of his Throat, lay on him a considerable while, and almost killed him. At length he remembered what Susanna

* From *Narratives of the Witchcraft Cases, 1648–1706,* ed. George Lincoln Burr (New York: Barnes and Noble, Inc., 1946), 229–36.

Martin had threatened the Day before; and with much striving he cryed out, "Avoid, though She-Devil! In the Name of God the Father, the Son, and the Holy Ghost, Avoid!" Whereupon it left him, leap'd on the Floor, and Flew out the Window.

And there also came in several Testimonies, that before ever Downer spoke a word of this Accident, Susanna Martin and her Family had related, How this Downer had been Handled! . . .

VIII. William Brown testify'd, that Heaven having blessed him with a most Pious and prudent wife, this wife of his one day mett with Susanna Martin; but when she approch'd just unto her, Martin vanished out of sight, and left her extremely affrighted. After which time, the said Martin often appear'd unto her, giving her no little trouble; and when she did come, she was visited with Birds that sorely peck'd and Prick'd her; and sometimes a Bunch, like a pullets egg, would Rise in her throat, ready to Choak her, till she cry'd out, "Witch, you shan't choak me!" While this good woman was in this Extremity, the Church appointed a Day of Prayer, on her behalf; whereupon her Trouble ceas'd; she saw not Martin as formerly; and the Church, instead of their Fast, gave Thanks for her Deliverance. But a considerable while after, she being Summoned to give in some Evidence at the Court, against this Martin, quickly thereupon this Martin came behind her, while she was Milking her Cow, and said unto her "For thy defaming me at Court, I'll make thee the miserablest Creature in the World." Soon after which, she fell into a strange kind of Distemper, and became horribly Frantick, and uncapable of any Reasonable Action; the Physicians declaring, that her Distemper was preternatural, and that some Devil had certainly Bewitched her; and in that Condition she now remained. . . .

Note, This Woman was one of the most Impugned, Scurrilous, wicked creates in the world; and she did now throughout her whole Trial discover herself to be such a one. Yet when she was asked, what she had to say for herself? her Cheef Plea was, That she had Led a most virtuous and Holy Life!

BENJAMIN WADSWORTH, *A Well-Ordered Family* (1712)

Within the Puritan community, the clergy provided the most advice on family governance. As a Congregational clergyman, Benjamin Wadsworth (1670–1737) emphasized that the husband was the "head" ordained by God to "rule and govern." Harmony between husbands and wives and family stability were considered essential to social order. How did Wadsworth try to enforce this? What particular advice did he offer husbands?*

About the Duties of Husbands and Wives

Concerning the duties of this relation we may assert a few things. *It is their duty to dwell together with one another.* Surely they should dwell together; if one house cannot hold them, surely they are not affected to each other as they should be. They should have a very great and tender love and affection to one another. This is plainly commanded by God. This duty of love is mutual; it should be performed by each, to each of them. When, therefore, they quarrel or disagree, then they do the Devil's work; he is pleased at it, glad of it. But such contention provokes God; it dishonors Him; it

---

* From Benjamin Wadsworth, *A Well-Ordered Family,* 2nd ed. (Boston, 1719), 4–5; 22–59.

is a vile example before inferiors in the family; it tends to prevent family prayer.

As to outward things. If the one is sick, troubled or distressed, the other should manifest care, tenderness, pity, and compassion, and afford all possible relief and succor. They should likewise unite their prudent counsels and endeavor comfortably to maintain themselves and the family under their joint care.

Husband and wife should be patient toward another. If both are truly pious, yet neither of them is perfectly holy, in such cases a patient, forgiving, forbearing spirit is very needful. You, therefore, that are husbands or wives, do not aggravate every error or mistake, every wrong or hasty word, every wry step as though it were a willfully designed intolerable crime; for this would soon break all to pieces: but rather put the best construction on things, and bear with and forgive one another's failings.

The husband's government ought to be gentle and easy, and the wife's obedience ready and cheerful. The husband is called the head of the woman. It belongs to the head to rule and govern. Wives are part of the house and family, and ought to be under the husband's government. Yet his government should not be with rigor, haughtiness, harshness, severity, but with the greatest love, gentleness, kindness, tenderness that may be. Though he governs her, he must not treat her as a servant, but as his own flesh; he must love her as himself.

Those husbands are much to blame who do not carry it lovingly and kindly to their wives. O Man, if your wife is not so young, beautiful, healthy, well-tempered, and qualified as you would wish; if she did not bring a large estate to you, or cannot do so much for you, as some other women have done for their husbands; yet she is your wife, and the great God commands you to love her, be not bitter, but kind to her. What can be more plain and expressive than that?

Those wives are much to blame who do not carry it lovingly and obediently to their own husbands. O woman, if your husband is not as young, beautiful, healthy, so well-tempered, and qualified as you could wish; if he has not such abilities, riches, honors, as some others have; yet he is your husband, and the great God commands you to love, honor and obey him. Yea, though possibly you have greater abilities of mind than he has, are of some high birth, and he of a more common birth, or did bring more estate, yet since he is your husband, God has made him your head, and set him above you, and made it your duty to love and revere him.

Parents should act wisely and prudently in the matching of their children. They should endeavor that they may marry someone who is most proper for them, most likely to bring blessings to them.

MARY JEMISON, *A Narrative of the Life of Mrs. Mary Jemison* (1724)

Captured by Indians when she was fifteen, Mary Jemison (1743–1833) subsequently chose to live most of her life among the Seneca of New York. Since she was unable to write, oral interviews formed the basis of her autobiography. Her long years among Indians make her testimony an important corrective to the Eurocentric views of male missionaries who supplied most of the written evidence about Indian customs. What does Jemison's phrase "treated by them like a real sister" mean? What was her greatest sorrow?*

---

* From James E. Seaver, *A Narrative of the Life of Mary Jemison; Deh-He-Wa-Mis,* 4th ed. (New York: Miller, Orton, and Mulligan, 1856), 52, 55–63, 67–70, 72–74.

The night was spent in gloomy fore-boding. What the result of our captivity would be, it was out of our power to determine, or even imagine. At times, we could almost realize the approach of our masters to butcher and scalp us; again, we could nearly see the pile of wood kindling on which we were to be roasted; and then we would imagine ourselves at liberty, alone and defenseless in the forest, surrounded by wild beasts that were ready to devour us. The anxiety of our minds drove sleep from our eyelids; and it was with a dreadful hope and painful impatience that we waited for the morning to determine our fate.

The morning at length arrived, and our masters came early and let us out of the house, and gave the young man and boy to the French, who immediately took them away. Their fate I never learned, as I have not seen or heard of them since.

I was now left alone in the fort, deprived of my former companions, and of every thing that was near or dear to me but life. But it was not long before I was in some measure relieved by the appearance of two pleasant-looking squaws, of the Seneca tribe, who came and examined me attentively for a short time, and then went out. After a few minutes' absence, they returned in company with my former masters, who gave me to the squaws to dispose of as they pleased.

The Indians by whom I was taken were a party of Shawnees, if I remember right, that lived, when at home, a long distance down the Ohio. . . .

It was my happy lot to be accepted for adoption. At the time of the ceremony I was received by the two squaws to supply the place of their brother in the family; and I was even considered and treated by them as a real sister, the same as though I had been born of their mother. During the ceremony of my adoption, I sat motionless, nearly terri-fied to death at the appearance and actions of the company, expecting every moment to feel their vengeance, and suffer death on the spot. I was, however, happily disappointed; when at the close of the ceremony the company retired, and my sisters commenced employing every means for my consolation and comfort.

Being now settled and provided with a home, I was employed in nursing the children, and doing light work about the house. Occasionally, I was sent out with the Indian hunters, when they went but a short distance, to help them carry their game. My situation was easy; I had no particular hardships to endure. But still, the recollection of my parents, my brothers and sisters, my home and my own captivity, destroyed my happiness, and made me constantly solitary, lonesome, and gloomy.

My sisters would not allow me to speak English in their hearing; but remembering the charge that my dear mother gave me at the time I left her, whenever I chanced to be alone I made a business of repeating my prayer, cate-chism, or something I had learned, in order that I might not forget my own language. By prac-ticing it that way, I retained it till I came to Genesee flats, where I soon became acquainted with English people, with whom I have been almost daily in the habit of conversing.

My sisters were very diligent in teaching me their language; and to their great satisfac-tion, I soon learned so that I could understand it readily, and speak it fluently. I was very fortunate in falling into their hands; for they were kind good-natured women; peaceable and mild in their dispositions; temperate and decent in their habits, and very tender and gentle toward me. I have great reason to respect them, though they have been dead a great number of years. . . .

In the second summer of my living at Wiishto, I had a child, at the time that the kernels of corn first appeared on the cob. When I was taken sick, Sheninjee was absent, and I was sent to a small shed on the bank of the river, which was made of boughs, where I was obliged to stay till my husband returned. My two sisters, who were my only com-panions, attended me; and on the second day of my confinement my child was born; but it lived only two days. It was a girl; and notwithstanding the shortness of time that I possessed it, it was a great grief to me to lose it.

After the birth of my child I was very sick, but was not allowed to go into the house for two weeks; when, to my great joy, Sheninjee returned, and I was taken in, and as comfortably provided for as our situation would admit. My disease continued to increase for a number of days; and I became so far reduced that my recovery was despaired of by my friends, and I concluded that my troubles would soon be finished. At length, however, my complaint took a favorable turn, and by the time the corn was ripe I was able to get about. I continued to gain my health, and in the fall was able to go to our winter quarters, on the Saratoga, with the Indians.

ELIZABETH SPRIGS, *Letter from an Indentured Servant* (1756)

Europeans too poor to pay their own passage to America often became indentured servants. Elizabeth Sprigs's letter is one of the few primary sources that describe the conditions of female indentured servants. As can be seen from her letter, servitude and poverty molded a miserable and precarious existence. Beyond this story of distress, we know nothing of her personal life and even whether she survived her ordeal. What evidence does Sprigs give of her desperation and helplessness? What does her style of the writing tell you about her education and social status?*

Maryland, Sept'r 22'd 1756

Honred Father

My being for ever banished from your sight, will I hope pardon the Boldness I now take of troubling you with these, my long silence has been purely owning to my undutifullness to you, and well knowing I had offended in the highest Degree, put a tie to my tongue and pen, for fear I should be extinct from your good Graces and add a further Trouble to you, but too well knowing your care and tenderness for me so long as I retain'd my Duty to you, induced me once again to endeavor if possible, to kindle up that flame again. O Dear Father, believe what I am going to relate the words of truth and sincerity, and Balance my former bad Conduct my sufferings here, and then I am sure you'll pity your Destress Daughter, What we unfortunate English People suffer here is beyond the probability of you in England to Conceive, let it suffice that I one of the unhappy Number, am toiling almost Day and Night, and very often in the Horses drudgery, with only this comfort that you Bitch you do not halfe enough, and then tied up and whipp'd to that Degree that you'd not serve an Animal, scarce any thing but Indian Corn and Salt to eat and that even begrudged nay many Negroes are better used, almost naked no shoes nor stockings to wear, and the comfort after slaving during Masters pleasure, what rest we can get is to rap ourselves up in a Blanket and ly upon the Ground, this is the deplorable Condition your poor Betty endures, and now I beg if you have any Bowels of Compassion left show it by sending me some Relief, Clothing is the principal thing wanting, which if you should condiscend to, may easily send them to me by any of the ships bound to Baltimore Town Patapsco River Maryland, and give me leave to conclude in Duty to you and Uncles and Aunts, and Respect to all Friends

Honored Father

Your undutifull and Disobedient Child
Elizabeth Sprigs

---

* From Elizabeth Sprigs, "Letter to Mr. John Sprigs in White Cross Street near Cripple Gate, London," September 22, 1756.

PHILLIS WHEATLEY, *Letter to the Reverend Samuel Occom* (Feb. 11, 1774)

Phillis Wheatley (c. 1753–1784) was brought to the colonies from Senegal, Africa, and purchased by John and Susannah Wheatly in Massachusetts when she was about eight years old. Her gift for poetry manifested itself when she was still a child. She was taught to read by one of her owner's daughters and also studied Latin and Greek. Women poets were almost unheard of during this time period. For an enslaved young woman, the production of poetry written in the classic or elegiac manner was completely unprecedented. Wheatley's example of poetic achievement defied white racist and gender assumptions about African women. Wheatley's poem commemorating the death of the well-known Methodist preacher George Whitney in 1770 received critical acclaim. A collection of her poetry was published in London in 1773. Unfortunately, hardship and poverty molded her adult life. Married to a free black man, she died at age thirty-one as a result of the complications of childbirth.

Although abolitionists appreciated her poetry, some contemporary scholars are critical of what they claim was her social acquiescence to white cultural standards. In fact, her poetry followed conventional British standards and themes, but as the following letter demonstrates she also condemned slavery. How would you interpret this letter?*

Phillis Wheatley (Library of Congress)

Rev'd and honor'd Sir,

I have this Day received your obliging kind Epistle, and am greatly satisfied with your Reasons respecting the Negroes, and think highly reasonable what you offer in Vindication of their natural Rights: Those that invade them cannot be insensible that the divine Light is chasing away the thick Darkness which broods over the Land of Africa; and the Chaos which has reign'd so long, is converting into beautiful Order, and [r]eveals more and more clearly, the glorious Dispensation of civil and religious Liberty, which are so inseparably Limited, that there is little or no Enjoyment of one Without the other: Otherwise, perhaps, the Israelites had been less solicitous for their Freedom from Egyptian slavery; I do not say they would have been contented without it, by no means, for in every human Breast, God has implanted a Principle, which we call Love of Freedom; it is impatient of Oppression, and pants for Deliverance; and by the Leave of our modern Egyptians I will assert, that the same Principle lives in us. God grant Deliverance in his own Way and Time, and get him honour upon all those whose Avarice impels them to countenance and help forward vile Calamities of their fellow Creatures. This I desire not for their Hurt, but to convince them of the strange Absurdity of their Conduct whose Words and Actions are so diametrically, opposite. How well the Cry for Liberty, and the reverse Disposition for the exercise of oppressive Power over others agree, —

I humbly think it does not require the Penetration of a Philosopher to determine.—

---

* *The Connecticut Gazette,* March 11, 1774.

CHAPTER 2

From Revolution to Republic:
Moral Motherhood and Civic Mission

The American Revolution transformed the lives of many women. For some, home front and battlefield merged, and war enveloped domestic life. They circulated petitions, and joined in the boycott of British goods. They raised funds and produced supplies for soldiers. Although the surviving documents contain mainly the voices of an educated elite, women's contributions to the Revolution bridged class divisions and blurred the distinction between public and private life. Esther deBerdt Reed defended women's claim to liberty and the right to participate in public events. She led women in a massive fund-raising drive, and under her leadership, countless women produced homespun and sewed the shirts desperately needed by General Washington's inadequately provisioned soldiers. Dressed in male clothing, Deborah Sampson, who came from a poor farm family in Massachusetts, completely crossed the boundary of prescribed gender roles and joined the Revolutionary troops. Paul Revere, a hero of the Revolution, eventually petitioned Congress in an effort to have her granted an invalid veteran's pension. The wounds she received in battle had caused permanent health problems.

Women also became involved in the pro-British loyalist cause. Ann Hulton, a resident of Boston and a loyalist, wrote letters with an observant eye and political awareness of the events leading to the Revolution. Mohawk Indian Molly Brant used her cross-cultural skills on behalf of the British and helped secure tribal loyalty.

The involvement of women in Revolutionary events did not redefine gender norms about women's subordination and the need to maintain male authority. Although some women, such as Abigail Adams, hoped that the men who were constructing the new nation would "remember the ladies," the Founding Fathers did not extend political rights to women. The common-law tradition of *femme covert* became part of the legal foundation of the new nation. The power and authority men possessed in the public realm also governed the private realm and created unequal relations between men and women. Husbands continued to own their wives' property and wages; they had a legal right to their wives' bodies. Although some states made wife beating illegal, the law was poorly enforced and the practice continued.

Revolutionary events and the rhetoric of equality heightened a consciousness among women of their own worth. Schoolgirl Molly Wallace alleged that female students had the right to speak before an audience of other women. Public speaking was a major form of communication, an important skill as well as a function claimed by men and denied to women. Judith Sargent Murray asserted that male and female minds were equal at birth and only the lack of education kept women from equal achievement. Her arguments failed to change social attitudes about the difference between male and female abilities, but a new social construction of what these differences meant gained acceptance. Those benefits women derived from inclusion in a republican nation occurred not within the framework of equal rights, but as republican wives and mothers. The new republic assigned to mothers the moral instruction of the nation's future male citizens. The concept of *republican motherhood* endowed maternity with a civic and patriotic mission that linked the personal and private responsibilities of mothers to national well-being.

Of course, behavior could depart from prescriptive ideals. In the case of Abigail Abbot Bailey's marriage and submission to her husband's brutality, the departure from prescribed family values was extreme. This family history provides a glimpse into the dysfunctional lives that existed despite the ideal of family discipline and moral values. Norms of well-ordered families, with wives submissive to their husband's authority, received the sanction of the Catholic Church in New Spain. In addition, marriage was a holy sacrament and divorce virtually nonexistent. Nonetheless, in 1775, in an outpost of Spanish control in California, Eulalia Callis submitted a petition of divorce from her husband, the military governor Pedro Fages. Although her appeal was denied, her example of defiance further illustrates the gap between prescriptive and actual behavior.

In post-Revolutionary America, prompted by ministers such as John Abbot, many middle-class women joined clergymen in promoting a mother's moral authority and the ideal of well-ordered families. The idealized view of well-ordered families contrasted sharply with the extreme dysfunction and distress of Abigail Bailey's family. The new emphasis on maternal guidance increased the significance of the domestic sphere and served to confine and insulate women within the home. At the same time, women's moral authority provided the rationale for participation in the public sphere. During the early 1800s, motherhood developed a community and civic dimension. In towns and urban centers throughout the young republic, countless women organized charitable and moral reform societies. Free African American women founded societies that linked religion and charitable action at a time when financial help may have been crucial to survival. The associational activities and community involvement of white and African American women gave a public dimension to their domestic roles. Other women, such as Emma Willard, founded schools for girls. Over time, women supplied the nation with the majority of its grammar school teachers; however, once elementary education became perceived as a female occupation, the pay scale dropped, and career advancement for women became unlikely.

For the majority of African American slaves, the Revolutionary era did not lead to freedom. After the war, the Northern states developed emancipation schedules ranging from immediate to gradual freedom for slaves. Judith Cocks's letter of appeal provides evidence of enslavement under Connecticut's gradual emancipation laws. Voluntary emancipation was a rarity in the South, where slavery was highly profitable and part of a patriarchal system of race and gender control. Nor was emancipation in the North accompanied by racial equality. Race and gender oppression damaged the lives and narrowed educational and employment opportunities for free black women. Despite formidable barriers, free African American women still took charge of their lives. Although they had limited resources, they engaged in civic improvement. In Salem, Massachusetts, they organized the Colored Female Religious and Moral Society that fused moral standards with charitable giving. Free African American women also joined the abolitionist movement. In Boston, freeborn Maria Stewart became the first woman abolitionist to lecture in public. Both her lectures and her role as public speaker promoted the empowerment of African American women (Chapter 6).

ANN HULTON, *Letter of a Loyalist Lady* (1774)

The following letter describes the opening days of the American Revolution from the perspective of a pro-British woman. Ann Hulton lived in Boston with her brother and his family. Henry Hulton was a British official who worked at the customs House in Boston. Ann Hulton is known to history mainly through the letters she wrote to her friend in England. She provides a firsthand account of the initial unfolding of Revolutionary events in Boston. Although the lives of late-eighteenth-century women centered on family activities, domesticity also intersected with the masculine realm of politics and public events. How does Hulton evaluate the rebel cause? What does this letter reveal about the writer's education and social status? Does she write from a gender-neutral or woman-focused perspective?*

I imagine you will be desirous to Know how the New Acts of Parliam^t operate here, & how y^r friends are affected by the Commotions, & disturbances of the Publick. I am sorry to say there appears no disposition yet in the People towards complying with the Port Bill,—They carry their Melasses & other Goods easily by Land from Salem, & find little inconvenience at present from its operation, The distress it will bring on the Town will not be felt very sever'ly before Winter, when the Roads will be impassible. There's little prospect of Boston Port being Opend this Year. The Leaders of the Faction are only more unwearied, & are pursuing every measure to draw the People onto resistance, & to irritate Governm^t more, & more and which probably will end in the total ruin of the Town & the Indivdials.

It is now a very gloomy place, the Streets almost empty, many families have removed from it, & the Inhabitants are divided into several parties, at variance, & quarreling with each other, some appear desponding, others full of rage. The People of Property of best sense & Characters feel the Tyranny of the Leaders, & foresee the Consequences of their proceedings, woud gladly extricate themselves from the difficulties, & distress they are involv^d in by makeing their peace with G: Britain, & speedily submiting to the Conditions & penalties required.

These who are well disposed towards Governm^t (more from interest than principle it's to be feard, as there are few will^g to acknowledge the Authority of Parliam^t) are termd Tories. They daily increase, & have

* From Ann Hulton, *Letters of a Loyalist Lady: Being the Letters of Ann Hulton, Sister of Henry Hulton, Commissioner of Customs at Boston, 1767–1776* (1927; New York: Arno Press, 1971). (Note: Editorial insertions that appear in square brackets are from the 1971 edition.)

made some efforts to take the power out of the hands of the Patriots, but they are intimidated & overpowerd by Numbers, & the Arts, & Machinations of the Leader, who Governs absolutely, the Minds & the Passions of the People—by publishing numberless falshoods to impose on their credulity, & various artifices to influence or terrify. The Ministers from the Pulpit & the Committee of Correspond^{ce} by writing inflame the Minds of the ignorant Country People. Their endeavors to engage the Other Colonies to shut up their Ports, & the Merch^{ts} here to joyn in a Nonimportation Agrement, proving without effect. The next plan is in opposition to the Merch^{ts} & which if it spreads must be attended wth the ruin of most of 'em here 'tis a Solemn League & Covenant, not to use any British Manufacturers, till the Port is opend, & the New Acts repeald. This is a deep & diabolical scheme, & some people are taken into the Snare, but it's to be hoped the progress of it will be stopd, Genl Gage who conducts himself with great good sense & spirit, issues a Proclaimation Against it to warn 'em of its Consequences, They are startled in general, however, the little Town of Marlborough has had the Audacity to burn the Genl in effigy wth the Proclaimation.

There are four Regiments & a Train of Artillery now encamped on the Common at Boston, & several Men of War [in] ye Harbor.

Tho' as yet we are in no wise humbled. We [expect] support from the other Colonies, & build much on a general Congress to be held in Septr or Octo^{r} of Deputies from all the [Colonies]. We are told that Blocking up the Port is the best thing that can be for Americans, that it will unite the Colonies against G: B:, distress ther Manufactorers and raise our friends, a numerous body as we have been informed by Dr Frankland, viz the Dissenters, & the Commercial part of the Nation, to exert themselves in our favor, & that we may expect a Rebellion there, which will answer our purpose, & we shall become intirely free & Independant. But if we now submit—Our Lands will be taxd—Popery introduced & we shall be Slaves for ever. I mention these as Some of the Artifices & Arguments which Keep up the spirit of opposition [by] wch the People are inflamed to the highest degree.

However I don't despair of seeing Peace & tranquility in America, tho' they talk very high & furious at present. They are all preparing their Arms & Amunition & say if any of the Leaders are seizd, they will make reprizals on the friends of Gover'ment. Three weeks will bring on the Crises.

Your Affectionate
Fr^{d} & Servt A H:

ESTHER DEBERDT REED, *Sentiments of an American Woman* (1780)

Esther DeBerdt Reed (1746–1780) arrived in the colonies in 1770 and died ten years later. During that brief time, she gave birth to seven children and played a key role in recruiting women to support the patriotic effort. This document was written to mobilize women to provide the army with homespun clothing. Because the war curtailed the importation of British cloth, women's production of homespun became a major priority. Reed's references to heroic women from the Old Testament and antiquity expressed an early effort to find alternative role models who would offset the belief that patriotism was a quality that belonged to men, not women. What did DeBerdt Reed mean by the phrase "Born for Liberty"? What evidence does she give that women are denied knowledge of their own history? What social purpose would such denial serve?*

* Esther DeBerdt Reed, *The Sentiments of an American Woman* (Philadelphia: John Dunlap, 1780).

On the commencement of actual war, the Women of America manifested a firm resolution to contribute as much as could depend on them, to the deliverance of their country. Animated by the purest patriotism, they are sensible of sorrow at this day, in not offering more than barren wishes for the success of so glorious a Revolution. They aspire to render themselves more really useful; and this sentiment is universal from the north to the south of the Thirteen United States. Our ambition is kindled by the fame of those heroines of antiquity, who have rendered their sex illustrious, and have proved to the universe, that, if the weakness of our Constitution, if opinion and manners did not forbid us to march to glory by the same paths as the Men, we should at least equal, and sometimes surpass them in our love for the public good. I glory in all that which my sex has done great and commendable. I call to mind with enthusiasm and with admiration, all those acts of courage, of constancy and patriotism, which history has transmitted to us: The people favoured by Heaven, preserved from destruction by the virtues, the zeal and the revolution of Deborah, of Judith, of Esther! The fortitude of the mother of the Machabees, in giving up her sons to die before her eyes: Rome saved from the fury of a victorious enemy by the efforts of Volumnia, and other Roman Ladies: So my famous siegers were the Women who have been seen forgetting the weakness of their sex, building new walls, digging trenches with their feeble hands, furnishing arms to their defenders, they themselves darting the missile weapons on the enemy, resigning the ornaments of their apparel and their fortune to fill the public treasury, and to hasten the deliverance of their country; burying themselves under its ruins; throwing themselves into the flames rather than submitt to the disgrace before a proud enemy.

Born for liberty, disdaining to bear the irons of a tyrannic Government, we associate ourselves to the grandeur of those Sovereigns, cherished and revered, who have held with so much splendor the scepter of the greatest States; the Matildas, the Elizabeths, the Maries, the Catherines, who have extended the empire of liberty, and contented to reign by sweetness and justice, have broken the chains of slavery, forged by tyrants in the times of ignorance and barbarity. The Spanish Women, do they not make, at this moment, the most patriotic sacrifices, to increase the means of victory in the hands of their Sovereign. He is a friend to the French Nation. They are our allies. We call to mind, doubly interested, that it was a French Maid who kindled up amongst her fellow-citizens, the flame of patriotism buried under long misfortunes: it was the Maid of Orleans who drove from the kingdom of France the ancestors of those same British, whose odious yoke we have just shaken off; and whom it is necessary that we drive from the Continent.

But I must limit myself to the recollection of this small number of achievements. Who knows if persons disposed to censure, and sometimes too severely with regard to us, may not disapprove our appearing acquainted even with the actions of which our sex boasts? We are at least certain, that he cannot be a good citizen who will not applaud our efforts for the relief of the armies which defend our lives, our possessions, our liberty? The situation of our soldiery has been represented to me; the evils inseparable from war, and the firm and generous spirit which has enabled them to support these. But it has been said, that they may apprehend, that, in the course of a long war, the view of their distresses may be lost, and their services be forgotten. Forgotten! Never; I can answer in the name of all my sex. Brave Americans, your disinterestedness, your courage, and your constancy will always be dear to America, as long as she shall preserve her virtue.

We know that at a distance from the theatre of war, if we enjoy any tranquillity it is the fruit of your watchings, your labours, your dangers. If I live happy in the midst of my family; if my husband cultivates his field and reaps his harvest in peace; if, surrounded with my children, I myself nourish the youngest, and press it to my bosom, without being afraid of seeing myself separated from it, by a ferocious enemy; if the house in which we dwell; if our barns, our orchards are safe at the present time from the hands of those incendiaries, it is to you that we owe it. And shall we hesitate to evidence to you our gratitude? Shall we hesitate to wear a clothing more simple; hair dressed less elegant, while at the price of this small privation, we shall deserve your benedictions. Who, amongst us, will not renounce with the highest pleasure, those vain ornaments, when she shall consider that the valiant defenders of America will be able to draw some advantage from the money which she may have laid out in these; that they will be better defended from the rigors of the seasons, that after their painful toils, they will receive some extraordinary and unexpected relief; that these presents will perhaps be valued by them at a greater price, when they will have it in their power to say: *this is*

the offering of the Ladies. The time is arrived to display the same sentiments which animated us at the beginning of the Revolution, when we renounced the use of teas, however agreeable to our taste, rather than receive them from our persecutors; when we made it appear to them that we placed former necessaries in the rank of superfluities, when our liberty was interested; when our republican and laborious hands spun the flax, prepared the linen intended for the use of our soldiers; when as exiles and fugitives we supported with courage all the evils which are the concomitants of war. Let us not lose a moment; let us be engaged to offer the homage of our gratitude at the altar of military valor, and you, our brave deliverers, while mercenary slaves combat to cause you to share with them the irons with which they are loaded, receive with a free hand our offering, the purest which can be presented to your virtue,

By an American Woman.

MOLLY BRANT, *Letter to Daniel Claus* (June 23, 1778)

During the pre-Revolutionary colonial era, there were borderland areas of cultural exchange between various Indian tribes and Europeans, as well as sexual unions between Indian women and white men. Molly Brant 's (1736–1796) relationship with Sir William Johnson, imperial administrator of the northern Indians, produced eight children. Brant played a major and highly successful role in her effort keep several of the Iroquois tribes in upstate New York loyal to the British during the American Revolution. When the Revolution ended, British cession of Indian lands opened floodgates to unrestricted American expansion.

Like other Indian women who played similar roles, she kept close ties with her family and tribe but also spoke English and selectively adopted certain English customs. During her relationship with Johnson, she lived in a manorial house that included servants and slaves. She continued to serve as cultural liaison between the British and Iroquois even after Johnson's death in 1774. The following brief letter expressed her close social ties with British officials in North America. The "Joseph" she refers to in her letter was her brother, Joseph Brant, Mohawk tribal leader who fought on the side of the British during the Revolution. After the war, Brant agreed to relocate her home and family to Kingston, Canada, in a house built at British expense, accompanied by a financial reward for her loyalist services. How would you describe the tone of Molly Brant's letter to Claus? In what way do they appear to be social equals?*

---

* Claus Papers, MG19 F1 2:29, transcribed by Wanda Burch.

Niagara 23d June
1778

Dear Sir

I have been favor'd with Yours, and the Trunk of parcels by Mr. Street; everything mentioned in the Invoice you sent me has come safe, except the pair of gold Ear rings, which I have not been able to find.

We have a report of Joseph having had a brush with the Rebels, but do not know at what place. A Cayuga Chief is said to be Wounded, one Schohary Indian/Jacob/killed, & one missing since when its reported that Colo Butler, & Joseph have joined; Every hour we look for a confirmation of this news.

I am much obliged to You for the care, & attention in sending me up those very necessary articles; & should be very glad if You have any accounts from New York that You would let me know them, as well as of the health of George & Peggy, whom I hope are agreably settled: My Children are all in good health, & desire their loves to You, Mrs. Claus, Lady & Sir John Johnson. I hope the Time is very near, when we shall all return to our habitations on the Mohawk River.

I am Dr. Sir ever

Affectionately Yours
Mary Brandt

ABIGAIL ADAMS, *Letters to John Adams and His Reply* (1776)

Abigail Adams's (1744–1818) plea that her husband "remember the ladies" was an initial appeal for a more equitable distribution of power. Feminists of a later era would spell out in detail Adams's statement on the potential of male tyranny. On what basis do you think Adams alleged that "all Men would be tyrants if they could"? How did the Revolution influence her request and the argument of her May 7 letter? How did John Adams who later became the second president of the United States, respond? What did he mean by the statement "we know better than to repeal our masculine systems"?*

Abigail Adams to John Adams

Braintree March 31 1776

—I long to hear that you have declared an independency—and by the way in the new Code of Laws which I suppose it will be necessary for you to make, I desire you would Remember the Ladies, and be more generous and favourable to them than your ancestors. Do not put such unlimited power into the hands of the Husbands. Remember all Men would be tyrants if they could. If particular care and attention is not paid to the Ladies we are determined to foment a Rebellion, and will not hold ourselves bound by any Laws in which we have no voice, or Representation.

That your Sex are Naturally Tyrannical is a Truth also thoroughly established as to admit of no dispute, but such of you as wish to be happy willingly give up the harsh title of Master for the more tender and endearing one of Friend. Why then, not put it out of the power of the vicious and the Lawless to use us with cruelty and indignity with impunity. Men of Sense in all Ages abhor those customs which treat us only as the vassals of your Sex. Regard us then as Being placed by providence under your protection and in imitation of the Supreme Being make use of that power only for our happiness.

---

* From *Adams Family Correspondence,* ed. L. H. Butterfield (Cambridge, MA: Harvard University Press, 1963), 76–402.

John Adams to Abigail Adams

Ap. 14 1776

As to Declarations of Independency, be patient. Read our Privateering Laws, and our Commercial Laws. What signifies a Word.

As to your extraordinary Code of Laws, I cannot but laugh. We have been told that our Struggle has loosened the bands of Government everywhere. That Children and Apprentices were disobedient—that schools and Colleges were grown turbulent—that Indians slighted their Guardians and Negroes grew insolent to their Masters. But your Letter was the first Intimation that another Tribe more numerous and powerful than all the rest were grown discontented.—This is rather too coarse a Compliment but you are so saucy, I wont blot it out.

Depend upon it, We know better than to repeal our Masculine systems. Altho they are in full Force, you know they are little more than Theory. We dare not exert our Power in its full Latitude. We are obliged to go fair, and softly, and in Practice you know We are the subjects. We have only the Name of Masters, and rather than give up this, which would compleatly subject Us to the Despotism of the Petticoat, I hope General Washington, and all our brave Heroes would fight. I am sure every good Politician would plot, as long as he would against Despotism, Empire, Monarchy, Aristocracy, Oligarchy, or Ochlocracy.

Abigail Adams to John Adams

B[raintree]e May 7 1776

I can not say that I think you are very generous to the Ladies, for whilst you are proclaiming peace and good will to Men, Emancipating all Nations, you insist upon retaining an absolute power over Wives. But you must remember that Arbitrary power is like other things which are very hard, very liable to be broken—and notwithstanding all your wise Laws and Maxims we have it in our power not only to free ourselves but to subdue our Masters, and without violence throw both your natural and legal authority at our feet—

"Charm by accepting, by submitting sway
Yet have our Humour most when we
obey."

MOLLY WALLACE, *The Young Ladies, Academy of Philadelphia* (1790)

The Philadelphia Academy, founded by a group of wealthy men, was one of the nation's first schools for girls. Academic objectives expressed the increased status attained by affluent white women during the post-Revolutionary era. Wallace's argument for the right of female students to learn public speaking skills represents an early example of the effort of educated women to surmount the gendered taboo that females were to remain silent and not engage in public speech. The effort to suppress women's voices was part of the larger objective of confining women to the domestic realm. How would you evaluate Wallace's arguments for women speaking before an audience? What does her statement about the need to speak before a "select," not a "promiscuous," audience tell you about the gender controls elite white women confronted in post-Revolutionary America?*

The silent and solemn attention of a respectable audience, has often, at the beginning of discourses intimidated even veterans in the art of public elocution. What then must my situation be, when my sex, my youth and inexperience all conspire to make me tremble

---

* From Molly Wallace, *The Rise and Progress of the Young Ladies, Academy of Philadelphia* (Philadelphia: Stewart and Cochran, 1794), 212–13.

at the task which I have undertaken? But the friendly encouragement, which I behold in almost every countenance, enables me to overcome difficulties, that would otherwise be insurmountable. With some, however, it has been made a question, whether we ought *ever* to appear in so public a manner. Our natural timidity, the domestic situation to which, by nature and custom we seem destined, as urged as arguments against what we have undertaken—many sarcastical observations have been handed out against female oratory: but to what do they amount? Do they not plainly inform us, that, because we are females, we ought therefore to be deprived of what is perhaps the most effectual means of acquiring a just, natural and graceful delivery? No one will pretend to deny that we should be taught to read in the best manner. And if to read, why not to speak? . . .

But yet it may be asked, what, has a female character to do with declamation? That she should harangue at the head of an Army, in the Senate, or before a popular Assembly, is not pretended, neither is it requested that she ought to be an adept in the stormy and contentious eloquence of the air, or in the abstract and subtle reasoning of the Senate—we look not for a female Pitt, Cicero, or Demothenes. . . .

Why is a boy diligently and carefully taught the Latin, the Greek, or the Hebrew language, in which he will seldom have occasion either to write or converse? Why is he taught to demonstrate the propositions of Euclid, when during his whole life, he will not perhaps make use of one of them? Are we taught to dance merely for the sake of becoming dancers? No, certainly. These things are commonly studied, more on account of the habits, which the learning of them establishes, than on account of any important advantages which the mere knowledge of them can afford. So a young lady, from the exercise of speaking before a properly selected audience, may acquire some valuable habits, which, otherwise she can obtain from no examples, and that no precept can give. But, this exercise can with propriety be performed only before a select audience: a promiscuous and indiscriminate one, for obvious reasons, would be absolutely unsuitable, and should always be carefully avoided.

JUDITH COCKS, *Letter to James Hillhouse* (1795)

Documents concerning the lives of enslaved women reveal the deep anguish felt by mothers who experienced the sale of their children to other owners. Mothers struggled to keep their families intact and developed deep bonds with their children. This particular letter to a former master describes Judith Cocks's effort to protect her son from his new owners. Cocks's letter is a rare personal glimpse of the impact of gradual emancipation on enslaved women: the promise of freedom combined with the present reality of enslavement and separation from children.

Although little is known about Judith Cocks beyond her letter, James Hillhouse was a political leader in the state of Connecticut and at the time of the letter a U.S. congressman as well as a slave owner who also supported gradual emancipation. Cocks reference to her son Juniper not receiving freedom until the age of 25 refers to the terms of Connecticut's gradual emancipation laws.

How would you describe the tone of Cocks's appeal to Hillhouse? What does the letter tell you about her ability to negotiate on behalf of her son and herself? What did she hope to achieve with this letter?*

---

* From the Hillhouse Family Papers, "Letter from Judith Cocks to James Hillhouse," dated March 8, 1795. From the Hillhouse Family Papers, Manuscripts and Archives, Yale University Library. Reprinted by permission.

Judith Cocks to James Hillhouse

Marietta, 8th March 1795

Sir

I have been so unhappy at Mrs. Wood-bridges that I was obliged to leeve thare by the consent of Mrs. Woodbridge who gave up my Indentures and has offen said that had she known that I was so sickly and expensive she would not have brought me to this Country but all this is the least of my trouble and I can truly say sir had I nothing else or no one but myself I am sure I should make any complaint to you But my Little son Jupiter who is now with Mrs. Woodbridge is my greatest care and from what she says and from the usage he meets with there is so trying to me that I am all

most distracted therefore if you will be so kind as to write me how Long Jupiter is to remain with them as she tells me he is to live with her untill he is twenty five years of age this is something that I had no idea of I all ways thought that he was to return with me to new england or at Longest only ten years these are matters I must beg of you sir to let me know as quick as you can make it convenient I hope you will excuse me of troubling you which I think you will do when you think that I am here in A strange country without one Friend to advise me [. . . .] I remain the greatest humil-ity you Humble servant

Judith Cocks

please [don't] show this to Mrs. Woodbridge

EULALIA CALLIS, *Petition to Divorce Her Husband Pedro Fages* (1784–1785)

It was highly unusual for a Spanish woman in New Spain to seek a divorce. Eulalia Callis's (1758–unknown) petition for a divorce may have reflected her own wishes to leave the remote, frontier outpost of Spanish-claimed Monterey, California, and return to Mexico City. Whether in New Spain or New England, pregnancy and giving birth were the constant occurrences that occupied a married woman's reproductive years. Callis already had four pregnancies in five years when she sought a divorce from her husband Pedro Fages. In seeking a divorce she struggled against the patriarchal power of her husband and the Catholic Church. Fages was the governor of California, a well-known army officer, and an Indian fighter. To suppress Callis's efforts to get a divorce, Fages, with the help of the priests, locked her up in the mission San Carlos. In seeking a divorce, Callis had made a public outcry against her husband that undermined both his authority and honor according to the norms of Spanish patriarchal culture. Later she withdrew her divorce petition, recanted her story about her husband's infidelity with an Indian girl, and agreed to remain married. Nonetheless her resistance and defiance subverted the fundamental gendered norm: wifely obedience and submission.

In what ways did the intersection of gender and class play a role in Callis's divorce petition? How would granting a wife a divorce alter the balance of power within marriage?*

Petition by Doña Eulalia Callis, the Wife of Don Pedro Fages, Governor of the Californias, that Her Case Be Heard and that She Be Freed from the Oppression from which She Is Suffering (Summary)

Doña Eulalia Callis, wife of Don Pedro Fages, the current Governor of the peninsula of the Californias, seeking Your Honor's most benevolent and superior protection, submits this petition for your fair ruling. She appeals

---

* From Lands of promise and despair, chronicles of early California, edited by Rose Marie Beebe and Robert M. Senkewicz, Santa Clara University, Heyday Books, Berkeley, CA. Copyright © 2006 Heyday Books. Reprinted by permission.

to your benevolence because she is a helpless woman. She calls upon your superior protection so that justice may be served. Justice seeks out the guilty parties and recognizes the one who has been wronged. Justice must protect the weaker party because that is the law.

It is the case that I found my husband physically on top of one of his servants, a very young Yuma Indian girl. Well-founded suspicions and the girl's easily obtained confession put me in the position of being the sentinel who discovered the incident. Even though prudence should have prevailed (this is my crime), I was overcome by passion, which fueled the flames of my rage, which caused me to cry out publicly against this infamy. Your Honor, what person would not acknowledge the wrong that had been done to them even though the pain had passed? A few hours later this guilty party besieged with an onslaught of advice and words of persuasion for her to return to her husband. It was all very well-meaning. However, the wound was still fresh and since the medicine was applied at the wrong time, it had no effect. Thus, drastic measures were taken. It is from the pain of these measures that I seek Your Honor's magnanimous mercy.

Reverend Father Fray Matias Antonio de Noriega, the priest at the nearby mission, ordered that the offended party be locked in a room guarded by soldiers from the troop. Placed there incommunicado, she began to prepare her case. The most important piece of evidence in this case was the girl's statement. Kneeling before the judge, the girl uttered what she could, constrained by her fear of the punishment she faced. This testimony was followed by cries to restore her [Callis's] husband's reputation (as if he had lost it with just that one woman). The judge forgot to obtain statements from everyone at the *presidio* who had evidence, according to the girl. In cases such as this, the law requires that the testimony be from credible witnesses,

such as midwives or others who have knowledge of the situation. The proceedings of this case have been drawn up as best as can be expected under the circumstances and they have been sent to the Illustrious Bishop of Sonora. We await news of his decision with regard to the offended party. Was it not important for Your Honor to allow this woman of sound mind to be heard? Apparently not. Perhaps one fears what she will say in her defense.

There is further evidence: on Ash Wednesday in the *presidio* church, the priest who celebrated Mass also was the judge on the case. After reading from the Gospel and preaching the sermon, he ended by vilifying me and had the soldiers throw me out of the church. This is what he said: "Detain that woman so I can put a gag over her mouth." He made it known that he would excommunicate anybody who spoke to me or who spoke about the matter. The error of these peoples' ways is due to their ignorance with regard to the matter. On my saint's day they tied me up and transferred me to Mission San Carlos. The cloister was rigorous. There were few candles. They stood watch over me and forced me to eat even though I was sick. I conclude this wretched tale of suffering with the threats of the aforementioned Father, who said he would have me flogged and placed in shackles.

I shall consider the first insult to my person as my cross to bear. I am told that the crimes committed against me were not that serious and my desires for satisfaction are merely earthly and transitory. Hence, I am told that I should forgive my husband and return to him, a surrender that would force the most innocent party to suffer the greatest losses. If he (Fages) insists that he has suffered from my outrage, then keep me imprisoned at the disposal of the priest who can restrain me more or less according to his nature. He will not, however, close the doors to my honor and noble birth. These doors shall remain open to receive a lawful defense and Your Honor's protection.

I humbly beg you to agree to hear this petition in the form that it is presented. Justice will grant me a pardon. I swear to accept what I am given. The laws that protect me will save me from poverty. I will not give up my rights during the course of the proceedings of my case.

Mission San Carlos
April 12, 1785

Eulalia Callis

ABIGAIL ABBOT BAILEY, Excerpt from *Memoirs* (1788–1789)

Abigail Bailey's (1746–1815) memoir is one of the very few female autobiographical accounts from this period. Her minister published it shortly after her death in 1815. The memoir provides the reader with a revealing personal account of domestic tyranny and family abuse. Bailey, who had fourteen children in twenty-six years, divorced her husband in 1793. The family lived on a farm in rural New Hampshire. During the marriage, her husband physically abused her, committed adultery with one woman, and attempted the rape of another. What completely drove Bailey to desperation and ultimately divorce was his incestuous relationship with their teenage daughter. Family dysfunction does not get much worse than this, but even after discovering the incestuous relationship, Bayley remained married for several more years. Deeply religious and introspective, she believed that God would not only indicate to her the path she should follow but would also deal with her husband's wickedness. After many years of trusting to God to resolve her difficulties, she realized that belief in God also necessitated her using her own free will. Wives were subordinate, but Puritan laws forbade husbands from inflicting physical harm. Adultery was grounds for a divorce, which Bailey eventually obtained.

What reasons did Bailey give for her reluctance to pursue a divorce? How did she deal with the issue of incest? In what ways might this narrative continue to resonate in twenty-first-century America?*

One result of all my examinations and prayers was, a settled conviction, that I ought to seek a separation from my wicked husband, and never to settle with him any more for his most vile conduct. But as sufficient evidence, for his legal conviction, had not yet offered itself, (though I as much believed his guilt, as I believed my own existence,) I thought God's time to bring Mr. B.'s conduct to public view had not yet arrived. But I was confident that such a time would arrive; that God would bring his crimes to light; and afford me opportunity to be freed from him.

Several months had passed, after Mr. B's last wicked conduct before mentioned, and nothing special took place. The following events then occurred. One of our young daughters, (too young to be a legal witness, but old enough to tell the truth,) informed one of her sisters, older than herself, what she saw and heard, more than a year before, on a certain sabbath. This sister being filled with grief and astonishment at what she had heard, informed her oldest sister. When this oldest sister had heard the account, and was prepared to believe it, (after all the strange things which she herself had seen and heard,) she was so shocked, that she fainted. She was then at our house, I administered camphire, and such things as were suitable in her case. She soon revived. She then informed me of the occasion of her fainting. I had long before had full evidence to my

---

* Abigail Abbot Bailey, *Memoirs of Mrs. Abigail Bailey, Who Had Been the Wife of Major Asa Bailey, Formerly of Landaff, (N.H.) Written by Herself.* Ed. Ethan Smith (Boston: Samuel T. Armstrong, 1815), 57–60.

mind of Mr. B's great wickedness in this matter; and I thought I was prepared to hear the worst. But verily the worst was dreadful! The last great day will unfold it. I truly at this time had a new lesson added, to all that ever I before heard, or conceived, of human depravity.

I was now determined to go and see the daughter, who had suffered such things. Mr. B. perceiving my design to go where she was, set himself to prevent it. But kind Providence soon afforded me an opportunity to go. She was living at the house of her uncle, a very amiable man, and one whom Mr. B. in his better days, esteemed most highly; but of whom he became very shy, after he abandoned himself to wickedness. Mr. B. now could not endure the thought of my going to his house. No doubt his guilty conscience feared what information I might there obtain, and filled him with terror.

With much difficulty, and by the help of her aunt, I obtained ample information. I now found that none of my dreadful apprehensions concerning Mr. B's conduct had been too high. And I thought the case of this daughter was the most to be pitied of any person I ever knew. I wondered how the author of her calamities could tarry in this part of the world. I thought that his guilty conscience must make him flee; and that shame must give him wings, to fly with the utmost speed.

My query now was, what I ought to do? I had no doubt relative to my living any longer with the author of our family miseries. This point was fully settled. But whether it would be consistent with faithfulness to suffer him to flee, and not be made a monument of civil justice, was my query. The latter looked to me inexpressibly painful. And I persuaded myself, that if he would do what was right, relative to our property, and would go to some distant place, where we should be afflicted with him no more, it might be sufficient; and I might be spared the dreadful scene of prosecuting my husband.

I returned home, I told Mr. B. I had heard an awful account relative to some man. I mentioned some particulars, without intimating who the man was; or what family

was affected by it. I immediately perceived he was deeply troubled! He turned pale, and trembled, as if he had been struck with death. It was with difficulty he could speak. He asked nothing, who the man was, that had done this great wickedness; but after a while said, I know you believe it to be true; and that all our children believe it; but it is not true! Much more he said in way of denying. But he said he did not blame me for thinking as I did.

He asked me, what I intended to do? I replied, that one thing was settled: I would never live with him any more! He soon appeared in great anguish; and asked what I could advise him to do? Such was his appearance, that the pity of my heart was greatly moved. He had been my dear husband; and had destroyed himself. And now he felt something of his wretchedness. I now felt my need of christian fortitude, to be firm in pursuing my duty. I was determined to put on firmness, and go through with the most interesting and undesirable business, to which God, in his providence, had called me, and which I had undertaken. I told him his case to me looked truly dreadful and desperate. That thought [though] I had long and greatly labored for his reformation and good, yet he had rejected all my advice. He had felt sufficient to be his own counsellor; and now he felt something of the result of his own counsels. . . .

I earnestly entreated him to break off his sins by unfeigned repentance, and make it his immediate care to become reconciled to God through Jesus Christ, who died for lost man, and even for the greatest of sinners. I suggested to Mr. B. that if he would reform, and would never injure his family relative to the interest, I could truly wish him well, and so much peace as was consistent with the holy and wise purposes of God. But that if he should undertake any farther to afflict our family, or any of his dear children, he might expect punishment in this life, and that the judgments of God would follow him. I begged of him to treat his family well, in relation to our property, and to treat all mankind, henceforth, well.

JUDITH SARGENT MURRAY, *On the Equality of the Sexes* (1790)

Judith Sargent Murray (1751–1820) wrote the essay "On the Equality of the Sexes" in 1790. A prolific writer of essays, poetry, and plays, she lived at a time when girlhood was little more than preparation for the roles of housewife and mother. A pioneer feminist, Murray argued that girls needed more than this one-dimensional domestic focus. An early advocate of educational equality, she believed the minds of men and women to be capable of equal intellectual attainment. She credited male prominence not to inborn sex differences but to the fact that from earliest youth, the minds of girls were "depressed," those of boys "exalted."

How does Murray reassure her readers that education would not interfere with women's domestic responsibilities? How does she evaluate women's "needle and kitchen" skills? In what ways does Murray provide a feminist perspective based on gender equality?*

Is it upon mature consideration we adopt the idea, that nature is thus partial in her distributions? Is it indeed a fact, that she hath yielded to one half of the human species so unquestionable a mental superiority? I know that to both sexes elevated understandings, and the reverse, are common. But, suffer me to ask, in what the minds of females are so notoriously deficient, or unequal. May not the intellectual powers be ranged under these four heads—imagination, reason, memory and judgment. The province of imagination hath long since been surrendered up to us, and we have been crowned undoubted sovereigns of the regions of fancy. Invention is perhaps the most arduous effort of the mind; this branch of imagination hath been particularly ceded to us, and we have been time out of mind invested with that creative faculty. Observe the variety of fashions (here I bar the contemptuous smile) which distinguish and adorn the female world; how continually are they changing, insomuch that they almost render the wise man's assertion problematical, and we are ready to say, *there is something new under the sun.* Now what a playfulness, what an exuberance of fancy, what strength of inventive imagination, doth this continual variation discover? Again, it hath been observed, that if the turpitude of the conduct of our sex, hath been

ever so enormous, so extremely ready are we, that the very first thought presents us with an apology, so plausible, as to produce our actions even in an amiable light. Another instance of our creative powers, is our talent for slander; how ingenious are we at inventive scandal? what a formidable story can we in a moment fabricate merely from the force of a prolifick imagination? how many reputations, in the fertile brain of a female, have been utterly despoiled? how industrious are we at improving a hint? suspicion how easily do we convert into conviction, and conviction, embellished by the power of eloquence, stalks abroad to the surprise and confusion of unsuspecting innocence. Perhaps it will be asked if I furnish these facts as instances of excellency in our sex. Certainly not; but as proofs of a creative faculty, of a lively imagination. Assuredly great activity of mind is thereby discovered, and was this activity properly directed, what beneficial effects would follow. Is the needle and kitchen sufficient to employ the operations of a soul thus organized? I should conceive not. Nay, it is a truth that those very departments leave the intelligent principle vacant, and at liberty for speculation. Are we deficient in reason? we can only reason from what we know, and if an opportunity of acquiring knowledge hath been denied us, the

* From Judith Sargent Murray, "On the Equality of the Sexes." First published in *Massachusetts Magazine,* 1790. Reprinted from *Selected Writings of Judith Sargent Murray* (New York: Oxford University Press, 1995).

inferiority of our sex cannot fairly be deduced from thence. . . . how is the one exalted, and the other depressed, by the contrary modes of education which are adopted! the one is taught to aspire, and the other is early confined and limitted. As their years increase, the sister must be wholly domesticated, while the brother is led by the hand through all the flowery paths of science. Grant that their minds are by nature equal, yet who shall wonder at the *apparent* superiority, if indeed custom becomes *second nature;* nay if it taketh place of nature, and that it doth the experience of each day will evince. At length arrived at womanhood, the uncultivated fair one feels a void, which the employments allotted her are by no means capable of filling. What can she do? to books she may not apply; or if she doth, *to those only of the novel kind,* lest she merit the appellation of a *learned lady;* and what ideas have been affixed to this term, the observation of many can testify. Fashion, scandal, and sometimes what is still more reprehensible, are then called in to her relief; and who can say to what lengths the liberties she takes may proceed. Meantime she herself is most unhappy; she feels the want of a cultivated mind. Is she single, she in vain seeks to fill up time from sexual employments or amusements. Is she united to a person whose soul nature made equal to her own, education hath set him so far above her, that in those entertainments which are productive of such rational felicity, she is not qualified to accompany him. She experiences a mortifying consciousness of inferiority, which embitters every enjoyment. . . .

Will it be urged that those acquirements would supersede our domestick duties? I answer that every requisite in female economy is easily attained; and, with truth I can add, that when once attained, they require no further *mental attention.* Nay, while we are pursuing the needle, or the superintendency of the family, I repeat, that our minds are at full liberty for reflection; that imagination may exert itself in full vigor; and that if a just foundation is early laid, our ideas will then be worthy of rational beings. If we were industrious we might easily find time to arrange them upon paper, or should avocations press too hard for such an indulgence, the hours allotted for conversation would at least become more refined and rational. Should it still be vociferated, "Your domestick employments are sufficient"—I would calmly ask, is it reasonable, that a candidate for immortality, for the joys of heaven, an intelligent being, who is to spend an eternity in contemplating the works of Deity, should at present be so degraded, as to be allowed no other ideas, than those which are suggested by the mechanism of a pudding, or the sewing the seams of a garment?

DEBORAH SAMPSON GANNETT, *Letter from Paul Revere on Behalf of Deborah Sampson Gannett* (1804)

The following letter written by Paul Revere, a Revolutionary War hero, supported Deborah Sampson Gannett's (1761–1827) appeal for a pension based on her seventeen months of active service in the Continental Army and the wounds she received in battle. Before she joined the Continental Army, Sampson, who came from an impoverished family, was an indentured servant. To enter the army, she wore a soldier's uniform, disguised her female identity, and assumed the name of Robert Shurtleff. The army did not require physical examinations on entering, and Sampson's disguise worked until a serious illness and a doctor's examination revealed her female identity. Earlier wounds that she received had not resulted in detection. After her release from the army, she married and became the mother of three children. As an invalid veteran, her petition for a pension from the U.S. government was finally approved in 1805 with a partial payment of four dollars a month. Subsequent petitions resulted in an increased payment and Sampson became the first woman to receive a veteran's pension.

Why would Revere emphasize that Sampson was not a "Masculine female"? In what ways did Sampson's behavior challenge gender roles?*

Canton, Feby 20 1804
William Eustis, Esq
Member of Congress
Washington

Sir

Mrs. Deborah Gannett of Sharon informes me, that she has inclosed to your Care a petition to Congress in favour of Her. My works for manufactureing of Copper, being at Canton, but a short distance from the Neighbourhood where She lives; I have been induced to enquire her situation, and Character, since she quitted the Male habit, and Soldiers uniform; for the more decent apparel of her own Sex; & Since she has been married and become a Mother.—Humanity, & Justice obliges me to say, that every person with whom I have conversed about Her, and it is not a few, speak of Her as a woman of handsom talents, good Morals, a dutifull Wife and an affectionate parent.—She is now much out of health; She has several Children; her Husband is a good sort of a man, 'tho of small force in business; they have a few acres of poor land which they cultivate, but they are really poor.

She told me, she had no doubt that her ill health is in consequence of her being exposed when She did a Soldiers duty; and that while in the Army, She was wounded.

We commonly form our Idea of the person whom we hear spoken of, whom we have never seen; according as their actions are described, when I heard her spoken off as a Soldier, I formed the Idea of a tall, Masculine female, who had a small share of understandg, without education, & one of the meanest of her Sex.—When I saw and discoursed with I was agreeably surprised to find a small, effeminate, and converseable Woman, whose education entitled her to a better situation in life.

I have no doubt your humanity will prompt you to do all in Your power to git her some releif; I think her case much more deserving than hundreds to whom Congress have been generous.

I am sir with esteem & respect your humble servant

Paul Revere

COLORED FEMALE RELIGIOUS AND MORAL SOCIETY OF SALEM, MASSACHUSETTS,
***Constitution* (1818)**

Free African American women also developed benevolent associations and societies. Limited employment opportunities for African Americans caused widespread poverty, and women made a major social contribution in providing aid to the poor and the sick. What evidence informs us that like their white counterparts, African American women also made moral behavior a requirement for assistance?**

---

* Massachusetts Historical Society. In the public domain.
** From the Constitution of the Female Anti-Slavery Society of Salem, Massachusetts. Reprinted in *We Are Your Sisters: Black Women in the Nineteenth Century,* edited by Dorothy Sterling, copyright © 1984 by Dorothy Sterling. Used by permission of W. W. Norton & Company, Inc.

Constitution

of the Colored Female Religious and Moral Society of Salem

Article I.—At the weekly meeting of the Society, when the appointed hour arrives, and a number are convened, the exercises shall begin by reading in some profitable book, till all have come in who are expected.

Art. II—A prayer shall then be made by one of the members, and after that, a chapter in the Bible shall be read, and religious conversation be attended to, as time will allow.

Art. III—Four quarterly days in the year, in January, April, July and October, beginning on the first day of every January, to be observed as a day of solemn fasting and prayer.

Art. IV—We promise not to ridicule or divulge the supposed or apparent infirmities of any fellow member; but to keep secret all things relating to the Society, the discovery of which might tend to do hurt to the Society or any individual.

Art. V—We resolve to be charitably watchful over each other; to advise; caution and admonish where we may judge there is occasion, and that it may be useful; and we promise not to resent, but kindly and thankfully receive such friendly advice or reproof from any one of our members.

Art. VI—Any female can become a member of this Society by conforming to the Constitution, and paying in fifty two cents per year.

Art. VII—This Society is formed for the benefit of the sick and destitute of those members belonging to the Society.

Art. VIII—If any member commit any scandalous sin, or walk unruly, and after proper reproof continue manifestly impenitent, she shall be excluded from us, until she give evidence of her repentance.

EMMA WILLARD, *Plan for Female Education* (1819)

Emma Willard (1787–1870) established one of the pre–Civil War's best-known schools for women in Troy, New York. In her effort to obtain funding from the New York legislature, Willard linked women's education to the role of mothers in the new republic and the virtues of hard work and thrift. Willard's emphasis on the need to avoid frivolity and idleness was addressed to privileged women. It would have little relevance to the harsh, work-filled lives of the poor. How does Willard relate "housewifery" to her educational objectives? What emphasis is placed on the maternal role?*

The inquiry to which these remarks have conducted us is this: what is offered by the plan of female education here proposed, which may teach or preserve, among females of wealthy families, that purity of manners which is allowed to be so essential to national prosperity, and so necessary to the existence of republican government.

1. Females, by having their understandings cultivated, their reasoning powers developed and strengthened, may be expected to act more from the dictates of reason and less from those of fashion or caprice.

2. With minds thus strengthened they would be taught systems of morality, enforced by the sanctions of religion; and they might be expected to acquire juster and more enlarged views of their duty, and stronger and higher motives to its performance.

3. This plan of education offers all that can be done to preserve female youth

---

* From *An Address to the Public; Particularly to the Members of the Legislation of New York, Proposing a Plan for Improving Female Education* (1819); in John Lord, *The Life of Emma Willard* (New York: Appelton, 1873), 76–84.

from a contempt of useful labor. The pupils would become accustomed to it, in conjunction with the high objects of literature and the elegant pursuits of the fine arts; and it is so to be hoped that, both from habit and association, they might in future life regard it as respectable.

4. To this it may be added that, if housewifery could be raised to a regular art and taught upon philosophical principles, it would become a higher and more interesting occupation; and ladies of fortune, like wealthy agriculturists, might find that to regulate their business was an agreeable employment.

5. The pupils might be expected to acquire a taste for moral and intellectual pleasures, which would buoy them above a passion for show and parade, and which would make them seek to gratify the natural love of superiority, by endeavoring to excel others in intrinsic merit, rather than in the extrinsic frivolities of dress, furniture, and equipage.

6. By being enlightened in moral philosophy, and in that which teaches the operations of the mind, females would be enabled to perceive the nature and extent of that influence which they possess over their children, and the obligation which this lays them under, to watch the formation of their characters with unceasing violence, to become their instructors, to devise plans for their improvement, to weed out the vices from their minds, and to implant and foster the virtues. And surely there is that in the maternal bosom which, when its pleadings shall be aided by education, will overcome the seductions of wealth and fashion, and will lead the mother to seek her happiness in communing with her children and promoting their welfare, rather than in heartless intercourse with the votaries of pleasure: especially when, with an expanded mind, she extends her views to futurity, and sees her care to her offspring rewarded by peace of conscience, the blessings of her family, the prosperity of her country, and finally with everlasting pleasure to herself and them.

JOHN S. C. ABBOTT, *The Mother at Home* (1833)

Ministers became a major force in the exaltation of motherhood. Protestant ministers such as John S. C. Abbott (1805–1870) constructed and publicized the concept of virtuous motherhood through child-rearing manuals. Abbot assigned mothers the sole responsibility for the moral instruction of their young sons. Earlier Christian tradition linked Eve's fall to women's sinful nature, but nineteenth-century ministers such as Abbott endowed motherhood with the moral redemption of the nation's sons. Abbott linked the failure of mothers to provide moral education for their children with the misery of the human race.

What social purposes would it serve to endow motherhood with such awesome responsibility? In what ways would a mother's influence differ from political power? How would this description of maternal influence relate to the gendered effort to limit women's roles to their maternal functions?*

---

* From John S. C. Abbott, *The Mother at Home; or the Principles of Maternal Duty, Familiarly Illustrated* (New York: The American Tract Society, 1833), 159–66.

Mothers have as powerful an influence over the welfare of future generations, as all other earthly causes combined. Thus far the history of the world has been composed of the narrations of oppression and blood. War has scattered its unnumbered woes. The cry of the oppressed has unceasingly ascended to heaven. Where are we to look for the influence which shall change this scene, and fill the earth with the fruits of peace and benevolence? It is to the power of divine truth, to Christianity, as taught from a mother's lips. In a vast majority of cases the first six or seven years decide the character of the man. If the boy leave the paternal roof uncontrolled, turbulent, and vicious, he will, in all probability, rush on in the mad career of self-indulgence. There are exceptions; but these exceptions are rare. If, on the other hand, your son goes from home accustomed to control himself, he will probably retain that habit through life. If he has been taught to make sacrifices of his own enjoyment that he may promote the happiness of those around him, it may be expected that he will continue to practice benevolence, and consequently will be respected, and useful, and happy. If he has adopted firm resolutions to be faithful in all the relations of life, he, in all probability, will be a virtuous man and an estimable citizen, and a benefactor of his race.

When our land is filled with pious and patriotic mothers, then will it be filled with virtuous and patriotic men. The world's redeeming influence, under the blessing of the Holy Spirit, must come from a mother's lips. She who was first in the transgression, must be yet the principal earthly instrument in the restoration. Other causes may greatly aid. Other influences must be ready to receive the mind as it comes from the mother's hand, and carry it onward in its improvement. But the mothers of our race must be the chief instruments in its redemption. This sentiment will bear examining; and the more it is examined, the more manifestly true will it appear. It is alike the dictate of philosophy and experience. The mother who is neglecting personal effort, and relying upon other influences from the formation of virtuous character in her children, will find, when it is too late, that she has fatally erred. The patriot, who hopes that schools, and lyceums, and the general diffusion of knowledge, will promote the good order and happiness of the community, while family government is neglected, will find that he is attempting to purify the streams which are flowing from a corrupt foundation. It is maternal influence, after all, which must be the great agent, in the hands of God, in bringing back our guilty race to duty and happiness. O that mothers could feel this responsibility as they ought! Then would the world assume a different aspect. Then should we less frequently behold unhappy families and brokenhearted parents. A new race of men would enter upon the busy scene of life, and cruelty and crime would pass away. O mothers! Reflect upon the power your Maker has placed in your hands! There is no earthly influence to be compared with yours. There is no combination of causes so powerful in promoting the happiness or the misery of our race, as the instructions of home. In a most peculiar sense God has constituted you the guardians and the controllers of the human family.

CHAPTER 3

Gendered Opportunity and Occupations:
Industrial and Educational Expansion

The majority of Americans still lived on farms, when industrial growth began in the 1800s. Early factory owners hired women. In fact, female operatives, mainly from New England farms, provided the nation with a major source of factory laborers in the area's textile mills. With a wider range of employment opportunities as well as the management of family farms, Anglo-American men rejected factory labor. In contrast, women, particularly young unmarried women such as the teenager Barilla Taylor, as well as widows, chose factory work as a welcome alternative to domestic service, the major source of employment for women during the nineteenth century. Female factory laborers exposed the class dimension of gender norms. Middle-class women could afford to stay in their "proper place" at home. Poor women needed paid employment. Textile factory owners in Lowell, Massachusetts, ignored the growing emphasis on female domesticity in order to recruit a labor force. The factory system eventually grew to employ a large number of women, but for many years it coexisted with preindustrial labor patterns in which women worked at home sewing and binding shoes. New England's female shoe workers were part of a male-centered crafts tradition that viewed women's work as supplemental to that of men, and lower pay expressed women's subordinate status regardless of quality and need for their labor.

Women who juggled child and home care with paid work faced a pervasive belief system that demeaned women's work, whether domestic or home production, as non-burdensome chores. Even the meager wages they received for home manufacture legally belonged to their husbands, and their subordinate status within the family unit strengthened employers' resolve to keep women's wages low. The middle-class prescriptive model of male-only earners has obscured the large number of working wives and daughters and their contributions to the family economy. In many cases, household production for market income was necessary for family survival. The majority of American women continued to live on farms and their paid and unpaid labor was vital. Nevertheless, the significance of women's labor stretched beyond home, farm, and factory production and had major implications for the national economy.

Free African American women encountered the intertwined obstacles of racial and gender barriers that further limited educational and employment opportunities. Domestic service and laundry work provided the major fields of employment. White abolitionist Prudence Crandall's attempt to open a school in Canterbury, Connecticut, for African American girls and young women met with outrage on the part of the town's residents.

At first thankful for an opportunity to earn money at the Lowell textile mills, women, such as Harriet Robinson and Sarah Bagley soon confronted their employers over issues of low pay, long hours, and poor working conditions. Proud and assertive, the first generation of textile workers claimed their republican heritage, and as daughters of "freemen," they struggled for greater control over the workplace. At Lowell, women workers lived in a close-knit community, and their labor protests expressed their collective bond as "sister operatives." They organized labor associations; participated in strikes; and some, including Sarah Bagley and members of the Female Labor Reform Association, spoke out before a state investigative committee about poor factory conditions and the need for a ten-hour day. In 1860, labor agitation again surfaced, this time among shoe workers, both those who labored in factories and those who worked binding shoes at home. The liberty rhetoric that reinforced the equal rights promise of republican ideals continued to mold protest rhetoric during the 1860 shoe workers' strike.

All factory employees faced the harsh conditions of industrialization, but gender assumptions kept women's wages even lower than men's, created far fewer opportunities for advancement, and limited employment options. The increasingly contested view that women's essential domestic identity was as a wife and mother still rationalized her wage work as supplemental to that of men and provided the justification for gender-based workplace discrimination. In contrast to the limited domestic identity of women, Betty Cowles promoted women's rights and gender equality. She compiled lengthy reports that documented not only oppressive labor conditions encountered by working women, but also the enormous wage gap between male and female workers in all occupations. From the early-nineteenth-century grievances of factory worker and telegraph operator Sarah Bagley to the present day, one aspect of the struggle for women's rights has been to overcome prescribed workplace barriers, including the sustained effort over the decades to attain pay equity.

The cultural ideal of full-time mothers who did not need paid work, gained relevance within the white middle class and hid the reality of the many other women who needed paid work for their own and their family's survival. Within the middle class, widening commercial opportunities for white men increased the gap between the wife's domestic functions and the realm of male business activity. Increasing numbers of husbands successfully sought paid employment away from the home and became the family "breadwinners." The cultural expectation that husbands were their families' sole economic providers became a status symbol for the emerging middle class of the pre-Civil War era.

As manufactured goods became more widely available, middle class women became consumers rather than producers of household goods. In towns and cities, the household began to decline as a unit of economic production. Women assumed the status of housewife and performed the unpaid, although vitally necessary, functions of home and family care. Many had servants to help with the more burdensome household functions. Whether as a housewife's unpaid labor or as wages paid to servants, domestic labor was seen as less significant than the "real" work performed by men. The middle-class home assumed new importance as a refuge and a haven for men returning from their business activities. Middle-class, gendered assumptions that wives would not need to work depended on adequate wages for husbands and obscured the actual life experience of the thousands of married women who took in boarders and worked at home stitching gloves, binding shoes, or performing other types of labor that added to the family income.

African American families faced racial discrimination that made it particularly difficult for husbands to obtain adequate wages for family support. Immigrants provided a ready supply of "cheap" labor that further depressed wages for African Americans and placed middle-class domestic norms beyond their reach.

Even as factories recruited female labor, educational opportunities for white women also advanced. Freed from the hardships faced by most working women, middle-class women advocated for labor reforms and expanded female employment opportunities. Dismayed that unhealthy factory conditions undermined female physical and moral well-being, Catharine Beecher, the nation's leading proponent of female education, proposed the remedy of transforming a woman's role from factory operative to elementary school teacher. Sarah Hale, the editor of the popular *Godey's Lady's Book,* promoted teacher training for women with government financial assistance in the rapidly expanding West. Mary Lyon founded Mt. Holyoke Seminary in 1837. Its curriculum combined rigorous academic standards including required courses in chemistry and Latin with a heavy infusion of religious inculcation that facilitated future missionary work. Beecher, Hale, and Lyon adhered to domestic norms but also expanded the parameters of women's gendered roles.

During the pre–Civil War era, educational opportunities for females expanded in all sections of the nation. However, racial as well as gender and class patterns of discrimination molded unequal opportunity. In Macon, Georgia, Wesleyan College, affiliated with the Methodists, became the nation's first female institution chartered to grant women college degrees. Not surprisingly, given the racial norms of the era, African American women faced far greater obstacles than did white women. Schooling for African Americans did exist in the free states, but segregation and inequality of resources shaped the educational experience. Before the Civil War, colleges were almost entirely a white male preserve. Oberlin College founded in Ohio in 1833 was the first co-ed, degree-granting institution to admit a few white and even fewer African American women to a restricted curriculum.

BARILLA TAYLOR, *Letter from Barilla Taylor to Her Family* (1844)

Barilla Taylor (1828–1845) was fifteen when she came to work in Lowell, Massachusetts, at the Hamilton Mills. One of twelve children, she left her family in Roxbury, Maine. Work at the mill, despite the twelve-hour days, provided her with a chance to earn wages and purchase new clothing and jewelry. Near the end of her letter, she casually reports that she might not see her family again because she plans to go out West. She also mentions a doctor's bill. Unfortunately for Taylor, she never fulfilled her plans. She died two years after her arrival at the mill. She was only seventeen.

How did Taylor evaluate conditions in the mill? What evidence does the letter provide of her independent outlook on life?*

Lowell, Mass. Sunday July 14, 1844

Distant Parents,

It is with pleasure that I seat myself this morning to write to you to let you know of my health which is very good at present. Having few leisure hours, I improve them in writing and I have a chance to send it by Mrs. Walker. I don't know as I can write half a letter as my mind is not upon it, but I will write what I can.
        . . . I like in the mill, but my overseer is not the best, or I might say, the cleverest. I do not make much. I did not make only six and a quarter last month beside my board. I pay five dollars for my board a month. I don't know but you will think strange that I have changed my boarding place again. But I will tell you a few of the reasons why I changed so much. The first place I went to was on the Corporation. It was a very good place indeed. They kept about thirty boarders all the time. They kept six in one room. Else had some trouble with two girls she roomed with and she would not stay. We went to the second place. Our boarding woman was done very well for about three weeks. If I may say it, she was cross, lazy and nasty. She would build up a fire just before she went to bed, put on her coffee and let it steep all night. In the morning she would get up, build up a fire and go to bed again. We would get up get our breakfast and go into the mill. . . . When we came out for dinner we would have what coffee was left from the morning for dinner. We would have a little dry bread, a cracker or two a piece and that was our dinner. We would have a piece of pie once a week and that was our living for about three months. I was sick there and I don't wonder, do you? I left there in about a week after I got able to work. I now board with Mr. and Mrs. Elston on

Central Street. They are first rate folks. Judith, Else, and I are all the boarders they keep. I have as much as I want and just when I want it. That is all I have to say about my boarding places. . . .

        Ann Graham, if you know her, has got her hand tore off. It was done in the card room. I heard she has got to have it taken off above the elbow. We don't know but she will lose her life by it. . . . I have received two letters from you since I left home. The first I got about two months after it was written, the second in about ten days. Write to me as soon as you can. . . . If mother would like to have me buy her something and send her, I will. Or I will buy her something and fetch her when I come. I think likely I shall have more then. I should like to have her write what she would like to have me get her. Though if I stay till spring I think it a doubt if you ever see me again if my health is as good as it is now for I think of joining the Association and going to the west next spring. I have got me three dresses within two months. Two of them cost me three dollars a piece. Six yards and ½ in the black, double width. Ten in the other, single width. I have a large cape like them both. I sent you a small piece of them and a piece of my cloak. The stripe is like my dress, the plain like my cloak.

        I hope these lines will find you well. I should like to see all of you very much. . . . If I cannot see you, I hope I shall hear from you. . . . I want you to write as much as I have. Fill up your letters full. I bid you all farewell as I don't know as I shall see any of you again.

        I have a small bill to pay to the doctor in the course of two or three weeks.

From your absent daughter,
Barilla A. Taylor

---

* From the personal collection of Virginia Taylor.

HARRIET HANSON ROBINSON, *Lowell Textile Workers* (1898)

Harriet Hanson Robinson (1825–1911) began to work in Lowell as a child and left in the 1840s to get married. An advocate of women's rights, Robinson, in her memoir, describes conditions in the Lowell mills during the early years when poor farm women flocked to the mills to take advantage of economic opportunity and the possibility of upward mobility. Although many of the women were young and considered their work temporary, the mills also provided older women with a chance to develop an independent life. Robinson's description of her experience at Lowell relied on more than a half-century of memories.

Read in conjunction with the contemporaneous Lowell accounts that follow, do you find Robinson's memories accurate or blurred? From a late-nineteenth-century perspective, Robinson presents an overview of rights that women gained. What rights did late-nineteenth-century women possess that those millworkers of Lowell lacked? What role did the lack of women's rights play in the Lowell protest and its outcome? What role did Robinson play in the 1836 strike or "turn out"?*

In 1831 Lowell was little more than a factory village. Several corporations were started, and the cotton mills belonging to them were building. Help was in great demand; and stories were told all over the country of the new factory town, and the high wages that were offered to all classes of workpeople—stories that reached the ears of mechanics' and farmers' sons, and gave new life to lonely and dependent women in distant towns and farmhouses. Into this Yankee El Dorado, these needy people began to pour by the various modes of travel known to those slow old days. The stagecoach and the canal boat came every day, always filled with new recruits for this army of useful people. The mechanic and machinist came, each with his homemade chest of tools, and oftentimes his wife and little ones. The widow came with her little flock and her scanty housekeeping goods to open a boarding-house or variety store, and so provided a home for her fatherless children. Many farmers' daughters came to earn money to complete their wedding outfit, or buy the bride's share of house-keeping articles. . . .

The laws relating to women were such, that a husband could claim his wife wherever he found her, and also the children she was trying to shield from his influence; and I have seen more than one poor women skulk behind her loom or her frame when visitors were approaching the end of the aisle where she worked. Some of these were known under assumed names, to prevent their husbands from trusteeing their wages. It was a very common thing for a male person of a certain kind to do this, thus depriving his wife of *all* her wages, perhaps, month after month. The wages of minor children could be trusteed, unless the children (being fourteen years of age) were given their time. Women's wages were also trusteed for the debts of their husbands, and children's for the debts of their parents. . . .

It must be remembered that at this date woman had no property rights. A widow could be left without her share of her husband's (or the family) property, a legal "encumbrance" to his estate. A father could make his will without a reference to his daughter's share of the inheritance. He usually left her a home on the farm as long as she remained single. A woman was not supposed to be capable of spending her own or of using other people's money. In Massachusetts, before 1840, a woman could not

* From Harriet Hanson Robinson, *Loom and Spindle or Life Among the Early Mill Girls* (New York: T.Y. Crowell, 1898), 16–22, 37–43, 51–53.

legally be treasurer of her own sewing society, unless some man were responsible for her.

The law took no cognizance of woman as a money spender. She was a ward, an appendage, a relict. Thus it happened, that if a woman did not choose to marry, or, when left a widow, to re-marry, she had no choice but to enter one of the few employments open to her, or to become a burden on the charity of some relative.

In almost every New England home could be found one or more of these women, sometimes welcome, more often unwelcome, and leading joyless, and in many instances unsatisfactory, lives. The cotton factory was a great opening to these lonely and dependent women. From a condition approaching pauperism they were at once placed above want; they could earn money and spend it as they please; and could gratify their tastes and desires without restraint, and without rendering an account to anybody. . . .

Among the older women who sought this new employment were very many lonely and dependent women, such as used to be mentioned in old wills as "encumbrances" and "relicts," and to whom a chance of earning money was indeed a new revelation. How well I remembered some of these solitary ones! As a child of eleven years, I often made fun of them—for children do not see the pathetic side of human life—and imitated them for their limp carriage and inelastic gait. I can see them now, even after sixty years, just as they looked—depressed, modest, mincing, hardly daring to look one in the face, so shy and sylvan had been their lives. But after the first pay-day came, and they felt the jingle of silver in their pockets, and had begun to feel its mercurial influence, their bowed heads were lifted, their necks seemed braced with steel, they looked you in the face, and moved blithely among their looms or frames, and walked with elastic step to and from their work. And when Sunday came, homespun was no longer their only wear; and how sedately gay in their new attire they walked to church, and how proudly they dropped their silver fourpences into the contribution-box! It seemed as if a great hope impelled them—the harbinger of the new era that was about to dawn for them and for all woman-kind.

One of the first strikes of cotton-factory operatives that ever took place in this country was that in Lowell, in October, 1836. When it was announced that the wages were to be cut down, great indignation was felt, and it was decided to strike, *en masse.* This was done. The mills were shut down, and the girls went in procession from their several corporations to the "grove" on Chapel Hill, and listened to "incendiary" speeches from early labor reformers.

One of the girls stood on a pump, and gave vent to the feelings of her companions in a neat speech, declaring that it was their duty to resist all attempts at cutting down the wages. This was the first time a woman had spoken in public in Lowell, and the event caused surprise and consternation among her audience.

Cutting down the wages was not their only grievance, nor the only cause of this strike. Hitherto the corporations had paid twenty-five cents a week towards the board of each operative, and now it was their purpose to have the girls pay the sum; and this, in addition to the cut in wages, would make a difference of at least one dollar a week. It was estimated that as many as twelve or fifteen hundred girls turned out, and walked in procession through the streets. They had neither flags nor music, but sang songs, a favorite (but rather inappropriate) one being a parody on "I won't be a nun."

> *"Oh! isn't it a pity, such a pretty girl as I—*
> *Should be sent to the factory to pine*
> *away and die?*
> *Oh! I cannot be a slave,*
> *I will not be a slave*
> *For I'm so fond of liberty*
> *That I cannot be a slave."*

My own recollection of this first strike (or "turn out" as it was called) is very vivid. I worked in a lower room, where I had heard the proposed strike fully, if not vehemently, discussed; I had been an ardent listener to what was said against this attempt at "oppression" on the part of the corporation, and naturally I took sides with the strikers. When the day came on which the girls were to turn out, those in the upper rooms started first, and so many of them left that our mill was at once shut down. Then, when the girls in my room stood irresolute, uncertain what to do, asking each other, "Would you?" or "Shall we turn out?" and not one of them having the courage to lead off, I, who began to think they would not go out, after all their talk, became impatient, and started on ahead, saying, with childish bravado, "I don't care what you do, *I* am going to turn out, whether anyone else does or not"; and I marched out, and was followed by the others.

Letters to the Voice of Industry (1846)

The following letters written to the *Voice of Industry,* a publication for factory workers, express growing dissatisfaction over Lowell's worsening conditions. Women argued that capitalist greed had undermined their well-being through management's insistence that they produce more yet receive a lower wage. What evidence do the women provide about worsening conditions? Why do they refer to themselves as part of the "toiling classes"? How do they justify their protest? What does the term "sister operatives" imply?*

March 13, 1846

The Female Department

NOTICE

The Female Labor Reform Association will meet every Tuesday evening, at 8 o'clock, at their Reading Room, 76 Central Street, to transact all business pertaining to the Association, and to devise means by which to promote the common interests of all the Laboring Classes. Also to discuss all subjects which shall come before the meeting. Every *Female* who realizes the great necessity of a *Reform* and improvement in the condition of the worthy, toiling classes, and who would wish to place woman in that elevated status intellectually and morally, which a bountiful Creator designed her to occupy in the scale of being, is most *cordially* invited to attend and give her influence on the side of *virtue* and *suffering humanity.*

Huldah J. Stone, Sec'y

April 24, 1846

To the Female Labor Reform Association In Manchester

SISTER OPERATIVES

As I am now in the "City of Spindles," out of employment, I have taken the liberty to occupy a few of your leisure moments in addressing the members of your Association, and pardon me for giving you a few brief hints of my own experiences as a factory Operative, before proceeding to make some remarks upon the glorious cause in which you are so arduously engaged. It would be useless to attempt to portray the hardships and privations which are daily endured, for all that have toiled within the factory walls, must be well acquainted with the present system of labor, which can be properly termed slavery.

I am a peasant's daughter, and my lot has been cast in the society of the humble laborer.

I was drawn from the home of my childhood at an early age, and necessity obliged me to seek employment in the Factory . . . I have heard with the deepest interest, of your flourishing Association of which you are members, and it rejoices my heart to see so many of you contending for your rights, and making efforts to elevate the condition of your fellow brethren, and raising them from their oppressed and degraded condition, and seeing rights restored which god and Nature designed them to enjoy. Do you possess the principles of Christianity? Then do not remain silent; but seek to ameliorate the condition of every fellow being. Engage laboriously and earnestly in the work, until you see your desires accomplished. Let the proud aristocrat who has tyrannized over your rights with oppressive severity, see that there is ambition and enterprise among the "spindles," and show a determination to have your plans fully executed. Use prudence and discretion in all your ways; act independently and no longer be a slave to petty tyrants, who, if they have an opportunity, will encroach upon your privileges.

Some say that "Capital will take good care of labor," but don't believe it; don't trust them. Is it not plain, that they are trying to deceive the public, by telling them that your task is easy and plead that there is no need of reform? Too many are destitute of feeling and sympathy, and it is a great pity that they are not obliged to toil one year, and then they would be glad to see the "Ten Hour Petition" brought before the Legislature. This is plain, but true language. . . .

Lowell Factory Workers (American Textile History Museum, Lowell, Mass)

Sarah Bagley, *Letter to Mrs. Martin* (March 13, 1848)

Sarah Bagley (1806–c.1884) was a leader of the organized protest movement at the Lowell Mills. She also testified to the Massachusetts legislature on behalf of the ten-hour day. At the time she wrote this letter, she had left the stressful and exhausting work of the Lowell factory and moved to Springfield, where she became a telegraph operator, the first women to have such a job. She wrote this letter shortly before the Seneca Falls Convention and the initial declaration of equal rights for women (see Chapter 7). Mrs. Martin was Angelique Martin, a member of a socialist commune in Ohio that believed in women's rights. As the letter indicates, Martin supported the effort of factory women to secure rights. As an unmarried woman, Bagley had to support not only herself, but also her elderly parents. She and other female factory workers experienced not only low wages and unremitting, toil but also the low value placed on their labor compared to that placed on work performed by men. Gender discrimination followed Bagley, and her experience as a telegraph operator provides a direct example of widening opportunity for women combined with gender inequity.

How would you describe the tone of her letter? How did Bagley describe her experience of receiving less pay than a man for performing the same work?*

Springfield, Mass March 13

Mrs. Martin

Dear Madam—You will pardon my long, delay when I tell you that your arrived in Lowell during my absence from the City to attend the sick bed of our aged father, who I am happy to inform you has, recovered. I would offer an apology for my long silence but be assured that you have given no offence in writing but I have always felt a great interest in your communications. I feel that I am deeply indebted for your generosity and hope you will let me hear often from you. My duties have been very pressing of late, and the business of my office has almost made me ungrateful to my correspondents. I left Lowell about three months since and am in charge of the magnetic telegraph in this place during the present year. I have an aged father and mother to support, to whom my duty is first and greatest. I regret to say to you, that the "Voice of Industry" is quite conservative and must be with its present conductor. The present editor thinks that a middle ground or half and half in our opinions is good policy. He thinks that truth ought to be spoken in such honeyed words that if it hits any one, it shall not affect him unfavorably. He found fault with my communications and I would not remain on the committee of publication with him for editor. He does not want a female department it would conflict with the opinions of the mushroom aristocracy that he seeks to favor, and beside it would not be dignified.

I am sick at heart when I look into the social world and see woman so willingly made a dupe to the beastly selfishness of man. A mere donkey for his use and no right, even to her own person.

I most fervently thank Heaven that I have never introduced into existence a being to suffer the privations that I have endured. For instance—the man who tended this office before me had four hundred dollars per year. I three and still the business has been on the increased all the time. But I am a woman and it is not worth so much to a company for *me* to write a letter as it would be for a man.

Well, the world is quite satisfied with the present arrangement, and we can only protest against such a state of things, and strive to arouse the minds of others to their state of servitude and dependence on the caprice and whims and selfishness of man. I feel as though my labors for the public good are nearly ended. It takes time and that is my only means. It takes money that I can ill afford. My father has had two severe fevers the last year. I am their only dependence and it has called for every shilling I could earn more than my absolute wants. Still I shall toil on with the little in my power until my task on earth is ended which will soon be.

Pardon me dear Mrs. Martin for writing so sadly. I feel so, and am only giving expression to my depressed soul.

To labor year after year and have only an ungrateful return from those you are striving to bless, is truly discouragy. But it is the way of the world, and to think a thought that has not been in stereotype for forty years is so ultra that it can be hardly countenanced in *refined* society.

Let us trust on and try to leave a little seed on earth that shall bear fruit when we shall pass away. I hope to see Father Owen this spring I am anxious to have some kind word of encouragement from him. Do write some kind word to me on the reception of

---

* Courtesy: Ohio Historical Society, Lilly Martin Spencer Collection. Transcribed: University of Massachusetts Lowell, Center for Lowell History.

this, it will be gratefully received. I will not neglect to answer you so long again. I had no time today but sit up an hour later to say to you, that you are kindly remembered.

Accept my best wishes and let me hear from you often.

yours Sarah G. Bagley

FEMALE LABOR REFORM ASSOCIATION, *Testimony Before the Massachusetts Legislature* **(1845)**

The testimony of Lowell factory women who represented the Female Labor Reform Association before the Massachusetts legislature was an early appeal for state intervention. Although they failed to achieve a ten-hour workday, their activism led to a state investigation of factory conditions. Not until the Progressive Era would female factory workers secure protective legislation.

What specific factory conditions do the women cite as detrimental to their health? Sarah Bagley played a key role in the organization. What evidence does she give about the women's health?*

The first petitioner who testified was Eliza R. Hemmingway. She had worked 2 years and 9 months in the Lowell Factories; 2 years in the Middlesex, and 9 months in the Hamilton Corporations. Her employment is weaving—works by the piece. The Hamilton Mill manufactures cotton fabrics. The Middlesex, woolen fabrics. She is now at work in the Middlesex Mills, and attends one loom. Her wages average from $16 to $23 a month exclusive of board. She complained of the hours for labor being too many, and the time for meals too limited. In the summer season, the work is commenced at 5 o'clock, a.m., and continued till 7 o'clock, p.m., with half an hour for breakfast and three-quarters of an hour for dinner. During eight months of the year, but half an hour is allowed for dinner. The air in the room she considered not to be wholesome. There were 293 small lamps and 61 large lamps lighted in the room in which she worked, when evening work is required. These lamps are also lighted sometimes in the morning. About 130 females, 11 men, and 12 children (between the ages of 11 and 14) work in the room with her. She thought the children enjoyed about as good health as children

generally do. The children work but 9 months out of 12. The other 3 months they must attend school. Thinks that there is no day when there are less than six of the females out of the mill from sickness. Has known as many as thirty. She, herself, is out quite often, on account of sickness. There was more sickness in the Summer than in Winter months; though in the Summer, lamps are not lighted. She thought there was a general desire among the females to work but ten hours, regardless of pay. Most of the girls are from the country, who work in the Lowell Mills. The average time there is about three years. She knew one girl who had worked there 14 years. Her health was poor when she left. Miss Hemmingway said her health was better where she now worked, than it was when she worked on the Hamilton Corporation.

She knew of one girl who last winter went into the mill at half past 4 o'clock, a.m., and worked til half past 7 o'clock p.m. She did so to make more money. She earned from $25 to $30 per month. There is always a large number of girls at the gate wishing to get in before the bell rings. On the Middlesex Corporation one-fourth part of the females go

---

* From "Report of the Special Committee on Hours of Labor," House Report No. 50, Massachusetts General Court Legislative Document 1845, House 1–65, 2–4.

into the mills before they are obliged to. They do this to make more wages. A large number come to Lowell and work in the mills to assist their husbands to pay for their farms. The moral character of the operatives is good. There was only one American female in the room with her who could not write her name.

Miss Sarah G. Bagley said she had worked in the Lowell Mills eight years and a half—six years and a half on the Hamilton Corporation, and two years on the Middlesex. She is a weaver, and works by the piece. She worked in the mills three years before her health began to fail. She is a native of New Hampshire, and went home six weeks during the summer. Last year she was out of the mill a third of the time. She thinks the health of the operatives is not so good as the health of females who do housework or millinery business. The chief evil, so far as health is concerned, is the shortness of time allowed for meals. The next evil is the length of time employed—not giving them time to cultivate their minds. She spoke of the high moral and intellectual character of the girls. That many were engaged as teachers in the Sunday schools. That many attended the lectures of the Lowell Institute; and she thought, if more time was allowed, that more lectures would be given and more girls attend. She thought that the girls generally were favorable to the ten hour system. She had presented a petition, same as the one before the Committee, to 132 girls, most of whom said that they would prefer to work but ten hours. In a pecuniary point of view, it would be better, as their health would be improved. They would have more time for sewing. Their intellectual, moral, and religious habits would also be benefited by the change.

Miss Bagley said, in addition to her labor in the mills, she had kept evening school during the winter months, for four years, and thought that this extra labor must have injured her health.

PRUDENCE CRANDALL, *Advertisement in* The Liberator, *"Regarding the Opening of a High School for Young Colored Ladies and Misses"* (March 2, 1833)

Prudence Crandall (1803–1890) was an abolitionist and advocate not only of emancipation but also of equal rights for African American women. In an era of expanding educational opportunity for white girls, education for free African American females was severely restricted. In defiance of community opinion and racist laws, Crandall opened a boarding school for young African American women. In 1833, she placed an advertisement in the abolitionist newspaper *The Liberator*, describing her objectives and stating that the school was for "Young Ladies and Little Misses of Color." Racial segregation was widespread in the Northeast and Midwest. In areas such as Canterbury, Connecticut, where gradual emancipation from slavery was still in progress, African Americans encountered widespread racism. Many white Northerners believed that the inclusion of African Americans in society could only occur in the context of enforced subordination and racial separation. Crandall's conflict with the community emerged over her efforts to provide a quality education and remove racial barriers. She was brought to trial on the grounds of encouraging students of color from outside the state to enter Canterbury. Trial records spelled out white residents' racial fears.

Given the intensity of race-based hostility, perhaps it is not surprising that Crandall was briefly imprisoned and put on trial for violating local laws restricting the educational access of African American students. Crandall was forced to abandon her project after repeated harassment of her students and an attempt to burn down the school building. What do you believe motivated Crandall to defy racial prejudice? How did her activism challenge male authority and the racial status quo?*

---

* Advertisement and Notice Regarding the Opening of a "High School for Young Colored Ladies and Misses," *The Liberator* (March 2, 1833).

High School for Young Colored Ladies and Misses

It is with a rush of pleasurable emotions that we insert, in another column, the advertisement of Miss P. CRANDALL, (a white lady) of Canterbury, Connecticut, for a High School for young colored Ladies and Misses. This is a seasonable auxiliary to the contemplated Manual Labor School for Colored Youth. An interview with Miss C. has satisfied us that she richly deserves the patronage and confidence of the people of color; and we doubt not they will give her both. The following extract from a letter, received by us from a highly respectable gentleman, contains all that need by said in her favor:

> Miss C. has, for a number of years, been principal of a high school for the education of Females, and has earned great credit to herself and school, as well as for her untiring zeal for the improvement of those entrusted to her charge. Miss C. possessing naturally a great share of the excellent virtue, viz. *Philanthropy,* has been provoked by the benevolent exertions of the day towards ameliorating the condition of the wretched suffering African, in this country, and to cast her mite into the treasury; and, sir, for myself, I have no doubt, knowing as I do her rare qualifications and firmness of purpose, that she would prove a most valuable auxiliary to the African cause.

In making the alteration in her School, Miss C. runs a great risk; but let her manifest inflexible courage and perseverance, and she will be sustained triumphantly. Reproach and persecution may assail her, at the commencement, but they will soon expire. Her terms are very low—the branches which she proposes to teach are various—she has a large and commodious house—and the village of Canterbury is central and pleasant.

Prudence Crandall,

Principal of the Canterbury, (Conn.) Female Boarding School,

Returns her most sincere thanks to those who have patronized her School, and would give information that on the first Monday of April next, her School will be opened for the reception of young Ladies and little Misses of color. The branches taught are as follows: —Reading, Writing, Arithmetic, English Grammar, Geography, History, Natural and Moral Philosophy, Chemistry, Astronomy, Drawing and Painting, Music on the Piano, together with the French language.

The terms, including *board, washing,* and tuition, are $25 per quarter, one half paid in advance. Books and Stationary will be furnished on the most reasonable terms.

Prudence Crandall (© Bettmann/CORBIS All Rights Reserved)

MARY LYON, *Letter to Mrs. Cooley* (Feb. 1843)

Mt. Holyoke Seminary opened in Massachusetts in 1837. Mary Lyon (1797–1849), its founder, was born and grew up on an isolated farm in rural Massachusetts. At seventeen, she began her lifelong career as a teacher and educator. Mt. Holyoke opened first as a seminary and attained college status after the Civil War. The school combined republican ideals for women's education with a heavy dose of religious devotion and instruction. The curriculum exemplified the way expanded educational and religious roles for Protestant women overlapped. Christian teachings and worship pervaded the educational experience and were designed to imbue young women with a sense of their own moral authority and Christian missionary purpose. Graduates from Mt. Holyoke traveled across the globe on conversion missions. In addition to religious instruction, academic requirements were rigorous and included chemistry as well as math and Latin. Mt. Holyoke made an education available for girls from poorer families. To keep tuition costs low, Lyon successfully solicited government support and the students performed most of the domestic labor on the campus.

Lyon wrote the following letter to the mother of a student who was either unwilling or unable to maintain the required academic standards. In what ways does the letter convey Lyon's sense of educational commitment? Why do you think Mt. Holyoke required students to learn algebra and Latin?*

The note you sent me was not given me till your niece left. I regretted it, as I should have talked with her on the subject. As she has not returned, I suppose it may be doubtful. I should advise about her returning just according to her wishes. She is not so much a lover of study as some. On this account, she is not inclined to be so happy & satisfied with what is done. I knew & advised, & planned about her studying Latin. Our scholars are of such a standing that it is very difficult for any who are late in getting through arithmetic, to go on well with Algebra, especially if they are not very good in arithmetic. Those of this description are always advised to study Latin. The classes get on in Algebra while they are going through arithmetic. Such scholars never do well in Algebra, if they are a little behind & a little discouraged. Such was the case with your niece and a few others. I thought she would have courage in Latin. Discipline is the great thing she needs, & on this account it matters but little which she studies. The

only thing in deciding the question is the clasping them to good advantage. Your niece did not study Latin long enough before she left to know at all how she should like it. We knew that she could not go on in our school without the discipline of Latin or Algebra. If we put her into Algebra, we knew she would not keep up with her class & would grow discouraged & I feared would find it very unprofitable. In Latin she could be classed with & after the first dislike was over, I had no doubt she would go on very happily. I attended to this case myself, & decided it myself, because I had so much anxiety about her doing well. I thought it best for her to study Latin. I should have done the same had she been my own child. I have a niece here, who is studying Latin instead of Algebra. If I can aid you at all, in deciding about her returning I shall be happy to do it. Give my love to your niece, if you think best, say to her, that I should like to have her do just as she pleases about returning. I think it best for young people to

---

* In the public domain.

have just as much education as they really want & no more.

Please let me hear from you when it is decided, & [crossed out words] mention whether she thinks she left any little bills unpaid, & how much money she thinks I let her have at different times.

Affectionately Yours,
Mary Lyon

CATHARINE BEECHER, *The Evils Suffered by American Women and American Children* (1846)

This document is part of Catharine Beecher's (1800–1878) campaign for the feminization of elementary school teaching. Although Beecher believed that women needed "healthful and productive labor," she did not advocate for women's rights. She limited her reform efforts to elevating women as mothers and teachers. Firmly faithful to a belief system that men and women occupied separate spheres, she argued that the factory environment was not appropriate for women.

What arguments does Beecher present that women rather than men should provide the nation with its elementary school teachers? What elements of her argument are based on gender assumptions? How would you describe her criticism of factory conditions?*

The immediate object which has called us together, is an enterprise now in progress, the design of which is *to educate destitute American children, by the agency of American women.* It is an effort which has engaged the exertions of a large number of ladies of various sects, and of all sections in our country, and one which, though commencing in a humble way and on a small scale, we believe is eventually to exert a most extensive and saving influence through the nation. . . .

Few are aware of the deplorable destitution of our country in regard to the education of the rising generation, or of the long train of wrongs and sufferings endured by multitudes of young children from this neglect.

The last twelve years I have resided chiefly in the West, and my attention has been directed to the various interests of education. In five of the largest western states I have spent from several weeks to several months—I have traveled extensively and have corresponded or conversed with well-informed gentlemen and ladies on this subject in most of the western states. And I now have materials for presenting the real situation of vast multitudes of American children, which would "cause the ear that heareth it to tingle." But I dare not do it. It would be so revolting—so disgraceful—so heartrending—so incredible—that in the first place, I should not be believed; and in the next place such an outcry of odium and indignation would be aroused, as would impede efforts to remedy the evil. The only thing I can safely do is to present some statistics, which cannot be disputed, because they are obtained from *official documents,* submitted by civil officers to our national or state legislatures. Look then at the census, and by its data we shall find that *now* there are nearly *a million* adults who cannot read and write, and more than *two million* children utterly illiterate, and entirely

---

* From Catharine Beecher, *The Evils Suffered by American Women and American Children: The Causes and the Remedy* (New York: Harper & Brothers, 1846), 3, 5–12.

without schools. Look at individual states, and we shall find Ohio and Kentucky, the two best supplied of our western states, demanding *five thousand* teachers each, to supply them in the same ratio as Massachusetts is supplied. *Ten thousand* teachers are now needed in Ohio and Kentucky alone, to furnish schools for more than two hundred thousand children, who otherwise must grow up in utter ignorance. . . .

Let us now turn to another class of our countrywomen—the *female operatives* in our shops and mills. Unfortunately, this subject cannot be freely discussed without danger of collision with the vast pecuniary and party interests connected with it. I therefore shall simply *state facts,* without expressing the impressions of my own mind.

Last year, I spent several days in Lowell, for the sole purpose of investigating this subject. I conversed with agents, overseers, clergymen, physicians, editors, ladies resident in the place, and a large number of the operatives themselves. All seem disposed to present the most favorable side of the picture; and nothing unfavorable was said except as drawn forth by my questions. . . .

Let me now present the facts I learned by observation or inquiry on the spot. I was there in mid-winter, and every morning I was wakened at *five,* by the bells calling to labor. The time allowed for dressing and breakfast was so short, as many told me, that both were performed hurriedly, and then work at the mills was begun by lamp-light, and proceeded without remission till twelve, and chiefly in the standing position. Then half an hour only allowed for dinner, from which the time for going and returning was deducted. Then back to the mills, to work till seven o'clock, the last part of the time by lamplight. Then returning, washing, dressing, and supper occupied another hour. Thus ten hours only remained for recreation and sleep. Now eight hours' sleep is required for laborers, and none in our country are employed in labor more hours than the female operatives in mills. Deduct eight hours for sleep and only *two hours* remain for shopping, mending, making, recreation, social intercourse, and *breathing the pure air.* For it must be remembered that all the hours of labor are spent in rooms where lamps, together with from forty to eighty persons, are exhausting the healthful principle of the air, where the temperature, both summer and winter, on account of the work, must be kept at $70\frac{1}{4}$ and in some rooms at $80\frac{1}{4}$, and where the air is loaded with particles of cotton thrown from thousands of cards, spindles, and looms. . . .

Now, without expressing any opinion as to the influence, on health and morals, of taking women away from domestic habits and pursuits, to labor with men in shops and mills, I simply ask if it would not be *better* to put the thousands of men who are keeping school for young children into the mills, and employ the women to train the children? . . .

Another cause of depression to our sex is found in the fact that there is no profession for women of education and high position which, like law, medicine, and theology, opens the way to competence, influence and honor, and presents motives for exertion. Woman ought never to be led to married life except under the promptings of pure affection. To marry for an establishment, a position, or for something to do, is a deplorable wrong. But how many women, for want of a high and honorable profession to engage their time, are led to this melancholy course. This is not so because Providence has not provided an ample place for such a profession for woman, but because custom or prejudice, or a low estimate of its honorable character, prevents her from entering it. The educating of children, that is the true and noble profession of a woman—that is what is worthy of the noblest powers and affections of the noblest minds.

SARAH JOSEPHA HALE, Godey's Lady's Book, *Editor's Table, Copy of Petition sent to Congress in 1855* (Jan. 1856)

As editor of *Godey's Lady's Book*, one of the nation's most popular women's magazines, Sarah Josepha Hale (1788–1879) upheld educational opportunity for girls and supported elementary school teaching as an employment opportunity for young unmarried women. Widowed at an early age with young children to support, Hale had to earn her own living. Although not an advocate for suffrage or gender equality, she became a proponent of the need for women's expanded economic opportunity within the gendered boundaries of what domestic advocates promoted as a woman's sphere.

Hale shared with the readers of *Godey's* a copy of the petition she had sent to Congress, enumerating the reasons why government should support schools for women to become teachers. In what ways did her advocacy for widening work opportunities for women fall within the parameters of gendered ideals? How did her petition complement the objectives of Catharine Beecher? Why did she stress the West as the location for new schools?*

Editors' Table

This *heart service* in the cause of humanity belongs naturally to women. We cannot take the sword to defend the right; we must aid by holier means. There are so many opportunities in our country both of improvement and of employment that we are in danger of forgetting the oppressions of our sex in the Old World. England we have always been in the habit of considering the bulwark of law and of freedom through the law in Europe; the injustice and cruelties which the law in England sanctions respecting women have never been sufficiently considered by us. We have lately had our attention called to this subject; and, partly to illustrate the blessings we American women enjoy under our better system of laws and usages, and partly to awaken public attention to the still existing defects in our own institutions, we show a glimpse of married life in England; and, while we commiserate the sufferings of our sister women on the other side of the Atlantic, we give a warmer grasp of friendship to the hands that are reaching out to us on all sides, and from every section of the Union, as we wish each household, where our influence enters a happy New Year! a *heart* happy New Year!

What Is Needed in America

Thanks to the spirit of Christian freedom, women in our land are favored above the sex in any other nation. The absurd and degrading customs or usages of the common law, and the partial and, therefore, unjust statutes of kings, brought by our forefathers from England, are fast passing away, or being rendered nugatory by new enactments, more in accordance with reason and righteousness. The Homestead laws, and the security given that the property of a married woman shall remain in her own possession, are great safeguards of domestic comfort. The efforts made to open new channels of industry and profitable professions for those women who have to support themselves are deserving of much praise; but one great act of public justice yet remains undone. Government, national or State, has never yet provided suitably for the education of women. Girls, as well as boys, have the advantages of the free school system; but no public provision has been made, no college or university endowed where young women may have similar advantages of instruction now open to young men in every State of the Union. True, there are very many private institutions devoted to female

---

* Transcribed from the original, Godey's Lady's Book, July 1855, pp. 29, 32 by Hope Greenberg. 11/21/95.

education; but these are defective for the want of a higher model than private enterprise has yet given. Of course, the better woman is educated the higher she will be estimated, and the more careful will legislators be to frame laws just and equitable which are to guard her happiness and protect her rights; men will thus improve their own *hearts* and elevate their views. The standard of woman is the moral thermometer of the nation.

Holding these sentiments, our "Book" has never swerved from its straight forward course of aiding women to improve themselves, while it has aimed to arouse public sentiment to help onward this improvement. For this, we give patterns and directions for feminine employment, we show the benefits of female education, and for this we have *twice* brought before congress our petition for aid; and now we come a *third* time, intending to persevere till some noble champion arises to advocate the cause and win the victory:—

Memorial

To the Honourable Senate and House of Representatives in Congress assembled.

Whereas, there are now more than *two millions* of children in our country destitute of the opportunity of education, demanding *sixty thousand teachers* to supply them at the same ratio as is common in our best educated sections, your memorialists beg to call your attention to these considerations:—

1. That, while the great West, California, and the wide ocean invite young men to wealth and adventure, and while the labors of the school-room offer so little recompense or honor, the sixty thousand teachers needed cannot be obtained from their ranks; and, therefore, the young women of our country must become teachers of the common schools, or these must be given up.

2. That the reports of common school education show that women are the *best*

teachers, and that in those States where education is most prosperous the average of female teachers to that of the other sex is *as five* to *one.*

3. That while, as a general rule, women are not expected to support families, nor to pay from their earnings to support the State, they can afford to teach for a smaller compensation than men; and, therefore, funds bestowed to educate female teachers gratuitously will in the end prove a measure of *economy,* and at the same time will tend to render education more universal and more elevated by securing the best class of teachers at a moderate expense.

4. That those most willing to teach are chiefly found in the industrial class, which as yet has received few favors from National or State Legislatures.

5. That providing for such gratuitous advantages for women to act as educators will secure a vast number of well-educated teachers, not by instituting a class of *celibates,* but by employing the unoccupied energies of thousands of young women from their school-days to the period of marriage, while, at the same time, they will thus be qualifying themselves for the most arduous duties of their future domestic relations.

In view of these considerations, your memorialists petition that THREE OR FOUR MILLIONS OF ACRES OF THE PUBLIC NATIONAL DOMAINS be set apart to endow at least one *Normal School* in every State for the gratuitous educations of female teachers. These institutions could be modelled and managed in each State to suit the wishes of its inhabitants; and young ladies of every section would be trained as instructors for children in their own vicinity; this would be found of immense advantage in the States where schools have hitherto been neglected.

While such vast portions of the national domains are devoted to national aggrandizements or physical advantages, we humbly petition that a moderate share may be conferred to benefit the daughters of our Republic, and thus at the same time to provide educators for two millions of its most neglected children.

SARAH JOSEPHA HALE, *Editor's Table, Twelve Reasons Why Women Should Receive a Medical Education* (1857)

In the following document, Hale provided twelve reasons for providing medical education to young women. Several reasons dealt directly with the role of women as family caregivers. Other reasons supported women moving beyond their own family and extending medical care to members of their own sex and to children. At a time when women's economic opportunities were limited, Hale stressed the significance of female doctors treating women too modest to seek help from male medical practitioners. It is interesting to note how Hale creates a more expansive definition of women's roles. At no point does she pursue a feminist or equal rights argument for gender equality. Note how she interweaves foreign missionary objectives and Christianity as particular beneficiaries of women's expanded medical role. Frances Willard would use similar arguments in linking female virtue to the suffrage cause (Chapter 10). In the name of women's allegedly feminine and domestic attributes, both Beecher and Hale, and later Willard, argued for expanded roles. Hale's suggestion of female doctors won little support in an era when almost all medical colleges were united in their rejection of women. Civil War nurses would serve as the catalyst for opening the field of nursing, but barriers remained in place for women who wanted to become doctors long after the Civil War.

What are the specific arguments Hale provides in advocating for medical education for women? In what ways might this argument still have relevance today?*

TWELVE REASONS why more attention should be given to the more general diffusion of physiological and hygienic knowledge among the present and prospective mothers of our country; and why ladies should be educated for the practice of medicine among their own sex and children:—

1. Because to the mother is consigned the physical, as well as the moral training of infancy, childhood, and youth; hence she becomes the natural guardian of the health of the household.

2. Because the education of woman is not generally conducted with regard to her natural position as wife and mother.

3. Because to a want of correct information in reference to the laws of life and health may much the greater part of infantile suffering and early mortality be attributed.

4. Because the mother, when properly instructed, may early detect the approach of serious or perhaps fatal diseases and, by a judicious interference, avert, or so modify the threatened attack, as to render it harmless, and shorten its duration.

5. Because, by the observance of the laws of health, of which mothers, unfortunately, seldom have an expansive and philosophical comprehension, a corresponding degree of health and physical development would be attained by their offspring.

6. Because nowhere so the beauty and excellence of the feminine character stand out more prominently than in the sick-room.

---

* Editor's Table, *Godey's Lady's Book,* Jan. 1856. In the public domain.

7. Because to those philanthropic, Christian ladies, whose sense of duty calls them to labor in the cause of foreign missions, a medical education will be of inestimable value. As healers of the sick, they can be admitted to the harems of the east, which are inaccessible to the Christian *man;* and, while they administer to the physical necessities of the sick, a most fitting opportunity will be afforded for administering the consolations of our holy religion; and through their own women can the light of Gospel truths be made to shine upon the benighted minds of the other sex. A missionary woman, thus qualified, combines two essential elements of usefulness and success; she goes forth both a moral and religious instructor, and a scientific physician.

8. Because, from her quickness of perception, activity of mind, readiness to receive instructions, and the facility with which she applies what she learns to the practical purposes of life, woman is preeminently qualified to study the healing art to advantage and effect.

9. Because, from the very intuitions of her sex, her natural kindness and sympathy, her peculiar adaptation to the necessities of the sick, her patience, perseverance, and endurance in scenes of affliction, she is admirably suited to the *practice* of medicine, particularly in its more delicate departments.

10. Because she has already *demonstrated,* by her eminent success in practicing the healing-art in these departments, her peculiar fitness for this highly important vocation.

11. Because it opens an appropriate avenue for employment both honorable and profitable for women.

12. Because thoroughly educated female physicians can relieve and remove sufferings of a vast and increasing number of the most delicate and refined of their own sex, many of whom, from an instinctive sense of propriety, too often endure their tortures even unto death, rather than submit to the necessary treatment by the male physician.

BETSY COWLES, *Report on Labor, Proceedings of the Woman's Rights Convention, Akron, Ohio* (1851)

During the 1850s, middle-class women reformers protested against the abusive conditions that most women workers confronted. They crossed class lines in their empathetic understanding of the limited options and impoverished lives of most of America's working women. Even teaching, a recently opened field for women, displayed persistent gender inequity. Betsy Cowles (1810–1876), a teacher, abolitionist, and suffrage advocate, compiled the following *Report on Labor* for a Woman's Rights Conference held in 1851 in Akron, Ohio. Cowles's labor reform objectives express the equal rights rationale that women should have the same employment opportunities as men. Her report documents more than low pay, long hours, and poor working conditions. She also demonstrates the lack of gender equity that prevailed throughout the labor market.

What examples does Cowles cite of women being unfairly treated? What factors does she believe account for the disparate gender-based pay scale? What evidence does she provide that the lowest paid women workers barely made enough to survive?*

---

* From Betsy Cowles, "Report on Labor" from *The Proceedings of the Woman's Rights Convention,* Akron, Ohio, May 28–29, 1851.

"The rights of woman"—what are they?
"The right to labor and to pray;
"The right to watch while others sleep.
"The right to tread the path of patience
under wrong.
"Such are woman's rights."

That the right to suffer and to labor has been fully granted to woman, no person whose vision is not bounded by the limits of his or her own domestic circle, town or county, will attempt to deny. That this right has been given to woman, history fully affirms. No nation in the past has stood too high or too low in the scale of civilization, to deny to woman the right to labor. The present as well as the past, extends to her the same code of rights, enough to satisfy every wish, every demand.

Turn our eyes wherever we may, and we find this assertion verified in the condition of woman in all nations. . . .

Could we to-day but look upon the patient plier of the needle, who works on for eighteen or twenty hours of the twenty-four; could the metropolis of that nation, which in the scale of civilization and christianity claims to look down upon all other nations, but pour forth in one congregated mass its 30,000 seamstresses, with their toil-worn visages; could the metropolis of our own enlightened nation join her twenty or forty thousand; these, by their haggard countenances, tell us, in language unmistakable, that "the right to watch while others sleep" is truly woman's.

But it may be said, what have we to do with the laboring women of Europe and other parts of the world? In reply to this, acknowledging as we do the unity of the human family,— "the world is our country"—neither boundaries or distance can isolate individuals or communities. The same causes which have produced the suffering and degradation of laboring classes in the old world, will produce—have already produced—like results in the new. . . .

But leaving Europe and coming to the land most highly favored under heaven, where as yet comparatively the hand of oppression rests lightly (save on the doomed race,) we find women engaged in needle-work, braiding straw, making artificial flowers, book-folding; in one department of shoe-making; millinery; huckstering, domestic service; only one of which, as will be seen, affords more than a mere pittance, barely sufficient to support life. The following statistics were originally published in the *New York Tribune:*

First Seamstresses: There are more than 10,000 who exist on what they can earn by the needle. The following are the prices for which they are compelled to work, such as are paid by the large depots for clothing in Chatham street and elsewhere: . . .

By working from fifteen to eighteen hours a day, these employed in these establishments can earn from 75¢ to $1.50 a week.

A large majority of these women are American born, many of whom have once been in comfortable and even in affluent circumstances, and have been reduced, by the death or bankruptcy of husbands and relatives, and other causes, to such straits. Others are the widows of mechanics and poor men, and have children, aged mothers and fathers, to support by their needle.

These women generally "keep house," that is, they generally rent a room in the upper story of some poor, ill-constructed, unventilated house, in a filthy street, breathing a most sickly and deadly atmosphere, which deposits seeds of debility and disease with every inspiration.

For these rooms the tenants never pay less than three to four and a half dollars per month, and pay they must and do. Some of the very worst single garrets, perhaps lighted by a single hole in the roof, rent as low as two dollars a month. Of course, every cent of their earnings are exhausted every week, and when winter comes, they have nothing with which to add to their scanty wardrobe, and nothing with which to purchase an ounce of fuel. Their work, too, at this season, is frequently cut off—leaving no resource but the alms-house or a pauper ticket for bread and coal.

The straw braiders, a large and ill-paid class of working females, begin work at seven in the morning, and continue until seven in the evening, with no intermission save to swallow a hasty morsel. They earn when in full employ, from $2 to $2.50 a week. Out of this, they pay for board and washing; and for the poorest accommodations must pay from $1.50 to $2.00 a week.

The artificial flower makers present a greater variety. Girls who have served a five years' apprenticeship can earn $3.50 a week. But most of the work is done by young girls who are serving apprenticeships, or who are paid 75¢ a week for their labor. As soon as they acquire skill sufficient to demand higher wages, they are pushed off and fresh ones obtained. Many a five-dollar wreath has been wrought into beauty by these little fingers, for perhaps 25 or 50 cents. There are about 2,000 engaged in this department in New York.

There are about 2,000 cap makers, who on an average earn about two shillings a day, although there are many who do not earn 18 cents a day. They are thrust into a dark room on an upper story, thirty or forty together, and work from sunrise to sundown. . . . Seventy-five years ago, it was quite if not entirely out of woman's sphere to engage professionally in teaching. Time, in effecting his magic changes, has wrought a wonderful revolution, and now "it is her *peculiar* province to teach, for this she seems expressly adapted by nature;" so omnipotent is public sentiment.

There are now in the State of Ohio, according to statistics obtained in 1849, 4,374 female teachers, receiving upon an average $21.49 a year, or in proportion of half as much as is paid to the same number of male teachers.

Report from Ashtabula county for the year 1850, gives the average wages of teachers per month—

- Of Males, . . . $16.50
- Females, . . . 6.85

Of the teachers employed in that county, two-thirds are females. The reason given for this, is that well qualified females can be obtained at half the expense necessary to obtain male teachers with equal qualifications, while the schools can be managed as well by the former as by the latter.

The sum paid to the principals of public schools in Cincinnati is—

- Males, per month, . . . $65.00
- To Females, do 35.00
- To Male Assistants, from . . . $35 to 45.00
- Female . . . 16 to 18.00
- And in one or two instances, . . . 25.00

In the city of Boston, the three grades of male teachers receive—

- Principal, . . . $15.00
- First Assistant, . . . 12.00
- Second do 8.00
- Females, . . . 3.00

In Connecticut, the average rate paid—

- Male teachers per month in summer, . . . $20.00
- DO. DO. DO. IN WINTER, . . . 17.50
- Female . . . 8.69
- In summer, . . . 6.50

This is the average and the difference in the wages, and may be considered a fair specimen of the East and the West.

CHAPTER 4

From Moral Reform to Free Love and Voluntary Motherhood:
Issues of Vulnerability and Sexual Agency

Between the early years of the republic and the opening decades of the nineteenth century, the civic virtue associated with the construct of republican motherhood became intertwined with Protestant religious values and benevolence. Women working within the Christian framework of moral reform adhered to gender beliefs that endowed white, Protestant, middle-class women with purity, piety, and moral authority. Controlling and changing male behavior, especially with reference to sex and drinking, shaped reform objectives, which also promoted protection for allegedly vulnerable women. In an era of limited women's rights and widespread gender inequality, reformers believed that vulnerable women required protection from the predatory behavior of men.

Gender norms based on class and race molded the behavior of white, Protestant, middle-class women and distanced them from poor white and African American women whose life experiences were vastly different. Gender norms depicted men as sexually dominant and their sexuality contrasted with that of allegedly pure, passionless, white women. Dichotomized views of male and female sexuality resulted in dual standards for judging sexual conduct and excused men for behavior that would ruin the reputations if not the lives of "respectable" women. The passionless construction of white female sexuality also reinforced submission and provided a rationale for men to pursue sex outside of marriage with women who were considered neither respectable nor pure. Yet, even within the privileged white, middle class, women confronted issues of sexual vulnerability, including coercive sex with their husbands, unwanted pregnancies, and venereal disease. Sex as danger rather than pleasure guided the mainstream discourse. Only the small group of female advocates for free love viewed sex from the perspective of pleasure.

Imbued with religious fervor and a desire to eradicate perceived immoral behavior, by the 1830s, middle-class white women began to organize moral reform societies, such as the New York City Female Moral Reform Society. Part of the reformers' anxiety over sexuality centered on the increasing growth of prostitution, as well as the developing working-class, urban youth culture. Addressing "Licentious Men," the New York City Moral Reform Society described its mission as a "terror to evil doers."

By the 1840s, female reform societies had spread to rural towns and villages mainly in the Northeast and Midwest. In addition to rescuing prostitutes, a particular objective of reformers was to hold "licentious" men accountable for the seduction and abandonment of young women. The image of seduced women as victims bolstered arguments for the need to rescue these "fallen" women and reinforced the stereotype of female weakness. Such cautionary stories as "Died in Jaffrey" sought to frighten young women from having premarital sex and also to publicize male sexual irresponsibility. The major objective was to hold men morally and socially accountable for predatory sexual behavior and to elevate them to the single standard of sexual purity that existed for respectable women.

Moral reformers connected seduction and abandonment as central causes of prostitution. They also believed that prostitution could be controlled only if male clients as well as prostitutes were held accountable. Over time, reformers shifted their argument about why women became prostitutes from moral weakness to economic necessity, a perspective expressed by women's rights advocate Caroline Healy Dall. Dall collected data on the near-starvation wages and lack of employment that confronted working-class women who drifted into prostitution as a means of survival. Dr. William Sanger's official investigation of prostitution in New York City revealed that some women gave "inclination" as their reason for becoming prostitutes. But in most cases, women cited poverty and the lack of alternative employment as the reasons that drove them into prostitution. The victim perspective made it difficult for reformers to see the exercise of agency as an explanation of why some women became prostitutes.

Antebellum moral reformers generally did not support women's rights. This was not the case after the Civil War. In the name of home protection, Frances Willard, the president of the Women's Christian Temperance Union tied together issues of temperance, social purity, and suffrage. Willard continued the public crusade to make men accountable for what women deemed to be morally irresponsible behavior (See Chapter 10). Efforts to control the sexual behavior of men complemented the growing concern of many wives in limiting the number of pregnancies. For example, Lucy Stone, in a letter to her friend and sister in-law Antoinette Brown Blackwell, and Paulina Wright, in a letter to the Woman's Rights Conference in Akron, Ohio, in 1851, disagreed with the assumption that wives had to submit to their husband's sexual desires. Stone considered the right of the wife to say no to sex to be the foundation for all other rights. She was not alone in her views. At a time when many women still believed that a husband's right to his wife's body was total, some women began to challenge the cultural assumption of masculine sexual entitlement. Moreover, an unknown number of women lived outside the norms of heterosexual marriage. A significant number of women avoided marriage and formed companionate and/or sexual relationships with other women, some that lasted a lifetime.

Protecting wives from abusive husbands also motivated many female temperance advocates. At the Whole World Temperance Convention held in New York City in 1853, Antoinette Brown Blackwell emphasized that temperance was a women's rights issue in terms of the damaging consequences of male drunkenness for wives and children. Within the temperance movement, men repeatedly tried to silence any arguments for linking temperance to women's rights and also tried to limit women to subordinate roles.

Women's rights advocates such as Elizabeth Cady Stanton and Susan B. Anthony carried the rights argument and its link to temperance even further. They promoted liberalizing divorce laws to empower women to end marriages to abusive, drunken husbands. Liberalizing divorce laws was part of Stanton's wider critique of marriage as an institution that she claimed promoted female dependence and facilitated male abuse. Few women agreed with her radical stance.

Health reform and free-love advocates, such as Mary Gove and Victoria Woodhull, emphasized the need for women to have control over their own bodies. Gove gave lectures about female anatomy, vitally important information if women were to control reproduction. Woodhull gained notoriety with her public proclamation that women had the right to choose their sexual partners and have sex without procreation. As a free-love advocate, she opposed the institution of marriage and stressed that loving relationships rather than a marriage contract should determine sexual intimacy. The free-love critique of conventional marriage described it as a corrupt bargain in which the wife trades the right to her body for a lifetime of her husband's economic support. Some argued that conventional marriage paralleled the prostitute's exchange of sex for cash. With their discussion of sexual pleasure as well as support for women's freedom to choose sexual relationships outside of marriage, free-love advocates gained notoriety rather than public approval. The mainstream movement for women's sexual rights remained within the reproductive constraints of what became known as "voluntary motherhood."

The rate of premarital sexual activity was high during the closing years of the eighteenth century, but it then declined, as did the birthrate within marriage. Historians believe that falling birthrates among married women occurred as a result of their gaining greater control over when and whether they would become pregnant. Frequent pregnancies took a toll on women's health, and medical complications resulting from childbirth could last a lifetime. Some married women, such as the unnamed woman in the document *The Unwelcome Child,* led lives of desperation because they found unplanned pregnancies and unwanted children intolerable. Post–Civil War advertisements for contraception and abortion indicate growing demand and availability. Congressional legislation passed in 1873, known as the Comstock Law, outlawed material classified as obscene from being sent through the U.S. mail. This included contraceptive information, advertisements, or products. Different states also passed similar restrictive legislation. For decades, individual states and the federal government attempted to control female sexuality and reproductive choice. Not until 1965 did the Supreme Court overturn the last vestiges of state control over contraception. In the twentieth century, women's struggle for contraceptive access and reproductive rights would have major significance. However, at this point in the discourse a woman's right to reproductive control remained muted. Women would not publicly defend the right to contraception even if they privately used or supported its use. Women's rights advocates, including Harriot Stanton Blatch and Winnifred Harper Cooley, advocated voluntary motherhood but avoided public discussion of contraception. The Comstock Law reinforced public reticence. The social construction of motherhood as central to female identity also made it difficult for some nineteenth-century women to dissolve the link between having sex and becoming a mother. Family limitation meant marital restraint. Some feared contraception would interfere with their choice for restraint. Not until the twentieth century would women who supported contraception openly address female sexuality in terms of reproductive freedom and sexual pleasure.

FEMALE MORAL REFORM SOCIETY, NEW YORK CITY, Excerpt from *First Annual Report: "Licentious Men"* (1835)

After the founding of the Female Moral Reform Society in New York City in 1834, women mobilized not only to protect female sexual purity and rescue "fallen women," they were equally intent upon punishing men for their sexual misconduct. What particularly angered the reformers was the double standard of sexual conduct that prescribed sexual purity for women but forgave men for sexual transgressions. The excerpt that follows, "Licentious Men," expresses the reformers' moral outrage and determination to end what they perceived to be the predatory sexual behavior of men. Seeking to sway public opinion about the need for more coercive control over male sexuality outside of marriage, the women initiated a major petition campaign in New York State, and by 1848 the state legislature passed anti-seduction legislation. Previously, in 1845, Massachusetts had passed anti-abduction legislation to protect women. Female moral reform societies sprung up in both urban and rural areas in New England, New York, Pennsylvania, and Ohio.

How did the moral reformers characterize prostitution? What arguments do the reformers make in their effort to improve male sexual conduct?*

Licentious Men

One great object to be effected in the work of Moral Reform is, the formation of a public sentiment, that will place the licentious *man* on a level with the licentious woman. The crime is as great, and we venture to say in a majority of cases greater, in the male than in the female. We see no reason why *either* should be exempt from merited disgrace. When men are guilty of this sin, let them lose their character as women do, and much of this abominable vice would be done away at once. This change in public sentiment we humbly conceive it is in the power of virtuous females to effect; and the way to effect it is, to *induce virtuous females to look down on licentious men as virtuous men now look down on licentious women.* Let virtuous women band together to keep such men at a distance and the work is done. Until they will do this, they must expect to see their daughters ruined and covered with infamy, while the base villain who has done this work, is regarded as a *gentleman,* received into respectable society, and thus encouraged to go on in his deeds of villainy. We have heard of one young man who penned down the names of thirteen young ladies, whom he deliberately determined to

seduce in succession. He succeeded with the first, and then if he had lost his character in estimation of the virtuous twelve, his powers to harm them would have been at an end. But while the victim of his treachery would be spurned by the virtuous of her sex, they would receive and caress her betrayer as a gentleman. O, if woman would stand for her rights, and insist upon it that the licentious man should be put down on a level with his guilty paramour, what good to the human race and to the cause of Christ would be the result? Daughters of America, why not let this good work begin with you? Why not marshal yourselves in bands, and become a terror to evil doers? Already have more than 1444 virtuous females pledged themselves that they will not associate with licentious men. Let this number be increased so that it will include every virtuous female in the land, and then licentious men can associate only with their kind. If our efforts can be instrumental of awakening an interest in the minds of the virtuous daughters of America on this subject, and of inducing them to array their influence against a vice so destructive to the happiness of their sex as licentiousness, we shall feel that we have done a great and noble work.

---

* In the public domain.

Warning to the Country

The Board have ascertained that there are annually brought into the larger cities from the country, a large number of young women under various pretences, but really for the purpose of supplying the market of sin. Some are brought in under the promise of marriage; and here, friendless and destitute, their seducers abandon them to infamy to hide their own guilt. Others, in coming to the city, are committed by their anxious mothers, to some *gentleman* for protection, but who gives them the protection the vulture does the dove. And others on visits to their friends are drawn into *her* doors, whose "house is the way to hell, going down to the chambers of death." Our operations are bringing to light more and more of the secrets of this abominable traffic, carried on in all its departments almost as regular as the trade in dry goods. To every anxious mother and every virtuous daughter throughout the land, we would raise the loud note of alarm, and cry, Beware of unprincipled men in the garb of *gentlemen*. If the Advocate of Moral Reform can be made subservient to this warning, and thus save the exposed from being ensnared in an evil time, we shall feel that it is not published in vain. . . .

Constitution of the New York Female Moral Reform Society

Whereas, The sin of licentiousness has made fearful havoc in the world, "corrupting all flesh," drowning souls in perdition, and exposing us to the vengeance of a holy God, whose law in this respect has been trampled on almost universally, not only by actual transgression, but by the tacit consent of the virtuous, and by the almost perfect silence of those whom He has commanded to "cry aloud and spare not;"

And whereas, It is the duty of the virtuous to use every consistent moral means to save our country from utter destruction: We do, therefore, form ourselves into a Society for this object, to be governed by the following

Constitution

ARTICLE I   This Society shall be called "THE NEW-YORK FEMALE MORAL REFORM SOCIETY," auxiliary to the "American Society for Promoting the Observance of the Seventh Commandment."

ARTICLE II   This Society shall have for its object the prevention of licentiousness, by diffusing light in regard to the existence and great extent of this sin, by showing its fearfully immoral and soul-destroying influence; by pointing out the numberless lures and arts practiced by the unprincipled destroyer, to seduce and ruin the unsuspecting; by excluding from social intercourse with us, all persons of both sexes who are known to be of licentious habits; and by such other means as the Society shall from time to time deem expedient.

IMPORTANT LECTURES TO FEMALES (1839)

Female moral reformers embraced a wide agenda that included health reform. The following document is an excerpt from an editorial that appeared in the paper *Advocate of Moral Reform,* calling women's attention to a series of lectures by Mary Gove. An important health reformer, Gove gave women some initial understanding of the anatomy and functioning of their bodies. Health advocates such as Gove included dress reform among their objectives and held the popular beauty standards of the era as responsible for female health problems. What beauty standards does the document cite as particularly damaging to women's health? What is meant by the phrase "the long night of ignorance, and consequent abuse, is, we hope, passing away"?*

---

* From "Important Lectures to Females," Editorial, *Advocate of Moral Reform,* March 1, 1839, 44.

Mrs. M.S. Gove, formerly of Lynn, Mass., is now in this city, delivering a course of lectures to women on anatomy and physiology, or the structure and functions of the human body. These are subjects of which our sex have been, with very few exceptions, profoundly ignorant; and yet the want of knowledge has subjected us to ten thousand evils, and led to ten thousand fatal errors. From utter ignorance of the laws which govern the animal economy, they have been constantly transgressed; and when sickness and suffering ensued as the inevitable consequences, they were considered as a visitation of God, which must be patiently borne until his hand was removed. True it is, that as the effect our own wrong-doing, our sufferings should be patiently borne; but we ought nevertheless to seek to find out the cause, and apply a remedy. This is done most admirably by Mrs. Gove, in her lectures, and in a manner so plain, and simple, and philosophical that the youngest may be interested, while the wisest must gain additional instruction. By the disinterested kindness of some who stand at the head of the medical profession, she has been furnished with uncommon facilities for acquiring all necessary information, and the testimonials voluntarily given by these physicians to her character as a woman, and a thoroughly scientific lecturer, are ample and flattering. We have attended her course thus far and are prepared to express our unqualified approbation of the lectures, so far as we have heard them. Our only regret is, that but a few hundreds should hear what is so essential to the health and comfort of all, both parents and children. The fact cannot be denied, that our race is greatly degenerating from the ancient standard of health and vigor, and such a thing as a healthy, robust young person, particularly young lady, is hardly to be found. A pale face, wisp-like waist, and languid air, which speak of enduring, not of enjoying existence, are considered almost essential characteristics of elegance and beauty. Against all this destructive system of corsets, improper food, and enervating habits, Mrs. Gove wages war—but it is not a war of words, but of facts and principles demonstrated with the clearness and accuracy of a problem in mathematics. No one is required to believe a thing on her ipse dixit, but the plain story is told of our structure and conformation as we came from the hands of our Maker, and reason, common sense, and religious feeling left to do their own work. For ourself, we are truly thankful for the valuable knowledge already acquired, brought home as it has been to our own heart and soul, and we fervently wish all our readers could share the benefit. A series of articles on physiology, with practical deductions, will, we trust, be prepared for the Advocate, and we bespeak the serious and candid attention of every woman to their contents. Beings so fearfully and wonderfully made, ought surely to know something more about themselves than the mere fact that they are here, though for what purpose many seem never to have inquired. The long night of ignorance, and consequent abuse, is, we hope, passing away, and a bright day beginning to dawn upon us.

Those who wish to become acquainted with the first principles of anatomy and physiology, will find the little work published by Dr. Alcott, entitled "The House I live in," a very useful work. It is published by G.W. Light, Cornhill, Boston, and Fulton-street, New York.

Mary Gove Nichols (Library Company of Philadelphia)

FRIEND OF VIRTUE, *Died in Jaffrey, N.H., Aged 27* (1841)

In an effort to give women greater protection from male abuse, women moral reformers embarked on a crusade to change male behavior. They publicized the names of men who had sex with prostitutes, condemned male drunkenness, and sought to make men morally and even legally accountable for the seduction of "innocent" women.

The moral reform activist who wrote the following article for the *Friend of Virtue* describes the disgrace and grim punishment suffered by a woman who transgressed sexual norms for female respectability. The woman who died in Jaffrey, a small community in southern New Hampshire, goes to an "untimely and dishonoured grave." Although the dead woman is considered the "author of her own ruin," the document also attempts to expose and dishonor the man. In what ways is the woman portrayed but as a victim of male lust? How does the document express both pity for the woman as victim as well as moral outrage against her behavior?*

For the Friend of Virtue.
*"I could a tale unfold whose lightest word
Would harrow up thy soul."*

Died in Jaffrey, N.H. May 8, M. A. L. Aged 27.

When an event occurs, which, like the wild tornado, carries consternation and dismay in its progress, it is found exceedingly difficult to present in such a manner as that as deep and as salutary an impression be made upon the public as when the event took place. But the circumstances attending the death of Miss L. were so appalling, sending through the heart of the community a thrill of horror and detestation against the author of her destruction, that we have been induced to give a brief statement of facts, with the hope, at least, that the youthful reader of the Friend of Virtue will be admonished, and the natural guardians of our children would be incited to greater faithfulness in the training of their interesting charge.

Some nine or ten years ago, during a season of a revival of religion, enjoyed in this place, Miss L. professed to have found an interest in the Redeemer, and united with the church of Christ. The declaration of her pastor, with that of those best acquainted, was that "she appeared well."

The few years succeeding this event that she remained in town, she maintained a credible profession of religion. In character she was exceedingly diffident and retiring, in person prepossessing, so that the danger that might arise to a young and unsuspecting girl, from this latter advantage, would seem to be obviated by the former characteristic.

In 183— she went to work in the shop of a tailor, by the name of J.D. Pease, in Winchendon, Mass.

From this time her residence at home was short and unfrequent, and little is known of her Christian character, save that when she appeared among the friends of her youth the same modest and unobtrusive manner distinguished her as in early years.

But a change came over her. She no longer shrank from the addresses of the other sex, but suffered herself to be conducted to various places by the man who employed her. Her friends remonstrated against the impropriety of so doing, as he had a wife and children, but she was deaf to their admonitions, and averred that it was a matter of convenience, and therefore no impropriety could be attached to her accompanying him.

Last winter she was brought home in a declining state of health; but as her health

---

* From "Died in Jaffrey, N.H. May 8, M.A.L. Aged 27," *Friend of Virtue*, August 1, 1841, 227–28.

amended she resolved to return with Pease, who had called upon her, though contrary to the wishes of her friends. After the lapse of a few weeks, she was most unceremoniously brought back again, but under circumstances the most unequivocal. But how apparent soever her situation, her friends could gain no satisfactory reply to their inquiry as to the author of her ruin.

She accused no one—she complained of no one—but pondered upon the dreadful secret, til reason, which had from her first return, given signs of alienation, was, forever dethroned! In the bitterness of her feelings she would sometimes exclaim, stung by recollection of her former and present condition, "Can this be Mary Ann?"

After giving birth to a child, her frenzy increased,—convulsions ensued,—and lingering a few weeks in unutterable horror, the remains of the once innocent, lovely, and beloved M.A.L. were consigned to an untimely and dishonored grave.

Language fails to do justice to a scene like this, or to paint the reality as it fell upon the startled vision of agonized friends and sympathizing neighbors. There was no redress for wrongs like these. Even the poor satisfaction that the law allows in cases of seduction was denied, since no accusation escaped her lips. Suspicion was however afloat, but with how much justice that day that is to judge the secret things of iniquity will decide. This man, suspecting that suspicion might rest on him, had taken the precaution to procure from her a paper declaring his innocence, if that should be called in question in reference to herself. Such, however, was the sentiment prevailing among the citizens with whom he resided, that he found it utterly impossible to endure the withering influence of virtuous indignation, and he abruptly absconded.

A voice as from the grave of our young friends speaks in thunderous tones, BEWARE! It calls upon parents to be more vigilant in seeking to imbue the minds of their offspring with those pure and elevating principles that shall be as a talisman to shield and protect in the hour of temptation. It speaks to the youthful and the fair to beware of the seducer's wiles; to guard well their hearts, for against such the tempter hath no power. It were well for them to understand that in an important sense they are their own keepers; that the strength needful to secure them in virtue's path, is most freely imparted: for the promise to those that ask, is that they shall receive. It speaks to our young men, also, the hope and pride of our nation, to beware how they prostitute their noble powers to the destruction of female innocence. If they would not implant daggers in their own bosoms, call down the imprecations of an incensed community, and the vengeance of an angry God, they will beware how they arrive at this unenvied pre-eminence in guilt.

CAROLINE HEALY DALL, *Letter to Paulina Wright Davis and the Woman's Rights Convention* (1851)

Caroline Healy Dall (1822–1912) was the eighth child in a prosperous New England family. A women's rights advocate, she was particularly committed to gender equality in the workplace and in education. The following document is an excerpt from a lengthy letter Dall wrote to the 1850 Worcester, Massachusetts, Women's Rights Convention. Whereas most moral reformers focused on issues of character, Dall approached the issue of prostitution from an economic rather than a moral perspective. In this letter, she notes the links among minimal work options, near-starvation wages, and prostitution and seeks a feminist solution that looked to pay equity and widening workplace opportunity as ways to combat prostitution. Improving wages and work opportunities became her objective. Dall continued her study of employment discrimination and was one of the nation's first women to investigate gender discrimination in the workplace.

Prostitution was prevalent in European cities. How does Dall describe the evidence that prostitution also posed a problem in American cities? What does she propose as the remedy?*

First of all, I am desirous that the women of this country should claim fitting provision for their own education. It is a stale truth now, that the safety of a republic depends upon the intelligence of its citizens; for the time is coming when the means of education, being wholly inefficient, the welfare of this republic, and the character of its citizens, will depend chiefly upon its mothers. Few persons know how difficult it is for a woman to procure an education. What is barely possible to wealth, is wholly impossible to poverty. Even men who teach mathematics and the languages to both sexes, teach them superficially to women, and take no pains to lay a solid foundation for such superstructures as they may afterward wish to rear. I speak from experience, for no money was spent on my own education, and I am, to this hour, daily mortified by its insufficiency, and the bad modes of investigation into which I was allowed to fall. If the poorer class of females in a community could receive a good education, they would be able to earn a living more successfully than they are now, and many of them would be spared lives of ignominy and sin. Now that the laws of Massachusetts have been somewhat altered with regard to property, I think that the subject next in importance is that of the rates of remuneration paid to women. It seems to me that the men and women in this country should imperatively demand, that when women do the same work as men, and are even acknowledged to do it better, they should be paid at the same rate. *Why* I feel particularly interested in this matter, will partly appear from the following remarks.

In every large city, there is a class of women, whose existence is a terror and reproach to the land in which they are born; whose name no modest woman is supposed to know; whose very breath is thought to poison the air of the sanctuary. I pass over the fact, so generally ignored, that there is a class of men corresponding to these women, and far viler in the sight of God, I doubt not. I avoid dwelling on the social death which is the lot of these miserable creatures, and which is often the reward of their first efforts for a better life. I know that many whom I love will blame me bitterly for speaking on this subject at all, but that blame I must bear as God permits, for I feel bound to draw your attention to a few facts. Whatever elevates woman will diminish this class; but proper remuneration for her labor would draw many from it at once, almost all, in fact, who had not reached the lowest deep. Most women,—if they dare to think about them at all,—suppose that these miserable creatures are always the victims of their own bad natures, or want of principle; that they find their life a life of pleasure, and that they would not forsake it if they could, unless under the influence of religious conviction. If such thinkers would study their own unpolluted natures more closely, they would understand the position of the despised class far better than they do; and the more intelligent and religious they themselves become, the more distinctly will they perceive, that to undertake the regeneration of such, is imperatively the duty of the women rather than the men of the community.

Nine-tenths of the women of this class in any community will be found to consist of two sub-divisions. First, those who are born to this life as naturally and inevitably as the

* Worcester Women's History Project: 30 Elm Street, Worcester, MA 01609; info@wwhp.org (mailto:info@wwhp.org), 508-767-1852.

robin is born to cleave the air. Of such are foundlings, orphans, and the children of the extremely poor, whose habits of lodging are fatal to modesty, in most instances. Second, those who began life honestly, but were compelled to sell themselves for bread. Of such are young exposed persons afraid to die, widows with large families dependent upon them, and single women burdened with the care of the infirm or aged. Many of this class have been known to leave this wretched life for months together, when it became possible for them to earn what is called an honest livelihood. Again, instead of leading a life of pleasure, such women suffer intensely, and twelve out of every fifteen examined testify, that they could not sustain its physical horrors without their daily dram. It is stated on good authority, that the strongest constitutions sink under this life in less than three years, and the cases are numerous in which, after a much shorter period, the victim commits suicide.

I have stated these facts to show that no woman will remain in this life who can quit it, that there is hope for those who will hold out hope to them, and to show that inadequate remuneration for honest labor is one great reason why their number is so large. In making this statement, I depend not merely on the statistics published at Paris and London, but on my own observation in New England. Many persons imagine that the horrors detailed of foreign cities find no parallel here. This is not true. The public sense of decorum in Boston drives vice into close corners . . ., Passing the other evening through a street at the North end of the city, I saw three children, under ten years of age, cuddled close together for warmth, and sound asleep on the brick pavement, at the base of building erected to store flour. Returning, at a late hour, I found, not far from them, three of the most wretched of the women alluded to. They were scantily clothed and starving. Their breaths bore witness that, even in this extremity, they had preferred their daily dram to their daily bread; yet such was their eagerness for food and rest, that they almost clutched the garments of passers by. These children slept and these women walked within the compass of the Swedish singer's voice [Jenny Lind], and many times that night, as the latter trod their dreary round, her clear notes swelled full upon their ears, the waves of her spiritual song floated round their dishonored heads, like dreams of their far-gone childhood, and the wonderful echo of the Herdsman's Song thrilled through the soul of more than one, I doubt not, like the cattle-call of her early companions, or the twittering of the swallows under the eaves of her home. These women had no roof to call their own, and the children who slept under God's unwinking eye on that cold stone, inherit their homelessness and their sin.

Such women are redeemable, and better wages or a better education would save thousands from their fate. Need I say any more to induce women to strain every nerve to secure these two ends, at least?

CAROLINE W.H. DALL
Boston, Nov. 2, 1850.

Dr. William W. Sanger, Excerpt from *The History of Prostitution, Its Extent, Causes, Effects throughout the World* (1859)

Dr. William Sanger was the former chief resident physician at Blackwell's Island hospital in New York City. The hospital treated the destitute, including prostitutes who had contracted a venereal disease. Sanger compiled his study on prostitution with a specific focus on New York City in the 1850s, a time when public anxiety over the increasing numbers of prostitutes in the city was growing. Sanger was one of the pioneer researchers of prostitution, and his work coincided with the growth of American cities and the expansion of houses of prostitution. Sanger searched for reasons why women living in New York City became prostitutes. His findings generally revealed extreme economic hardship, although some prostitutes he interviewed noted their own "inclination." Many urban working-class women lived close to the edge of complete destitution. Occasional acts of prostitution were a survival strategy and for some women a preferable alternative to the barely sustainable wages of needle trades and laundry work. Some who became prostitutes were single mothers who could not find other sources of income. The dichotomy between the moral reformers' view of prostitutes as "fallen victims in need of rescue or women exercising economic choice" continues to resonate in the twenty-first century. Unlike reformers who championed the abolition of prostitution, Sanger believed prostitution could not be eradicated but could be regulated. He was particularly concerned with what he perceived to be the rapid spread of syphilis and other venereal diseases. What evidence did Sanger provide that prostitution could not be abolished? Why did he favor regulation?*

It is a mere absurdity to assert that prostitution can ever be eradicated. Strenuous and well-directed efforts for this purpose have been made at different times. The whole power of the Church, where it possessed not merely a spiritual but an actual secular arm, has been in vain directed against it. Nature defied the mandates of the clergy, and the threatened punishments of an afterlife were futile to deter men from seeking, and women from granting, sinful pleasures in this world. Monarchs victorious in the field and unsurpassed in the council-chamber have bent all their energies of will and brought all the aids of power to crush it out, but before these vice has not quailed. The guilty women have been banished, scourged, branded, executed; their partners have been subjected to the same punishment; held up to public opinion as immoral; denuded of their civil rights; have seen their offenses visited upon their families; have been led to the stake, the gibbet, and the block, and still prostitution exists. . . .

But if history proves that prostitution can not be suppressed, it also demonstrates that it can be regulated, and directed into channels where its most injurious results can be encountered, and its dangerous tendencies either entirely arrested or materially weakened. This is the policy to which civilized communities are tending.

Lucy Stone, *Letter from Lucy Stone to Antoinette Brown Blackwell* (July 11, 1855)

Lucy Stone (1818–1893), a Mt. Holyoke Seminary and Oberlin College graduate, was one of the nineteenth century's leading abolitionist and women's rights activist. Her marriage contract with her husband created an equal partnership and she kept her own name. Less well known, because not openly acknowledged in her public speeches and writings, was her deep commitment to planned pregnancies or voluntary motherhood. The issue of negotiating sexual restraint within marriage was central to Stone's wider effort of empowering wives and ending their dependence on their husbands and loss of self-identity. What are the major points in her letter to Antoinette Blackwell? Why does she believe the marriage issue should not be publicly discussed at the women's convention?**

---

* William Sanger, *The History of Prostitution: Its Extent, Causes and Effects Throughout the World,* 1858. In the public domain.
** Women's rights activist Lucy Stone to her sister in law, Antoinette Brown Blackwell. In Carol Lasser and Marlene Deahl Merrill, eds., *Friends and Sisters: Letters between Lucy Stone and Antoinette Brown Blackwell, 1846-93* (Urbana: University of Illinois Press, 1987) 143–44.

Dear Nettee

    . . . I expect to be at Saratoga, tho only for one day. But I do not think it is any sense good economy to have a meeting *there*—The people who congregate at Saratoga are not reformers, not workers and will *never* help forward our ideas. I would give more for a patient hearing in some country school-house. The rich and fashionable, move only when the masses that are behind and under them move. So that our real work is with the mass, who have no reputation to lose, no ambition to gratify, and who, as they do not depend upon the Public, need not smother their convictions for its favor— . . . .

    Paulina Davis has written me, that she wants the marriage question to come up at the National Convention (I hope she won't be here, with her vanity and her jealousy.) It seems to me that we are not ready for it. I saw that at Philadelphia, by private conversations. No two of us think alike about it. And yet it is clear to me, that question underlies, this whole movement and all our little skirmishing for better laws, and the right to vote, will yet be swallowed up, in the real question, viz, has woman, as wife, a right to herself? It is very little to me to have the right to vote, to own property & c. if I may not keep my body, and its uses, in my absolute right. Not one wife in a thousand can do that now, & so long as she suffers this bondage, all other rights will not help her to her true position—This question will *force* itself upon us some day, but it seems to me it is untimely now— . . . .

ever lovingly
Lucy

PAULINA WRIGHT DAVIS, *Letter to Women's Rights Conference, Akron, Ohio* (1851)

Paulina Wright Davis (1813–1876) was well known during her own lifetime as a leader in the struggle for women's rights. She presided at two conventions in Worcester, Massachusetts, in 1850 and 1851. Davis explicitly advocated the right of the wife "to the control her own person," as well as the need for women to have financial independence and not choose husbands because of financial dependency. Note her assertion that wives must not be led to believe that the husband's passion should mandate the wife's submission. At a time when sexual issues were not discussed in public, it was radical for Davis to address the intimate issue of marital relations. Even cautious advocacy of voluntary motherhood was considered a taboo topic for public presentation before the Civil War.

    As the following document demonstrates, Davis publicly addressed this issue as early as 1851 but in a letter, not as a public address. How does Davis contradict the assumption that sexual indulgence is necessary for the husband's well-being? In the context of her letter, what did she mean by her statement that marriage "annihilated" the wife? How would you evaluate her assertion that young women are desperate to marry because they lack the means for self-support?*

Providence, April 26, 1851.

Mrs. McMillan:

    Dear Madam: * * * * * * I have few apprehensions for your Convention, for I have great faith in woman, in her instincts, her delicacy and truth, and I have the greater faith in those who have but recently begun to work. There is always power in the first awakenings of enthusiasm; there is also a hopefulness that leads the actors to believe well of others; and in a struggle of this kind

---

* In the public domain.

it is essential that we look with charity upon the wrong doers; in fact, so involved are we all in the sin, that we cannot shift it all upon our brothers' shoulders; indeed I am sometimes half disposed to consider woman the more guilty one.

I know the answer is that man educates her and makes her what she is. But how have the duties of the mother been performed, that the son should go out from her influence without a just sense of the rights of her who bore him. In one family you will find mother and sister toiling like southern slaves, early and late, for a son who sleeps on the downiest couch, wears the finest linen, and spends his hundreds of dollars in a wild college life. How should he not feel that women were made purposely to minister to his happiness? On the other hand, a son is forced to labor, without stint or measure, for a sister's support who leads an idle, aimless life. Has not a foul wrong been done them both? To one, she is the drudging, patient slave; to the other, a toy to amuse in an idle hour, to be petted and flattered; but not the less is she a slave. Whose is the fault? Would not a wise mother have given to each an aim in life? Would she not have sought from their very infancy to prevent antagonisms of interest. While our relations in life are all so false, man is not more free than woman.

The happiness and truth of the marriage relation absolutely pivots itself on this very movement. In that relation woman must give the law, and redeem it from its present sensual and mental pollutions. She must not be taught to feel from her very girlhood, but man is so wholly unlike herself, governed not only by stronger passions, but of a character that it would be shameful for her to share, or even comprehend; and that when she marries, she must not presume that she has the right to the control of her own person, because, forsooth, indulgence is essential to the health of her husband, nay, even his very life is involved. Excessive maternity follows for a few years, then exhaustion, weariness

and death comes to close the drama. A sad winding up of a sad false theory and practice. Morally and physiologically false, as all know who are sufficiently unperverted to look at it calmly. I know this is a delicate question to probe, but it is not the less necessary. The mother has the teaching on all these questions; and I would here remark that if she has physiological knowledge, which is the positive root of all these other outgrowths of reform, she will find no difficulty in giving the requisite instruction to her sons as well as her daughters.

Woman is ideally annihilated in the marriage relation, and to all intents and purpose enslaved; so inwrought into the very textures and tissues of man's nature, even the noblest among them, is this subtle principle, that it has its influence upon them. Old ideas and old habitudes of mind long survive the causes which produced them. The shadows of night linger in the sheltered nooks and deep dells, till the sun is waning. So it will be the work of a whole creation day, to remove all the darkness that now obscures the light.

We ask that the thousands of strong young men who are crowding behind the counters, selling ribbons and laces, shall with a true manly spirit go forth and cultivate the broad, glorious prairies of the west, dam the rivers, fell the forests, "and make the wilderness to bud and blossom as the rose." Then he can with safety ask to share his home, a woman that has a pecuniary independence, for she will enter the holy relation from a natural attraction, and not as she does now, rushing with desperation from one false position to another, and performing its duties as slaves always do, with caution, cunning, fear, duplicity and management. * * * * In such false relations, neither man nor woman can be symmetrically developed, nor can they inherit lofty and pure organizations.

Yours, very truly,
P.W. DAVIS.

THE UNWELCOME CHILD (1845)

Very few documents from this era provide evidence about the private lives of married couples, and sexual issues were not discussed in public. In this letter, the wife's statements concern marital duties that include her sexual submission. Her claim to the "justice of her personal rights in regard to maternity" has remained basic to the argument for reproductive freedom. When this letter was written, women had limited options for controlling pregnancy. Women's rights advocates supported voluntary motherhood—the wife's right to abstain from sexual relations. The prevalence of abortion may also have been a factor in the decline of the birthrate that occurred during the nineteenth century. According to the evidence, how did the husband enforce his claim to his wife's body? How would you evaluate the husband's behavior? Why was the wife so desperate?*

Before we married, I informed him (the husband) of my dread of having children. I told him I was not yet prepared to meet the sufferings and responsibilities of maternity. He entered into an arrangement to prevent it for a specified time. This agreement was disregarded. After the legal form was over and he felt that he could now indulge his passion without loss of reputation, and under legal and religious sanctions, he insisted on the surrender of my person to his will. He violated his promise at the beginning of our united life. That fatal bridal night! . . . I can never forget it. It sealed the doom of our union, as it does of thousands.

He was in feeble health; so was I; and both of us mentally depressed. But the sickly germ was implanted, and conception took place. We were poor. . . . In September, 1838, we came to ———, and settled in a new country. In the March following my child . . . was born. After three months' struggle, I became reconciled to my, at first, unwelcome child. . . .

In one year I found I was again to be a mother. I was in a state of frightful despair. My first born was sickly and troublesome, needing constant care and nursing. My husband chopped wood for our support. . . . I felt that death would be preferable to maternity under such circumstances. A desire and determination to get rid of my child entered into my heart. I consulted a lady friend, and by her persuasion and assistance, killed it. Within less than a year, maternity was again imposed upon me, with no better prospect of doing justice to my child. It was a most painful conviction to me; I felt that I could not have another child at the time. . . .

I consulted a physician, and told him of my unhappy state of mind. . . . He told me how to destroy it. After experimenting on myself three months, I was successful. I killed my child about five months after conception. . . .

Soon after the birth of my [second] child, my husband insisted on his accustomed injustice. Without any wish of my own, maternity was again forced upon me. I dared no attempt to get rid of the child, abortion seemed so cruel, so inhuman, unnatural and repulsive. I resolved again, for my child's sake, to do the best I could for it. Though I could not joyfully welcome, I resolved quietly to endure its existence.

After the birth of this child, I felt that I could have no more to share our poverty, and to suffer the wrongs and trials of an unwelcome existence. I felt that I had rather die at once, and thus end my life and my power to be a mother together. My husband cast the entire care of the family on me. . . .

In this state, known as it was to my husband, he thrust maternity on me twice. I employed a doctor to kill my child, and in the

---

* From Henry C. Wright, *The Unwelcome Child* (Boston: B. Marsh, 1858), as cited in John Cowan, M.D., and W.R.C. Latson, *What All Married People Should Know* (Chicago: G.W. Ogilvie & Co., 1903), 214–18.

destruction of it, which should have been the vigor of my life, ended my power to be a mother. . . . I suffered, as woman alone can suffer, not only in body, but in bitter remorse and anguish of soul. . . .

Such has been my false religious and social education, that, in submitting my person to his passion, I did it with the honest conviction that in marriage my body became the property of my husband. He said so; all women to whom I applied for counsel said it was my duty to submit; that husbands expected it, had a right to it, and must have this indulgence whenever they were excited, or suffer; and that in this way alone could wives retain the love of their husbands. I had no alternative but silent, suffering submission to his passion, and then procure abortion or leave him, and thus resign my children to the tender mercies of one with whom I could not live myself. Abortion was most repulsive to every feeling of my nature. It seemed degrading, and at times rendered me an object of loathing to myself.

When my firstborn was three months old, I had a desperate struggle for my personal liberty. My husband insisted on his right to subject my person to his passion, before my babe was two months old. I saw his conduct then in all its degrading and loathsome injustice. I pleaded, with tears and anguish, for my own and my child's sake, to be spared; and had it not been for my helpless child I should then have ended the struggle by bolting my legal bonds. For its sake I submitted to that outrage, and to my own conscious degradation. For its sake, I concluded to take my chances in the world with other wives and mothers, who, as they assured me, and as I then knew, were, all around me subjected to like outrages and driven to the degrading practice of abortion.

But, even then, I saw and argued the justice of my personal rights in regard to maternity . . . insisted on my right to say when and under what circumstances I would accept of him the office of maternity, and become the mother of his child. I insisted that it was for me to say when and how often I should subject myself to the liability of becoming a mother. But he became angry with me; claimed ownership over me; insisted that I, as a wife, was to submit to my husband *"in all things";* threatened to leave me and my children, and declared I was not fit to be a wife. Fearing some fatal consequences to my child or to myself—being alone, destitute, and far from helpful friends, in the far West, and fearing that my little one would be left to want—I stifled all expression of my honest convictions, and ever after kept my aversion and painful struggles in my own bosom.

ANTOINETTE BROWN BLACKWELL, *Address: The Whole World's Temperance Convention* **(September 1853)**

Antoinette Blackwell (1825–1921) was the first woman to be ordained as a minister of a mainstream Protestant denomination in 1853. Earlier she had attended Oberlin College where she met Lucy Stone. The two became close friends and Blackwell married the brother of Stone's husband. As was the case with many women reformers of the pre–Civil War era, Blackwell supported multiple reforms, including women's rights, temperance, and abolition. Temperance advocacy represented the quintessential reform of white, middle-class women. Advocates linked a moral argument for temperance to one for women's rights: Their rallying cry was to control male drinking and protect women from abusive husbands. Family stability and domestic harmony, as well as economic security, required sober husbands and fathers. Blackwell's passionate outcry that temperance was a women's issue must be understood in the context of male temperance reformers' efforts to end all discussions about women's rights. As occurred with other reform movements, men attempted to control women's participation and limit them to distinctly subordinate or auxiliary roles. In the following rebuttal, Blackwell spoke on behalf of other rights advocates who refused to accept male efforts to silence them. Why does Blackwell insist that temperance is a women's rights issue? What specific evidence does she offer to support the link between women's rights and temperance?*

The President then introduced Rev. Miss Antoinette L. Brown, the Pastor of an Orthodox Congregational Church at South Butler, N. Y., who was enthusiastically received. She said:

The Whole World's Temperance Convention,—room on its broad platform for everybody! "Parthians, and Medes, and Elamites, and the dwellers in Mesopotamia, in Judea and Cappadocia, in Pontus and Asia, Phrygia, and Pamphylia, in Egypt and in the parts of Libya about Cyrene, and strangers about Rome, Jews and Proselytes, Cretes and Arabians"—every man who may come here speaks his own tongue wherein he was born, about one of the most needed reforms ever launched on the ocean of events. Here is Woman invited to speak into the great ear-trumpet of the world, that all may hear. No wonder that the Woman's Rights Convention should be called directly hereafter. It follows immediately on upon the present occasion. But I am reminded that in this Temperance gathering teetotalism is to be discussed in its length and breadth—nothing else and nothing more; not a word about Woman and her rights. This may be well, but there's a good time coming, friends; wait a little longer. The sun may be everywhere seen, though it is not yet up in the meridian. Milk for babes, but strong meat afterwards. Temperance and Woman's Rights, chopped up together, would be a potato and meal amalgamation, quite nauseous to many modern reformers, even by those who like either when served up by itself. Hash is an old fashioned dish used at large banquets. But any one has a right to speak of Temperance to the world, even though this right has been disputed and

virtually voted away. Who does not see this to have been in bad taste—and not a word here about any woman's right to vote, even in favor of a Maine Law, although the world disfranchises one-half of its inhabitants: although they are not recognized as belonging to its inhabitants, and although the other part are licensed to sell and to use what bring them desolation and ruin, with the exception of those who live in the darkness of heathenism, in a few Yankee States and a few imitators of Yankee States; not a word about all this. Say nothing about this, and not a breath either about a woman's owing service or labor to her intemperate husband, and his right to take her earnings. Are we not told that the great nations of the earth are sanctifying such a system of things? Do not let it be known that the father has the whole custody of the children, although a drunkard, and that he may take them away from the mother and apprentice them as a security for his own grog-bill; and that he may, in his last will and testament, give them over to the rum-seller for the whole term of their minority. Not a word about all this. Why, this belongs to Woman's Rights, and what has it to do with the temperance cause? It may be that this is after all a distinction without a difference; for we always find the degradation of women connected with the rum-traffic. The world will tell us that the drunken man may be expected to blend together his thoughts, and take up various subjects at the same time, while the wine he has drunk makes his brain to boil like a red hot hasty-pudding, or a boiling hodge-podge till you may no more expect an idea from his expressions, than you could pick out all the

---

* In the public domain.

particles of the apple or cabbage from the homogeneous mass of a heterogeneous stew. Wine dulls the brain, of course. . . . All this is well, and yet, since the regular old orthodox physicians have not succeeded in curing the evils of intemperance, I think we should turn to the innovator, who goes to work another way to cure these evils. I feel here, this morning, in attempting to speak, like John the Baptist; for I am only preparing the way for those who are "to come after me, the latchets of whose shoes I am not worthy to unloose." I appear here to speak at the request of our committee, who for a while have gone from us. Still there is enough to be said. But those who will come after me will take up the temperance question in its length and breadth, and will deal with it as it deserves.

A TEMPERANCE ACTIVIST (1853)

Women who advocated temperance were confined to supporting roles in male-dominated temperance societies. Until they actively protested, they were denied a public voice and leadership roles. Women's activism on behalf of temperance awakened male concern that women were stepping beyond their family and household roles. Although most female temperance advocates protested peacefully, this newspaper article describes a "novel case"—the actual destruction of property of a saloon owner. What personal factors motivated the woman's destructive behavior? What bearing on the case would her status as a "pious mother" have?*

A Heroic Woman—Mrs. Margaret Freeland, of Syracuse, was recently arrested upon a warrant issued on complaint of Emanuel Rosendale, a rum-seller, charging her with forcing an entrance to his house, and with stones and clubs smashing his doors and windows, breaking his tumblers and bottles, and turning over his whiskey barrels and spilling their contents. Great excitement was produced by this novel case. It seems that the husband of Mrs. Freeland was a drunkard—that he was in the habit of abusing his wife, turning her out of doors, etc., and this was carried so far that the police frequently found it necessary to interfere to put a stop to his ill-treatment of his family. Rosendale, the complainant, furnished Freeland with the liquor which turned him into a demon. Mrs. Freeland had frequently told him of her sufferings and besought him to refrain from giving her husband the poison. But alas! she appealed to a heart of stone. He disregarded her entreaties and spurned her from his door. Driven to desperation she armed herself, broke into the house, drove out the base-hearted landlord and proceeded upon the work of destruction.

She was brought before the court and demanded a trial. The citizens employed Charles B. Sedgwick, Esq., as her counsel, and prepared to justify her assault upon legal grounds. Rosendale, being at once arrested on complaint of Thomas L. Carson for selling liquor unlawfully, and feeling the force of the storm that was gathering over his head, appeared before the Justice, withdrew his complaint against Mrs. Freeland, paid the costs, and gave bail on the complaint of Mr. Carson, to appear at the General Sessions and answer to an indictment should there be one found.

Mrs. Freeland is said to be "the pious mother of a fine family of children, and a highly respectable member of the Episcopal Church."

---

* From *The Lily,* June 1853, in Elizabeth Cady Stanton, Susan B. Anthony, and Matilda J. Gage, eds., *History of Woman Suffrage* (New York: Fowler and Wells, 1881), I: 475.

VICTORIA WOODHULL, *And the Truth Shall Make You Free* (1871)

Victoria Woodhull (1838–1927), an advocate of free love and a rebel against what she perceived as the sexual hypocrisy of her era, briefly crossed paths with the Stanton-Anthony faction of the women's suffrage movement. The first woman to argue for suffrage before a congressional committee in 1871, Woodhull impressed Anthony and Stanton with her pro-suffrage argument. Using her suffrage connections, in 1872, Woodhull announced her candidacy for president of the United States on the newly formed People's Party. Her campaign amounted to little more than self-promotion.

By November 1872, Woodhull found herself jailed for allegedly violating the recently passed antiobscenity Comstock Law. Her published allegation that the Rev. Henry Ward Beecher, president of the American Woman's Suffrage Association, had committed adultery eventually led to a courtroom drama that involved suffrage advocates and gave the era its defining sex scandal. It also tarnished the entire suffrage movement. For years, anti-suffrage opponents equated women's rights with free love and family destruction.

The following excerpt is from a free-love speech Woodhull made in New York City in 1871. She was the era's most outspoken advocate of free love and in the following speech covered the major arguments against conventional monogamous marriage and in favor of commitment based on love not legality. What evidence does Woodhull give that the institution of marriage has failed? How does she distinguish between free love and promiscuity? Discuss whether Woodhull's free-love views would be considered radical today.*

The tenth commandment of the Decalogue says: "Thou shalt not covet thy neighbor's wife." And Jesus, in the beautiful parable of the Samaritan who fell among thieves, asks: "Who is thy neighbor?" and answers his own question in a way to lift the conception wholly out of the category of mere local proximity into a sublime spiritual conception. In other words, he spiritualizes the word and sublimates the morality of the commandment. In the same spirit I ask now, Who is a *wife?* And I answer, not the woman who, ignorant of her own feelings, or with lying lips, has promised, in hollow ceremonial, and before the law, to love, but *she who really loves most,* and *most truly,* the man who commands her affections, and who in turn loves her, with or without the ceremony of marriage; and the man who holds the heart of such a woman in such a relation is "thy neighbor," and *that woman is "thy neighbor's wife" meant in the commandment;* and whosoever, though he should have been a hundred times married to her by the law, shall claim, or *covet* even, the possession of that woman as against the true lover and husband in the spirit, sins against the commandment.

We know positively that Jesus would have answered in that way. He has defined for us "the neighbor," not in the paltry and commonplace sense, but spiritually. He has said, "He that looketh on a woman to lust after her hath committed adultery with her already in his heart." So, therefore, he spiritualized the idea of adultery. In the kingdom of heaven, to be prayed for daily, to come on earth, there is to be no "marrying or giving in marriage," that is to say, formally and legally; but spiritual marriage must always exist, and had Jesus been called on to define a wife, can anybody doubt that he would, in the same spirit, the spiritualizing tendency and character of all his doctrine, have spiritualized the marriage relation as absolutely as he did the breach of it? that he would, in other words, have said in meaning precisely what I now say? And when Christian ministers are no longer afraid or ashamed *to be Christians* they

---

* From Victoria C. Woodhull, "And the Truth Shall Make You Free." A speech on the principles of social freedom, delivered in Steinway Hall, November 20, 1871.

will embrace this doctrine. Free Love will be an integral part of the religion of the future.

It can now be asked: What is the legitimate sequence of Social Freedom? To which I unhesitatingly reply: Free Love, or freedom of the affections. "And are you a Free Lover?" is the almost incredulous query.

I repeat a frequent reply: "I am; and I can honestly, in the fullness of my soul, raise on my voice to my Maker, and thank Him that *I am,* and that I have had the strength and the devotion to truth to stand before this traducing and vilifying community in a manner representative of that which shall come with healing on its wings for the bruised hearts and crushed affections of humanity."

And to those who denounce me for this I reply: "Yes, I am a Free Lover. I have an *inalienable, constitutional* and *natural* right to love whom I may, to love *as long* or as *short* a period as I can; to *change* that love *every day* if I please, and with *that* right neither *you* nor any *law* you can frame have *any* right to interfere. And I have the *further* right to demand a free and unrestricted exercise of that right, and it is *your duty* not only to *accord* it, but, as a community, to see that I am protected in it. I trust that I am fully understood, for I mean *just* that, and nothing less!

To speak thus plainly and pointedly is a *duty I owe* to myself. The press have stigmatized me to the world as an advocate, theoretically and practically, of the doctrine of Free Love, upon which they have placed their stamp of moral deformity; the vulgar and inconsequent definition which they hold makes the theory an abomination. And though this conclusion is a no more legitimate and reasonable one than that would be

which should call the Golden Rule a general license to all sorts of debauch, since Free Love bears the *same* relations to the moral deformities of which it stands accused as does the Golden Rule to the Law of the Despot, yet it obtains among many intelligent people. But they claim, in the language of one of these exponents, that "Words belong to the people; they are the common property of the mob. Now the common use, among the mob, of the term Free Love, is a synonym for promiscuity." Against this absurd proposition I oppose the assertion that words *do not* belong to the mob, but to that which they represent. Words are the exponents and interpretations of ideas. If I use a word which exactly interprets and represents what I would be understood to mean, shall I go to the *mob* and *ask of them* what interpretation *they* choose to place upon it? If lexicographers, when they prepare their dictionaries, were to go to the mob for the rendition of words, what kind of language would we have?

I claim that freedom means *to be free,* let the mob claim to the contrary as strenuously as they may. And I claim that love means an exhibition of the affections, let the mob claim what they may. And therefore, in compounding these words into Free Love, I claim that united they mean, and should be used to convey, their united definitions, the mob to the contrary notwithstanding. And when the term Free Love finds a place in dictionaries, it will prove my claim to have been correct, and that the mob have not received the attention of the lexicographers, since it will not be set down to signify sexual debauchery, and that only, or in any governing sense.

HARRIOT STANTON BLATCH, *"Voluntary Motherhood," Transactions of the National Council of Women* (1891)

In the final years of the suffrage struggle, Harriot Stanton Blatch (1856–1940), the daughter of Elizabeth Cady Stanton, brought new and dramatic strategies to rally public opinion and support across class lines. In contrast to her suffragist activism, her support of voluntary motherhood showed her caution over the issue of contraception. Many women's rights activists found contraception unnatural. They promoted the wife's right to control reproduction by limiting sex. In the context of the era, any form of family planning was a departure from the assumption that nature and God destined women for motherhood with multiple births. How does Blatch justify voluntary motherhood as preferable to pregnancies without choice? In what way does she apply evolutionary observations to her view of the mother's role in parenting? How does her argument relate to women's rights?*

The difficulty of approaching the subject of the relation of the sexes is tenfold, if the prerogatives of the dominant sex are challenged. . . .

In animal life, as soon as we get conscious motherhood, the strides in evolution become greater and more rapid. . . .

Below the birds "the animal takes care of himself as soon as he begins to live. He has nothing to learn, and his career is a simple repetition of the careers of countless ancestors." Among higher birds and mammals a great change takes place; the life of the creature becomes so varied and complex that habits cannot be fully organized in the nervous system before birth. The antenatal period is too short to allow of such development. So we get a period of infancy, a time of plasticity, of teachableness. Of this time Fiske truly says, "The first appearance of infancy in the animal world heralded the new era which was to be crowned by the development of man." From this point in evolution the period of infancy lengthens,—indeed, this is the condition of progress. To reach a higher stage of development a longer time must be given to immaturity or growth, and that period will be one of greater or less dependence according as the adult being is of higher or lower species. What chiefly distinguishes the human being from the lower animals is the increase in the former of cerebral surface and organization, and the necessary accompaniment of this development, a lengthened period of infancy.

Now, this increased time of immaturity is a direct tax upon the mother in any species; so to her is due each step in evolution. Men

talk of the sacredness of motherhood, but judging from their acts it is the last thing that is held sacred in the human species. Poets sing and philosophers reason about the holiness of the mother's sphere, but men in laws and customs have degraded the woman in her maternity. Motherhood is sacred,—that is, voluntary motherhood; but the woman who bears unwelcome children is outraging every duty she owes the race. The mothers of the human species should turn to the animals, and from the busy caretakers, who are below them in most things, learn the simple truths of procreation. Let women but understand the part unenforced maternity has played in the evolution of animal life, and their reason will guide them to the true path of race development. Let them note that natural selection has carefully fostered the maternal instinct. The offsprings of the fondest females in each animal species, having of course the most secure and prolonged infancy, are "naturally selected" to continue their kind. The female offspring gains by inheritance in philoprogenitiveness, and thus is built up the instinct which prepares the females of a higher species for a more developed altruism. Through countless ages mother-love has been evolved and been working out its mission; surely women should recognize the meaning of the instinct, and should refuse to prostitute their creative powers, and so jeopardize the progress of the human race. Upon the mothers must rest in the last instance the development of any species.

In this work women need not hope for help from men. The sense of obligation to

---

* In the public domain.

offspring, men possess but feebly; there has not been developed by animal evolution an instinct of paternity. They are not disinherited fathers; they are simply unevolved parents. There is no ground for wonder that this is so; for in but a few species among the lower animals is even a suggestion of paternal instinct found. The male bird often occupies itself with the hatching and feeding of the brood, and the lion is a pattern father; but usually we find no hint of paternal instinct in the male, and sometimes antagonism towards the young of the species. Evidently nature tried her hand on paternity, it did not fulfil the hopes she had of it, and she returned a cold shoulder upon its development. The paternal instinct is not a factor in evolution.

If, then, the law of natural selection is of weight, we should expect to find very little, if any, instinct of paternity in the male of the human species. Not only by such a *priori* reasoning is this conclusion reached, but a *posteriori* reasoning emphasizes the same truth. Men like to accumulate, and hand down their accumulations with their name. This is a method of securing some sort of immortality, and gives rise to the neglect of illegitimate children, the preference of male to female offspring, the law of primogeniture, and the selection, in case of male heirs failing, of some distant relation to inherit the property provided he will adopt the name of his benefactor. The masculine tendencies which have crystallized themselves in these customs bear no resemblance to paternal love. A woman does not discriminate between her legitimate and illegitimate child; and had mothers been instrumental in making legal codes there would not have been a law of entail.

WINNIFRED HARPER COOLEY, *The New Womanhood* (1904)

Winnifred Harper Cooley (1874–1967), like Harriot Stanton Blatch, was a second-generation women's rights activist and suffragist. Her mother, Ida Husted Harper, was a close friend of Susan B. Anthony and also coauthored some of the volumes of the *History of Woman's Suffrage.* Cooley's book, *The New Womanhood,* helped define the construct of the "new woman," the term used to describe the turn-of-the-century's younger women as more modern in outlook and behavior than their mothers' generation. One section of her book dealt with "The Bachelor Maiden" and how women's increasing financial independence removed the economic pressure to marry.

In the following excerpt dealing with "The Problem of Human Propagation," Cooley describes the need for voluntary motherhood as a fundamental component for women's progress and rights. Although her reference is mainly to middle-class women, her observations also include the working class. How would you compare her defense of family limitation to that of Harriot Stanton Blatch? In the context of early-twentieth-century women's history, what significance would Cooley's statement that "the modern woman is regarded of some use besides reproducing the species" have?*

Modern America does not recognize the necessity for large families. Modern America is said to produce the most charming women and also the best husbands in the world. Nowhere to-day (unless in England) has the recent experiment of educating women had opportunity to flower. It will require several generations to estimate the real results, but we have had one generation of college-bred mothers, of women and men upon a fairly equal social

---

plane. The son of such parents does not condescendingly explain some subject to "dear, stupid old mater," nor can the daughter relegate the blooming matron to the realm of pots and kettles, while she entertains company.

The modern married couple, whether from love of ease and luxury, from selfishness, from high motives of wishing to bring into existence only those children for whom they can provide bountifully and educate,—from whatsoever motive, do not have more than two or three children, if any. To assume that this condition is due to disinclination upon the part of the woman only is to cast aspersions upon the will of the husband, and it is manifestly absurd to presuppose that the wife rules in every household. The facts, without regard to whether or not we approve them, are that the average couple do not desire a numerous offspring.

An inquiry into the various probable motives of people in abstaining from prolific reproduction may be of value, for that small families are voluntarily small can scarcely be doubted by any one who studies the sudden drop in the birth-rate of this from the last few decades.

1. *The economic struggle of the modern world is beginning to be viewed seriously by a vast number of people, with an effort to ameliorate conditions.*

There is no question in the mind of the sober, industrious citizen that the economic struggle for existence crowds out the overburdened as well as the incompetent. The problem of living upon a small salary is increased ten-fold if there are ten human beings dependent upon the one salary. Actual necessities are difficult to procure for more than two or three, upon the salary of the average man, not to speak of the small pleasures and luxuries his habits and training demand; and his very self-respect is lost if he is powerless to provide these for those he loves. Seeing that he alone can do little

toward controlling the cruel conditions of industry, he no longer weakly cries out against "the Lord," nor curses his employer, but looks to his own life, and conscientiously decides not to make manifold his poverty and lack of opportunities by increasing the number of consumers when powerless to increase the supply of food and clothing. Often, if the wife of the poor man is not burdened by numerous small children and the numerous ills of child-bearing, she too can earn a salary, and thus the combined income will lighten their distress. This course of reasoning, more or less imperfectly formulated, is found with increasing frequency among the better class of people of small incomes. If it were considered oftener, many worthy and congenial young people might marry who now live in loneliness because they know that they dare not bring up a family upon the salary of the man.

Even the young professional man, whose salary does not preclude a few small luxuries, finds that he has so many obligations attendant upon his position that his actual living income is not much better than that of the "day laborer." He and his congenial young wife wish to save a little money for travel, for books; they feel the necessity of investing in life insurance and building and loan associations, to insure against calamity, and they dare not and desire not to add voluntarily to their financial burdens, and rob life of its few aesthetic pleasures, by rearing a large family. They know that to do this would bring about illness and drudgery, and *they see no necessity for it.*

2. *The modern woman is regarded as of some use besides that of reproducing the species.* With the industries taken out of the home, and with opportunities for education and activity, woman has been able to develop many latent energies and tastes. She sees beyond her home and church. This does not imply that she is any less important in either of these. As "love divided doubles," so energies and functions exercised in many directions, increase many times. Only the woman with a poor sense of proportion and discrimination plunges into public work, civic or philanthropic, at the expense of duties near at hand. Man's very assumption of the support of the family should make him welcome relief from many civic duties, such as those relating to schools and charities, when he becomes convinced that women are intelligent and willing. The orphans, cripples, paupers, criminals, all the dependent and defective classes, are a dead weight upon society, and should be the especial study and care of women who

have not assumed the gaining of a livelihood, and are no longer weighted down by the extensive cares of domesticity. Both men and women are groping for these new sociological phenomena, and the very belief which intelligent men hold that woman is worth something as an individual, and should share the peculiar burdens of civilization, and woman's feeling that for countless ages she has wanted to do these things, develop a sense in both man and woman that all virtue does not consist in the thoughtless begetting of numerous offspring.

CHAPTER 5

Enslaved Women:
Race, Gender, and the Plantation Patriarchy

In the context of the enslavement process, a gendered racial ideology was constructed that rationalized the physical and sexual abuse of enslaved African and African American females. Socially constructed racial and gender stereotypes portrayed enslaved women as promiscuous and overly sexual. The social construction of these gender assumptions were used to justify the primacy of reproduction and sexual exploitation. As a result, enslaved women not only lacked freedom, they also encountered interlocking and simultaneous gender and racial oppression, which scholars have referred to as a "racialized" gender construct.

Analysis of white and black as racial constructs enables us to better understand the dynamics of the hierarchic race relations that existed in an extreme form on Southern plantations, as well as the power imbalance that governed the relationship between enslaved black women and their white male plantation owners. Although accurate statistics are not available, extensive evidence documents sexual exploitation. The sexual harassment experienced by Harriet Jacobs and Elizabeth Keckley's brutal assault are representative of the sexual vulnerability of enslaved women. In addition to the evidence from slave narratives and slave interviews conducted during the 1930s, plantation mistresses' private journals testify to widespread sexual exploitation of enslaved women. Under slavery, rape by the master was not an offense. The enslaved female, was not legally defined as a woman but as property. Rape by the owner was a non-offense and by a white male nonowner a trespass against property.

Given the extent of the power imbalance, all interracial unions between owners and enslaved women made the element of sexual choice for the women problematic. Nonetheless, examples of successful resistance to sexual exploitation, as in the case of Harriet Jacobs, did occur. Some enslaved women also were able to negotiate special privileges and even freedom for their biracial children. Not only women's field and domestic labor but also their reproductive labor were vital to plantation profitability.

Racially embedded gender norms ascribed to elite and middle-class white women the delicacy, purity, and dependence on white male protection that was denied to all women of color. Despite gender barriers that constricted opportunity and attempted to limit their lives to domestic roles, white women, particularly the elite, still shared a degree of privilege stemming from their social and racial status. Racial and gender constructs created contrasting categories for enslaved black and free white women: in place of white purity, black sexuality; in place of white delicacy, black brute strength; and in place of white maternal sensitivity, black breeding of children. This polarized construction widened the social difference between the white mistress and the enslaved black woman and added to the hierarchic imbalance of power.

Although some plantation mistresses had empathy for the enslaved, this empathy was offset by the fact that the plantation mistress joined her husband in upholding the institution of slavery. The narratives of enslaved women provide examples of the plantation mistress inflicting beatings as well as sadistic treatment. Plantation mistress Fanny Kemble's journal reveals that kindness and concern also could exist. But Kemble's empathy was unusual; she was a British abolitionist married to a Southern slave owner, and she was shocked by the cruelty and degradation of enslavement.

Gender expectations made it clear that the planter's wife was to submit to her husband's authority even if it caused her personal discomfort. Gertrude Clanton Thomas and Mary Boykin Chestnut believed that planters' sexual relations with slave women damaged the family life of whites. Yet their subordinate status as women and wives also made it clear that they had no authority to openly criticize, let alone change, the behavior of the plantation patriarchy. They confined their criticism and pain to the private pages of their journals.

Scholarly interpretations differ on how far patriarchal control extended over enslaved families' relationships, particularly over marriage and motherhood. Whereas some scholars emphasize the ability of enslaved women to exert considerable autonomy within their own families, others remind us that ultimate power remained with owners, who broke families apart, sold children, and exerted control over the most intimate aspects of the lives of their slaves. The sale of slaves was, in fact, a routine part of the slave owners' economic balance sheet. Letitia Burwell, the daughter of a Virginia plantation owner, acknowledged that even her "kind" father sold slave children when he needed money. Enslaved women such as Bethany Veney struggled to prevent the sale of their children, and slave narratives describe their post-emancipation search for missing children and sorrow for lost family members that lasted a lifetime.

Despite oppression and cruelty, enslaved women were not passive victims. They engaged not only in daily acts of resistance, but also in remarkable acts of defiance and courage. Harriet Tubman's escape to freedom and her repeated efforts to rescue others, despite the risk to her own life, made her a legend even in her own lifetime. Bethany Veney recounted the strategy that prevented her sale to a different owner and separation from her only daughter. Elizabeth Keckley's sense of self-worth and the value she place on her own dressmaking skills infused her desire to purchase her own freedom. Documents in this chapter illuminate various forms of resistance and outright defiance, including escape, refusal to submit to sexual violation, and as in the case of Harriet Jacobs the exercise of sexual choice within the constrained boundaries of bondage.

BENJAMIN DREW, *Narrative of an Escaped Slave* (1855)

Enslaved women encountered both sexual exploitation and physical abuse. Benjamin Drew, an abolitionist, recorded the stories of fugitive slaves who had escaped to Canada. Since most slaves could not write, their oral testimony is of particular historical value. Thousands of slaves risked their lives escaping from slavery and settling in Canada. For Jane Howard and others, Canada became a desirable place of refuge from the Fugitive Slave Act and the possibility of re–enslavement.

Because of the difficulty of fleeing slavery with small children, fewer enslaved women than men made the dangerous journey to freedom. What abuses convinced Howard to risk her life and escape first from enslavement and then to Canada?*

Mrs. Nancy Howard

I was born in Anne Arundel county, Maryland — was brought up in Baltimore. After my escape, I lived in Lynn, Mass., seven years, but I left there through fear of being carried back, owing to the fugitive slave law. I have lived in St. Catherine's less than a year.

The way I got away was—my mistress was sick, and went into the country for her health. I went to stay with her cousin. After a month, my mistress was sent back to the city to her cousin's, and I waited on her. My daughter had been off three years. A friend said to me—"Now is your chance to get off." At last I concluded to go—the friend supplying me with money. I was asked no questions on the way north.

My idea of slavery is, that it is one of the blackest, the wickedest things everywhere in the world. When you tell them the truth, they whip you to make you lie. I have taken more lashes for this, than for any other thing, because I would not lie.

One day I set the table, and forgot to put on the carving-fork—the knife was there. I went to the table to put it on a plate. My master said,—"Where is the fork?" I told him "I forgot it." He says,—"You d——d black b——, I'll forget you!"—at the same time hitting me on the head with the carving knife. The blood spurted out—you can see. (Here the woman removed her turban and showed a circular cicatrices denuded of hair, about an inch in diameter, on the top of her head.) My mistress took me into the kitchen and put on camphor, but she could not stop the bleeding. A doctor was sent for. He came but asked no questions. I was frequently punished with raw hides—was hit with tongs and poker and anything. I used when I went out, to look up at the sky, and say, "Blessed Lord, oh, do take me out of this!" It seemed to me I could not bear another lick. I can't forget it. I sometimes dream that I am pursued, and when I wake, I am scared almost to death.

HARRIET TUBMAN, Excerpts from *A Biography by Her Contemporaries* (c. 1880)

Based on a series of interviews by abolitionists, Harriet Tubman's (1820–1913) biography described her escape from slavery, as well as her vital role in the Underground Railroad. Known as "Moses, the deliverer of her people," Tubman personally risked death and repeatedly returned to the South to lead as many as three hundred slaves to freedom. In what ways did Tubman's life contradict stereotypes about female weakness?**

One of the teachers lately commissioned by the New England Freedmen's Aid Society is probably the most remarkable woman of this age. That is to say, she has performed more wonderful deeds by the native power of her own spirit against adverse circumstances than any other. She is well known to many by the various names

---

* From *A Northside View of Slavery: The Refuge, or The Narratives of Fugitive Slaves in Canada, Related by Themselves*, ed. Benjamin Drew (Boston: John P. Jowett, 1856), 41–3; 50–51, 138, 140–41, 224–27.
** In the public domain.

which her eventful life has given her; Harriet Garrison, Gen. Tubman, &c; but among the slaves she is universally known by her well-earned title of *Moses*—Moses the deliverer. She is a rare instance, in the midst of high civilization and intellectual culture, of a being of great native powers, working powerfully, and to beneficent ends, entirely unaided by schools or books.

Her maiden name was Araminta Ross. She is the granddaughter of a native African, and has not a drop of white blood in her veins. She was born in 1820 or 1821, on the Eastern Shore of Maryland. Her parents were slaves, but married and faithful to each other, and the family affection is very strong. She claims that she was legally freed by a will of her first master, but his wishes were not carried into effect.

She seldom lived with her owner, but was usually "hired out" to different persons. She once "hired her time," and employed it in rudest farming labors, ploughing, carting, driving the oxen, &c., to so good advantage that she was able in one year to buy a pair of steers worth forty dollars.

When quite young she lived with a very pious mistress; but the slaveholder's religion did not prevent her from whipping the young girl for every slight or fancied fault. Araminta found that this was usually a morning exercise; so she prepared for it by putting on all the thick clothes she could procure to protect her skin. She made sufficient outcry, however, to convince her mistress that her blows had full effect; and in the afternoon she would take off her wrappings, and dress as well as she could. When invited into family prayers, she preferred to stay on the landing, and pray for herself; "and I prayed to God," she says "to make me strong and able to fight, and that's what I've allers prayed for since." It is in vain to persuade her that her prayer was a wrong one. She always maintains it to be sincere and right, and it has certainly been fully answered.

In her youth she received a severe blow on her head from a heavy weight thrown by her master at another slave, but which accidentally hit her. The blow produced a disease of the brain which was severe for a long time, and still makes her very lethargic. She cannot remain quiet for fifteen minutes without appearing to fall asleep. It is not a refreshing slumber; but a heavy, weary condition which exhausts her. She therefore loves great physical activity, and direct heat of the sun, which keeps her blood actively circulating. She was married about 1844 to a free colored man named John Tubman, but never had any children. Owing to changes in her owner's family, it was determined to sell her and some other slaves; but her health was so much injured, that a purchaser was not easily found. At length she became convinced that she would soon be carried away, and she decided to escape. . . .

She remained two years in Philadelphia, working hard and carefully hoarding her money. Then she hired a room, furnished it as well as she could, bought a nice suit of men's clothes, and went back to Maryland for her husband. But the faithless man had taken to himself another wife. Harriet did not dare venture into her presence, but sent word to her husband where she was. He declined joining her. At first her grief and anger were excessive. She said, "she did not care what massa did to her, she thought she would go right in and make all the trouble she could, she was determined to see her old man once more" but finally she thought "how foolish it was just for temper to make mischief" and that, "if he could do without her, she could without him," and so "he dropped out of her heart," and she determined to tie her life to brave deeds. Thus all personal aims died out of her heart; and with her simple brave motto "I can't die but once," she began the work which has made her Moses—the deliverer of her people. Seven or eight times she has returned to the neighborhood of her former home, always at the risk of death in the most terrible forms, and each time has brought away a company of fugitive slaves, and led them safely to the free States, or to Canada. Every time she went, the dangers increased. In 1857 she brought away her old parents, and, as they were too feeble to walk, she was obliged to hire a wagon, which added greatly to the perils of the journey. In 1860 she went for the last time, and among her troop was an infant whom they were obliged to keep stupefied with laudanum to prevent its outcries. This was a period of great excitement and Moses was not safe even in the New York states; but her anxious friends insisted upon her taking refuse in Canada.

Harriet Tubman (Courtesy of the Library of Congress)

BETHANY VENEY, *The Narrative of Bethany Veney, A Slave Woman* (1890)

In 1858, Bethany Veney (1815–1912) moved from Virginia and enslavement to Rhode Island and freedom with the Adams family, who had purchased her. At this point, she was forced to separate from her daughter, Charlotte. After the Civil War, Veney returned to the South on different occasions to bring Charlotte and other family members to the North. For most of her life, Veney lived in Worcester, Massachusetts. Charlotte and her family lived next door. Much of Veney's slave narrative deals with the dread of family loss: her ever-present fear of sale and separation. Her narrative is a potent reminder of the centrality to the U.S. economy of the domestic slave trade and its impact on the lives of enslaved individuals and the emotional anguish of mothers who suffered the loss of their children.

In the following excerpt, from her autobiography, Veney describes how she thwarted her master's effort to sell her. Her sale would have resulted in permanent separation from her beloved daughter. What was Veney's reaction to her prospective sale? What role did religion play in her life? What evidence does this excerpt offer about enslaved resistance and women helping one another?*

My dear white lady, in your pleasant home made joyous by the tender love of husband and children all your own, you can never understand the slave mother's emotions as she clasps her new-born child, and knows that a master's word can at any moment take it from her embrace; and when, as was mine, that child is a girl, and from her own experience she sees its almost certain doom is to minister to the unbridled lust of the slave-owner, and feels that the law holds over her no protecting arm, it is not strange that, rude and uncultured as I was, I felt all this, and would have been glad if we could have died together there and then.

The Narrative of Bethany Veney, a Slave Woman (Worcester, MA: 1890; repr., Lauray, VA: Page County Heritage Association, 1998).

Master Kibbler was still hard and cruel, and I was in constant trouble. Miss Lucy was kind as ever, and it grieved her to see me unhappy. At last, she told me that perhaps, if I should have some other home and some other master, I should not be so wretched, and, if I chose, I might look about and see what I could do. I soon heard that John Prince, at Luray, was wanting to buy a woman. Miss Lucy told me, if it was agreeable to me, I might go to him and work for a fortnight, and if at the end of that time he wanted me, and I chose to stay, she would arrange terms with him; but, if I did not want to stay, not to believe anything that any one might tell me, but come back at once to her.

At the end of two weeks, Master John said he was going over to have a talk with Miss Lucy; and did I think, if he should conclude to buy me, that I should steal from him? I answered that, if I worked for him, I ought to expect him to give me enough to eat, and then I should have no need to steal. "You wouldn't want me to go over yonder, into the garden of another man, and steal his chickens, when I am working for you, would you, Master John? I expect, of course, you will give me enough to eat and to wear, and then I shall have no reason to steal from anybody." He seemed satisfied and pleased, and bargained with Miss Lucy, both for me and my little girl. Both master and Mrs. Prince were kind and pleasant to me, and my little Charlotte played with the little Princes, and had a good time. I worked very hard, but I was strong and well, and willing to work; and for several years there was little to interrupt this state of things.

At last, I can't say how long, I was told that John O'Neile, the jailer, had bought me; and he soon took me to his home, which was in one part of the jail. He, however, was not the real purchaser. This was David McCoy, the same who had grabbed Jerry on that fatal morning; and he had bought me with the idea of taking me to Richmond, thinking he could make a speculation on me. I was well known in all the parts around as a faithful,

hard-working woman, when well treated, but ugly and wilful, if abused beyond a certain point. McCoy had bought me away from my child; and now, he thought, he could sell me, if carried to Richmond, at a good advantage. I did not think so; and I determined, if possible, to disappoint him.

The night after being taken in charge by John O'Neile, as soon as I was sure everybody was asleep, I got up and crawled out of the house, and went to my old Methodist friend, Jerry Kibbler. I knew the way into his back door; and, though I presumed he would be asleep, I was sure he would willingly get up and hear what I had to say. I was not mistaken. He heard my voice inquiring for him, and in a very few minutes dressed himself, and came out, and in his pleasant, kind manner said: "Aunt Betty, what is the matter? What can I do for you?" I told him McCoy had bought me, away from my child, and was going to send me to Richmond. I *couldn't* go there. *Wouldn't* he buy me? I saw he felt very badly; but *what*, he said, could *he* do with me? He didn't believe in buying slaves,—and, finally, he hadn't "money enough to do it." I begged so hard that he said he would see what he could do, and I went back to the jail. Mrs. O'Neile had discovered my absence, and was on the watch for me. The next day, she told me I was to start for Richmond the day after, and it was no use for me to make a fuss, so I might as well bring my mind to it first as last.

The day was almost gone, and I had had no word from Mr. Jerry. As it was growing dark, I saw a colored man whom I knew, and I managed to make him see, through the jail windows, that I wanted to speak with him. I induced him to find Master Jerry; but he came back with word from him that he had seen both O'Neile and McCoy, and could make no kind of an arrangement with them. He had not come to me, because he felt so sorry for me, and had waited, in the hope that some one else would tell me. So there seemed nothing else before me; and when, on the next morning, Mrs. O'Neile told me to make myself ready for the journey, I tried to be submissive, and dressed myself in a new calico dress that Miss Lucy had given me long before.

I had never in my life felt so sad and so completely forsaken. I thought my heart was really breaking. Mr. O'Neile called me; and, as I passed out of the door, I heard Jackoline, the jailer's daughter, singing in a loud, clear voice,—

"When through the deep waters I call thee to go,
The rivers of woe shall not thee overflow;
For I will be with thee, and cause thee to stand,
Upheld by my righteous, omnipotent hand."

I can never forget the impression these *words* and the *music* and the tones of Jackoline's voice made upon me. It seemed to me as if they all came directly out of heaven. It was my Saviour speaking directly to me. Was not *I* passing the deep waters? What rivers of woe could be sorer than these through which I was passing? Would not this righteous, omnipotent hand uphold me and help me? Yes, here was His word for it. I would trust it; and I was comforted.

We mounted the stage, and were off for Charlotteville, where we stopped over night, and took the cars next morning for Richmond.

Arrived in Richmond, we were again shut up in jail, all around which was a very high fence, so high that no communication with the outside world was possible. I say we, for there was a young slave girl whom McCoy had taken with me to the Richmond market.

The next day, as the hour for the auction drew near, Jailer O'Neile came to us, with a man, whom he told to take us along to the dressmaker and to charge her to "fix us up fine." This dressmaker was a most disagreeable woman, whose business it was to array such poor creatures as we in the gaudiest and most striking attire conceivable, that, when placed upon the auction stand, we should attract the attention of all present, if not in one way, why, in another. She put a white muslin apron on me, and a large cape, with great pink bows on each shoulder, and a similar rig also on Eliza. Thus equipped, we were led through a crowd of rude men and boys to the place of sale, which was a large open space on a prominent square, under cover.

I had been told by an old negro woman certain tricks that I could resort to, when placed upon the stand, that would be likely to hinder my sale; and when the doctor, who was employed to examine the slaves on such occasions, told me to let him see my tongue, he found it coated and feverish, and, turning from me with a shiver of disgust, said he was obliged to admit that at that moment I was in a very bilious condition. One after another of the crowd felt of my limbs, asked me all manner of questions, to which I replied in the ugliest manner I dared; and when the auctioneer raised his hammer, and cried, "How much do I hear for this woman?" the bids were so low I was ordered down from the stand, and Eliza was called up in my place. Poor thing! there were many eager bids for her; for, for such as she, the demands of slavery were insatiable.

HARRIET JACOBS (LINDA BRENT), Excerpt from *Incidents in the Life of a Slave Girl* (1861)

Harriet Jacobs (1813–1897) assumed the name "Linda Brent" to disguise her own identity. Her autobiography did not fit the conventional pattern of enslaved victim narratives, but rather it described a resourceful and successful survivor whose determination to escape her married owner's sexual advances led her to hide for seven years in a small attic. One of the few personal accounts written by an enslaved woman, Jacobs's autobiography of her life in slavery has become a classic narrative. Jacobs also revealed how she chose an unmarried white man for her lover. Middle-class women who embraced the code of female purity addressed nonmarried female sexuality within the context of female victims and male predators. Jacobs's experience expressed her own successful effort to avoid becoming a victim of coerced sex. But the fact that she also had chosen a lover may have made it more difficult for her to publish her autobiography. Eventually, after Harriet Beecher Stowe refused to assist her, the abolitionist Lydia Maria Child helped Jacobs with publication.

How did Jacobs deal with her master's continual sexual harassment? How does she justify taking a lover of her own choosing? How would you describe her resistance to enslavement?*

The slaveholder's sons are, of course, vitiated, even while boys, by the unclean influences every where around them. Nor do the master's daughters always escape. Severe retributions sometimes come upon him for the wrongs he does to the daughters of the slaves. The white daughters early hear their parents quarrelling about some female slave. Their curiosity is excited, and they soon learn the cause. They are attended by the young slave girls whom their father has corrupted; and they hear such talk as should never meet youthful ears, or any other ears. They know that the women slaves are subject to their father's authority in all things; and in some cases they exercise the same authority over the men slaves. I have myself seen the master of such a household whose head was bowed down in shame; for it was known in the neighborhood that his daughter had selected one of the meanest slaves on his plantation to be the father of his first grandchild. She did not make her advances to her equals, nor even to her father's more intelligent servants. She selected the most brutalized, over whom her authority could be exercised with less fear of exposure. Her father, half frantic with rage, sought to revenge himself on the offending black man; but his daughter, foreseeing the storm that would arise, had given him free papers, and sent him out of the state.

In such cases the infant is smothered, or sent where it is never seen by any who know its history. But if the white parent is the *father*, instead of the mother, the offspring are

unblushingly reared for the market. If they are girls, I have indicated plainly enough what will be their inevitable destiny.

You may believe what I say; for I write only that whereof I know. I was twenty-one years in that cage of obscene birds. I can testify, from my own experience and observation, that slavery is a curse to the whites as well as to the blacks. It makes the white fathers cruel and sensual; the sons violent and licentious; it contaminates the daughters, and makes the wives wretched. And as for the colored race, it needs an abler pen than mine to describe the extremity of their sufferings, the depth of their degradation.

Yet few slaveholders seem to be aware of the widespread moral ruin occasioned by this wicked system. Their talk is of blighted cotton crops—not of the blight on their children's souls. If you want to be fully convinced of the abominations of slavery, go on a southern plantation, and call yourself a negro trader. Then there will be no concealment; and you will see and hear things that will seem to you impossible among human beings with immortal souls.

X.

A Perilous Passage in the Slave Girl's Life

After my lover went away, Dr. Flint contrived a new plan. He seemed to have an idea that my fear of my mistress was his greatest obstacle. In the blandest tones, he told me that he was

---

* Harriet A. Jacobs, *Incidents in the Life of a Slave Girl: Written by Herself* (Cambridge, MA: Harvard University Press, 1987). Jean Yellin, Distinguished Professor Emerita, Pace University, authenicated Jacob's narrative and retrieved her experience and literary achievement.

going to build a small house for me, in a secluded place, four miles away from the town. I shuddered; but I was constrained to listen, while he talked of his intention to give me a home of my own, and to make a lady of me. Hitherto, I had escaped my dreaded fate, by being in the midst of people. My grandmother had already had high words with my master about me. She had told him pretty plainly what she thought of his character, and there was considerable gossip in the neighborhood about our affairs, to which the open-mouthed jealousy of Mrs. Flint contributed not a little. When my master said he was going to build a house for me, and that he could do it with little trouble and expense, I was in hopes something would happen to frustrate his scheme; but I soon heard that the house was actually begun. I vowed before my Maker that I would never enter it. I had rather toil on the plantation from dawn till dark; I had rather live and die in jail, than drag on, from day to day, through such a living death. I was determined that the master, whom I so hated and loathed, who had blighted the prospects of my youth, and made my life a desert, should not, after my long struggle with him, succeed at last in trampling his victim under his feet. I would do any thing, every thing, for the sake of defeating him. What *could* I do? I thought and thought, till I became desperate, and made a plunge into the abyss.

And now, reader, I come to a period in my unhappy life, which I would gladly forget if I could. The remembrance fills me with sorrow and shame. It pains me to tell you of it; but I have promised to tell you the truth, and I will do it honestly, let it cost me what it may. I will not try to screen myself behind the plea of compulsion from a master; for it was not so. Neither can I plead ignorance or thoughtlessness. For years, my master had done his utmost to pollute my mind with foul images, and to destroy the pure principles inculcated by my grandmother, and the good mistress of my childhood. The influences of slavery had had the same effect on me that they had on other young girls; they had made me prematurely knowing, concerning the evil ways of the world. I knew what I did, and I did it with deliberate calculation.

But, O, ye happy women, whose purity has been sheltered from childhood, who have been free to choose the objects of your affection, whose homes are protected by law, do not judge the poor desolate slave girl too severely! If slavery had been abolished, I, also, could have married the man of my choice; I could have had a home shielded by the laws; and I should have been spared the painful task of confessing what I am now about to relate; but all my prospects had been blighted by slavery. I wanted to keep myself pure; and, under the most adverse circumstances, I tried hard to preserve my self-respect; but I was struggling alone in the powerful grasp of the demon Slavery; and the monster proved too strong for me. I felt as if I was forsaken by God and man; as if all my efforts must be frustrated; and I became reckless in my despair.

I have told you that Dr. Flint's persecutions and his wife's jealousy had given rise to some gossip in the neighborhood. Among others, it chanced that a white unmarried gentleman had obtained some knowledge of the circumstances in which I was placed. He knew my grandmother, and often spoke to me in the street. He became interested for me, and asked questions about my master, which I answered in part. He expressed a great deal of sympathy, and a wish to aid me. He constantly sought opportunities to see me, and wrote to me frequently. I was a poor slave girl, only fifteen years old.

So much attention from a superior person was, of course, flattering; for human nature is the same in all. I also felt grateful for his sympathy, and encouraged by his kind words. It seemed to me a great thing to have such a friend. By degrees, a more tender feeling crept into my heart. He was an educated and eloquent gentleman; too eloquent, alas, for the poor slave girl who trusted in him. Of course

I saw whither all this was tending. I knew the impassable gulf between us; but to be an object of interest to a man who is not married, and who is not her master, is agreeable to the pride and feelings of a slave, if her miserable situation has left her any pride or sentiment. It seems less degrading to give one's self, than to submit to compulsion. There is something akin to freedom in having a lover who has no control over you, except that which he gains by kindness and attachment. A master may treat you as rudely as he pleases, and you dare not speak; moreover, the wrong does not seem so great with an unmarried man, as with one who has a wife to be made unhappy. There may be sophistry in all this; but the condition of a slave confuses all principles of morality, and, in fact, renders the practice of them impossible.

ELIZABETH KECKLEY, Excerpt from *Behind the Scenes, or Thirty Years a Slave and Four Years in the White House* (1868)

Elizabeth Keckley's (1818–1907) autobiography demonstrates her resilience and, despite enslavement, her development of dressmaking skills and an entrepreneurial work ethic. She describes beatings, as well as the sexual assault that led to the birth of her son and only child. What distinguished Keckley's life experience was her purchase of her freedom and subsequent service as official dressmaker to First Lady Mary Todd Lincoln. Keckley took great pride in her dressmaking, entrepreneurial skills, and social interaction with elite individuals. In 1868, she published her life story with major emphasis on her White House years. She divulged a range of personal information about Mrs. Lincoln that she wrongly thought would redeem her own role in helping the former first lady sell her wardrobe to raise money to pay her debts. Keckley's behind-the-scenes disclosures of her White House role and friendship with the former first lady led to public outrage. Judged to have transgressed the line of confidentiality as well as those of race and class, Keckley's successful career as a dressmaker to the wives of politicians came to an abrupt end. Although she had other work opportunities, she ended her life in a home for "destitute colored women."

What role do you think Keckley's race and status as a former slave may have played in the public anger over her revelations about Mrs. Lincoln? How would you evaluate Keckley's rise from slavery to official White House dressmaker?*

Tuesday morning, at eight o'clock, I crossed the threshold of the White House for the first time. I was shown into a waiting-room, and informed that Mrs. Lincoln was at breakfast. In the waiting-room I found no less than three mantua-makers waiting for an interview with the wife of the new President. It seems that Mrs. Lincoln had told several of her lady friends that she had urgent need for a dressmaker, and that each of these friends had sent her mantua-maker to the White House. Hope fell at once. With so many rivals for the position sought after, I regarded my chances for success as extremely doubtful. I was the last one summoned to Mrs. Lincoln's presence. All the others had a hearing, and were dismissed. I went up-stairs timidly, and entering the room with nervous step, discovered the wife of the President standing by a window, looking out, and engaged in likely conversation with a lady, Mrs. Grimsly, as I afterwards learned. Mrs. L. came forward, and greeted me warmly.

"You have come at last. Mrs. Keckley, who have you worked for in the city?"

"Among others, Mrs. Senator Davis has been one of my best patrons," was my reply.

---

* Elizabeth Keckley, *Behind the Scenes, or Thirty Years a Slave and Four Years in the White House* (New York: G.W.Carleton & Co, 1868).

"Mrs. Davis! So you have worked for her, have you? Of course you gave satisfaction; so far, good. Can you do my work?"

"Yes, Mrs. Lincoln. Will you have much work for me to do?"

"That, Mrs. Keckley, will depend altogether upon your prices. I trust that your terms are reasonable. I cannot afford to be extravagant. We are just from the West, and are poor. If you do not charge too much, I shall be able to give you all my work." . . .

Mrs. Lincoln looked elegant in her rose-colored moire-antique. She wore a pearl necklace, pearl ear-rings, pearl bracelets, and red roses in her hair. Mrs. Baker was dressed in lemon-colored silk; Mrs. Kellogg in a drab silk, ashes of rose; Mrs. Edwards in a brown and black silk; Miss Edwards in crimson, and Mrs. Grimsly in blue watered silk. Just before starting down-stairs, Mrs. Lincoln's lace handkerchief was the object of search. It had been displaced by Tad, who was mischievous, and hard to restrain. The handkerchief found, all became serene. Mrs. Lincoln took the President's arm, and with smiling face led the train below. I was surprised at her grace and composure. I had heard so much, in current and malicious report, of her low life, of her ignorance and vulgarity, that I expected to see her embarrassed on this occasion. Report, I soon saw, was wrong. No queen, accustomed to the usages of royalty all her life, could have comported herself with more calmness and dignity than did the wife of the President. She was confident and self-possessed, and confidence always gives grace. . . .

I made fifteen or sixteen dresses for her during the spring and early part of the summer, when she left Washington; spending the hot weather at Saratoga, Long Branch, and other places. In the mean time I was employed by Mrs. Senator Douglas, one of the loveliest ladies that I ever met, Mrs. Secretary Wells, Mrs. Secretary Stanton, and others. Mrs. Douglas always dressed in deep mourning, with excellent taste, and

several of the leading ladies of Washington society were extremely jealous of her superior attractions.

Chapter XV.

The Secret History of Mrs. Lincoln's Wardrobe in New York.

In March, 1867, Mrs. Lincoln wrote to me from Chicago that, as her income was insufficient to meet her expenses, she would be obliged to give up her house in the city, and return to boarding. She said that she had struggled long enough to keep up appearances, and that the mask must be thrown aside. "I have not the means," she wrote, "to meet the expenses of even a first-class boarding-house, and must sell out and secure cheap rooms at some place in the country. It will not be startling news to you, my dear Lizzie, to learn that I must sell a portion of my wardrobe to add to my resources, so as to enable me to live decently, for your remember, what I told you in Washington, as well as what you understood before you left me here in Chicago. I cannot live on $1,700 a year, and as I have many costly things which I shall never wear, I might as well turn them into money, and thus add to my income, and make my circumstances easier. It is a humiliating to be placed in such a position, but, as I am in the position, I must extricate myself as best I can. Now, Lizzie, I want to ask a favor of you. It is imperative that I should do something for my relief, and I want you to meet me in New York, between the 30th of August and the 5th of September next, to assist me in disposing of a portion of my wardrobe."

I knew that Mrs. Lincoln's income was small, and also knew that she had many valuable dresses, which could be of no value to her, packed away in boxes and trunks. I was confident that she would never wear the dresses again, and thought that, since her need was urgent, it would be well enough to dispose of them quietly, and believed that New York was the best place to transact a delicate business of the kind. She was the wife of Abraham Lincoln, the man who had done so much for my race, and I could refuse to do nothing for her, calculated to advance her interests. I consented to render Mrs. Lincoln all the assistance in my power, and many letters passed between us in regard to the best way to proceed. It was finally arranged that I should meet her in New York about the middle of September. While thinking over this question, I remembered an incident of the White House. When we were packing up to leave Washington for Chicago, she said to me, one morning:

"Lizzie, I may see the day when I shall be obliged to sell a portion of my wardrobe. If Congress does not do something for me, then my dresses some day may have to go to bring food into my mouth, and the mouths of my children."

I also remembered of Mrs. L. having said to me at different times, in the years of 1863 and '4, that her expensive dresses might prove of great assistance to her some day.

"In what way, Mrs. Lincoln? I do not understand," I ejaculated, the first time she made the remarks to me.

"Very simple to understand. Mr. Lincoln is so generous that he will not save anything from his salary, and I expect that we will leave the White House poorer than when we came into it; and should such be the case, I will have no further need for an expensive wardrobe, and it will be policy to sell it off."

I thought at the time that Mrs. Lincoln was borrowing trouble from the future, and little dreamed that the event which she so dimly foreshadowed would ever come to pass.

Fanny Kemble, *Journal* Excerpt (1838)

A British actress and abolitionist, Fanny Kemble (1809–1893) married the plantation owner Pierce Butler in 1834. The two had met during Kemble's theatrical tour of the Atlantic states. She spent a year on the Georgia Sea Island plantation her husband inherited after their marriage. Producing rice and cotton, it was the second largest plantation in the state. The following excerpt from Kemble's journal, written in 1838, describes her eyewitness account of the treatment of ill and pregnant enslaved women. She also describes the brutal physical labor of the enslaved women who worked in the rice fields despite advanced pregnancy or physical illness. Kemble records a litany of deprivations and suffering. Understandably her marriage to Butler became oppositional. Their views diverged not only over slavery, but also over Butler's treatment of her: He expected her complete obedience and submission. Given Kemble's sense of agency and moral authority, wifely submission was impossible. The marriage dissolved and ended in divorce in 1849. Her journal, published in 1863 during the Civil War, expressed her effort to add to the abolitionist sentiment in Britain and negate any aid that the British government might send to the Confederacy.

What conditions of the enslaved women did Kemble find most intolerable? How did Kemble describe the physical distress of the women in the infirmary?*

The infirmary is a large two-story building, terminating the broad orange-planted space between the two rows of houses which form the first settlement; it is built of white washed wood, and contains four large-sized rooms. But how shall I describe to you the spectacle which was presented to me, on my entering the first of these? But half the casements, of which there were six, were glazed, and these were obscured with dirt, almost as

---

* *Fanny Kemble's Journals*, ed. Catherine Clinton (Cambridge, MA: Harvard University Press, 2000).

much as the other windowless ones were darkened by the dingy shutters, which the shivering inmates had fastened to, in order to protect themselves from the cold. In the enormous chimney glimmered the powerless embers of a few sticks of wood, round which, however, as many of the sick women as could approach, were cowering; some on wooden settles, most of them on the ground, excluding those who were too ill to rise; and these last poor wretches lay prostrate on the floor, without bed, mattress, or pillow, buried in tattered and filthy blankets, which, huddled round them as they lay strewed about, left hardly space to move upon the floor. And here, in their hour of sickness and suffering, lay those whose health and strength are spent in unrequited labour for us—those who, perhaps even yesterday, were being urged onto their unpaid task—those whose husbands, fathers, brothers and sons, were even at that hour sweating over the earth, whose produce was to buy for us all the luxuries which health can revel in, all the comforts which can alleviate sickness. I stood in the midst of them, perfectly unable to speak, the tears pouring from my eyes at this sad spectacle of their misery, myself and my emotion alike strange and incomprehensible to them. Here lay women expecting every hour the terrors and agonies of child-birth, others who had just brought their doomed offspring into the world, others who were groaning over the anguish and bitter disappointment of miscarriages—here lay some burning with fever, others chilled with cold and aching with rheumatism, upon the hard cold ground, the draughts and dampness of the atmosphere increasing their sufferings, and dirt, noise, and stench, and every aggravation of which sickness is capable, combined in their condition—here they lay like brute beasts, absorbed in physical suffering; unvisited by any of those Divine influences which may ennoble the dispensations of pain and illness, forsaken, as it seemed to me, of all good; and yet, O God, Thou surely hadst not

forsaken them! Now, pray take notice, that this is the hospital of an estate, where the owners are supposed to be humane, the overseer efficient and kind, and the negroes, remarkably well cared for and comfortable. As soon as I recovered from my dismay, I addressed old Rose, the midwife, who had charge of this room, bidding her open the shutters of such windows as were glazed, and let in the light. I next proceeded to make up the fire, but upon my lifting a log for that purpose, there was one universal outcry of horror, and old Rose, attempting to snatch it from me, exclaimed, "Let alone, missis—let be— what for you lift wood—you have nigger enough, missis, to do it!" I hereupon had to explain to them my view of the purposes for which hands and arms were appended to our bodies, and forthwith began making Rose tidy up the miserable apartment, removing all the filth and rubbish from the floor that could be removed, folding up in piles the blankets of the patients who were not using them, and placing, in rather more sheltered and comfortable positions, those who were unable to rise. It was all that I could do, and having enforced upon them all my earnest desire that they should keep their room swept, and as tidy as possible, I passed on to the other room on the ground floor, and to the two above, one of which is appropriated to the use of the men who are ill. They were all in the same deplorable condition, the upper rooms being rather the more miserable, inasmuch as none of the windows were glazed at all, and they had, therefore, only the alternative of utter darkness, or killing draughts of air, from the unsheltered casements. In all, filth, disorder and misery abounded; the floor was the only bed, and scanty begrimed rags of blankets the only covering. I left this refuge for Mr.——'s sick dependants, with my clothes covered with dust, and full of vermin, and with a heart heavy enough, as you will well believe. My morning's work had fatigued me not a little, and I was glad to return to the house, where

I gave vent to my indignation and regret at the scene I had just witnessed, to Mr.—— and his overseer, who, here, is a member of our family. The latter told me that the condition of the hospital had appeared to him, from his first entering upon his situation (only within the last year), to require a reform, and that he had proposed it to the former manager, Mr. K——, and Mr.——'s brother, who is part proprietor of the estate, but receiving no encouragement from them, had supposed that it was a matter of indifference to the owners, and had left it in the condition in which he had found it, in which condition it has been for the last nineteen years and upwards.

MARY BOYKIN CHESNUT, *A Confederate Lady's Diary* (1861)

The daughter and wife of wealthy Southern senators, Mary Boykin Chesnut (1823–1886) lived a plantation mistress's life of class and racial privilege. Her diary provides evidence of male slave owners' sexual exploitation of enslaved women. Chesnut's primary concern was the impact of the plantation owners' sexual misconduct on their wives. What evidence does Chesnut offer to support her allegation about interracial sexual relations between owners and enslaved women? What value judgments does she make? Why does she call slavery "a monstrous system"?*

I wonder if it be a sin to think slavery a curse to any land. Sumner said not one word of this hated institution which is not true. Men & women are punished when their masters & mistresses are brutes & not when they do wrong—& then we live surrounded by prostitutes. An abandoned woman is sent out of any decent house elsewhere. Who thinks any worse of a Negro or Mulatto woman for being a thing we can't name. God forgive *us*, but ours is a *monstrous* system & wrong & iniquity. Perhaps the rest of the world is as bad. This is *only* what I see: like the patriarchs of old, our men live all in one house with their wives & their concubines, & the Mulattos one sees in every family exactly resemble the white children—& every lady tells you who is the father of all the Mulatto children in everybody's household, but those in her own, she seems to think drop from the clouds or pretends so to think—. Good women we have, *but* they talk of *nastiness tho* they never do wrong; they talk day & night of—. My disgust sometimes is boiling over—but they are, I believe, in conduct the purest women God ever made. Thank God for my countrywomen—alas for the men! No worse than men everywhere, but the lower their mistresses, the more degraded they must be.

My mother-in-law told me when I was first married not to send my female servants in the street on errands. They were there tempted, led astray—& then she said placidly, "So they told *me* when I came here—& I was very particular, *but you see with what* result." Mr. Harris said it was so patriarchal. So it is—flocks & herds & slaves—& wife Leah does not suffice. Rachel must be *added,* if not *married* & all the time they seem to think themselves patterns—models of husbands & fathers.

Mrs. Davis told me "everybody described my husband's father as an old character, a Millionaire who did nothing for his son whatever, left him to struggle with poverty," &c. I replied, "Mr. Chesnut Senior thinks himself the

* In the public domain.

best of fathers—& his son thinks likewise. I have nothing to say—but it is true, he has no money but what he makes as a lawyer," &c.

Again I say, my countrywomen are as pure as angels—tho surrounded by another race who are—the social evil!

ELLA GERTRUDE CLANTON THOMAS, Excerpt from *The Secret Eye* (Sept. 17, 1864)

This excerpt from Ella Clanton Thomas's (1837–1907) journal was written in the context of Clanton's experience of the Civil War. Clanton implicitly corroborates Chestnut's belief of the prevalence of plantation owners' and their sons' sexual relations with enslaved women. Clanton kept her journal between 1849 and 1889. A member of the plantation elite, she developed doubts about the institution of slavery, but unlike those of the abolitionist Grimke sisters, her doubts were neither caused by her belief that slavery was a brutal institution nor by her sympathy for the enslaved. Like many slave owners, Clanton's racist values provided a rationale for ownership as not only necessary but as a benefit to the enslaved who came into contact with what Clanton believed to be superior white civilization. In this excerpt, Clanton describes the negative impact of slavery not on the enslaved but on the white owners.* What are the main points of her argument that slavery harms the owners?

Saturday, September 17, 1864 . . . How I do wish this war was over. I wish to breath free. I feel pent up, confined—cramped and shall I confess it am reminded of that Italian story of The Iron Shroud where daily—daily hourly and momently the room contracts, the victim meanwhile utterly impotent to avert the impending doom. Never have I so fully realised the feeble hold upon this world's goods as I do now. I don't think I have ever enjoyed that peculiarly charming season the Indian Summer more than I have during the past few weeks. Looking up the three Avenues and at the Goats Cows and Horses so quietly walking about, listening at the cooing of Pigions, the chirping of the different fowls in the yard—I imagine this contrasted with men clad in Yankee uniform rudely violating the privacy of my home. I imagine the booming of Yankee cannon and the clash of Yankee sabres and I ask myself how soon shall this thing be?? Nor does it require an imaginative mind to foretell such an event but the last page of my Journal must bear no such cowardly record.

I have sometimes doubted on the subject of slavery. I have seen so many of its evils chief among which is the terribly demoralising influence upon our men and boys but of late I have become convinced the Negro as a race is better off with us as he has been than if he were made free, but I am by no means so sure that we would not gain by his having his freedom given him. I grant that I am not so philanthropic as to be willing voluntarily to give all we own for the sake of the principle, but I do think that if we had the same invested in something else as a means of support I would willingly, nay gladly, have the responsibility of them taken off my shoulders.

This Journal was commenced July 13th 1861 and I am ashamed that three years of the most eventful period of my life should have had so poor a record but I find that the absorbing theme of war is one to be talked of better than written about and what I write is so commonplace when contrasted with the stirring events to which I allude that I shrink

---

* *The Secret Eye: The Journal of Ella Gertrude Clanton Thomas, 1848–1889*, edited by Virginia Ingraham Burr. Copyright © 1990 by Virginia Ingrahm Burr and Gertrude T. Despeau. Used by permission of the publisher.

from making a record of them. I have cut out for the scrap books (which I cannot buy) an account of all the important events which have taken place. . . . Again political events have absorbed so much of my Journal to the exclusion of domestic matters that one might readily suppose that I was not the happy mother of four darling children.

In this plantation memoir, Letitia Burwell (1838–1905) recalled the delights of childhood on her father's Virginia plantation and the contentment of the slaves. She stated that she wrote about her experience to provide her own nieces with the truth that slave owners were not cruel and monstrous. In the context of the justification of slavery literature, Burwell's narrative supports the depiction of kindly owners and docile slaves. This depiction of mutual harmony survived until the mid-twentieth century in popular culture and in movies such as *Gone with the Wind* and was repeated in many academic texts. Only in the 1950s did historians begin to undertake the serious scholarship needed to correct this mythic Southern plantation past. Yet even in Burwell's depiction, the cruelty inherent in slave ownership is demonstrated. The sale of slaves and separation of children from family members was a business transaction and exposed the pretense that slaves were part of their owners' extended family. What information does Burwell give to try to convince the reader that slaves benefited from their ownership by whites? How do Burwell's views of white superiority mold the narrative?*

At such establishments one easily acquired a habit of being waited upon, there being so many servants with so little to do. It was natural to ask for a drink of water when the water was right at hand, and to have things brought which you might easily have gotten yourself. But these domestics were so pleased at such errands, one felt no hesitation in requiring them. A young lady would ask black Nancy or Dolly to fan her, whereupon Nancy or Dolly would laugh good-naturedly, produce a large palm-leaf, and fall to fanning her young mistress vigorously, after which she would be rewarded with a bow of ribbon, some candy, or sweet cakes. The negroes made pocket-money by selling their own vegetables, poultry, eggs, etc.,—produced at the master's expense, of course. I often saw my mother take out her purse and pay them liberally for fowls, eggs, melons, sweet potatoes, brooms, shuck mats, and split baskets. The men made small crops of tobacco or potatoes for themselves on any piece of ground they chose to select.

My mother and grandmother were almost always talking over the wants of the negroes,—what medicine should be sent, whom they should visit, who needed new shoes, clothes, or blankets,—the principal object of their lives seeming to be in providing these comforts. The carriage was often ordered for them to ride around to the cabins to distribute light-bread, tea, and other necessaries among the sick. And besides employing the best doctor, my grandmother always saw that they received the best nursing and attention. . . .

When I reflect upon the degree of comfort arrived at in our homes, I think we should have felt grateful to our ancestors; for, as Quincy has written: "In whatever mode of existence man finds himself, be it savage or civilized, he perceives that he is indebted for the greater part of his possessions to events over which he had no control; to individuals

* Letitia M. Burwell, *A Girl's Life in Virginia before the War* (New York: F. A. Stokes, 1895).

whose names, perhaps, never reached his ear; to sacrifices which he never shared. How few of all these blessings do we owe to our own power or prudence! How few on which we cannot discern the impress of a long past generation!" So we were indebted for our agreeable surroundings to the heroism and sacrifices of past generations, which not to venerate and eulogize betrays the want of a truly noble soul. For what courage, what patience, what perseverance, what long suffering, what Christian forbearance, must it have cost our great-grandmothers to civilize, Christianize, and elevate the naked, savage Africans to the condition of good cooks and respectable maids! They—our great-grandmothers—did not enjoy the blessed privilege even of turning their servants off when inefficient or disagreeable, but had to keep them through life. The only thing was to bear and forbear, and

> *Be to their virtues very kind,*
> *Be to their faults a little blind.*

If in heaven there be one seat higher than another, it must be reserved for those true Southern matrons, who performed conscientiously their part assigned them by God—civilizing and instructing this race. I have searched missionary records of all ages, but find no results in Africa or elsewhere at all comparing with the grand work accomplished for the African race in out Southern homes.

Closing the last chapter of "Explorations in the Dark Continent," the thought came to me that it would be well if our African friends in America would set apart another anniversary to celebrate "the landing of their fathers on the shores of America," when they were bought and domiciled in American homes. This must have been God's own plan for helping them, although a severe ordeal for our ancestors.

In God's own time and way the shackles have been removed from this people, who are now sufficiently civilized to take an independent position in the great family of man. However we may differ in the opinion, there is no greater compliment to Southern slaveowners than the idea prevailing in many places that the negro is already sufficiently elevated to hold the highest positions in the gift of our government.

I once met in traveling an English gentleman who asked me: "How can you bear those miserable black negroes about your houses and about your persons? To me they are horribly repulsive, and I would not endure one about me."

"Neither would they have been my choice," I replied. "But God sent them to us. I was born to this inheritance and could not avert it. What would you English have done," I asked, "if God had sent them to you?"

"Thrown them to the bottom of the sea!" he replied.

Fortunately for the poor negro this sentiment did not prevail among us. I believe God endowed our people with qualities peculiarly adapted to taking charge of this race, and that no other nation could have kept them. Our people did not demand as much work as in other countries is required of servants, and I think had more affection for them than is elsewhere felt for menials.

CHAPTER 6

Abolitionist Women and the Controversy over Racial Equality

During the 1830s, some women developed an abolitionist sisterhood that united white and free black women across the racial divide. Initially women were barred from membership in the American Anti-Slavery Society (AASS), the nation's leading abolitionist organization. In 1832, in Salem, Massachusetts, African American women organized the nation's first female antislavery society. Female Anti-Slavery Society (PFASS) under Lucretia Mott's leadership and a similar society in Boston led by Maria Weston Chapman. Within a few years, there was a proliferation of female abolitionist societies, some segregated, others racially inclusive. In these female-only organizations, women acquired the skill and confidence to speak out, formulate objectives, write antislavery petitions to Congress, and sponsor fund-raising events. In Boston, African American abolitionist Maria Stewart set a precedent and became the first woman to engage in public speaking to a mixed audience of men and women.

This was not, however, a sisterhood based on racial equality. Relatively few white abolitionist women supported the struggle of their black "sisters" to attain civil rights and racial equality. Racist policies and segregation blanketed the Northeast and Midwest, and most white women shared the belief in the superiority of whites over blacks. Sisterhood as rhetoric and symbol linked the abolitionist communities in England and America. For some white women, it was easier to cross the Atlantic divide than the racial one. A trans-Atlantic sisterhood also would characterize the women's rights movement. Nonetheless white female abolitionists in the context of their time and the national experience were progressive, even radical, particularly those who advocated immediate emancipation and supported integrated organizations. Their efforts at "sisterhood," although flawed and incomplete as judged by contemporary standards, moved well beyond the social norms of the antebellum era.

For free African American women, the link between antislavery agitation and civil rights was vital, based in part on their own pain and outrage over their experience of racial discrimination in the North and Midwest that restricted their access to libraries, first-class accommodations, schools, housing, theaters, and restaurants. Sarah Mapps Douglass, to her dismay, found that her Quaker meetinghouse in Philadelphia enforced segregated seating, and she had to sit in the back on a bench restricted to African Americans. Sarah Remond, despite her academic ability, could not attend the school of her choice in Salem, Massachusetts, and some time later she was forcibly ejected from a Boston theater after refusing to sit in the balcony. A century before Rosa Parks defied racial subordination on public transportation, African American schoolteacher Elizabeth Jennings boarded a for whites-only horse-drawn bus in New York City, and was dragged out by the driver who received help from a policeman. She sued the bus company and won the case. The verdict in her favor facilitated the desegregation of the city's transportation system.

Free African American women experienced the intertwined oppression of racial and gender discrimination. Not only did they encounter the racism of white women who embraced emancipation but endorsed segregation, but they also confronted gender assumptions about women's "proper" domestic roles. Although the abolitionist sisterhood splintered over the issue of racial equality, there were notable white women who promoted both emancipation and racial equality. Lydia Maria Child, as early as 1833, wrote a lengthy but passionate appeal to end slavery and also racial discrimination. Angelina Grimké in 1838 implored white women to change their behavior and allow black women to live on equal terms with whites. Prudence Crandall put her belief in equality into action and despite community outrage admitted black female students to her private school in Canterbury, Connecticut (see Chapter 3), A trans-Atlantic American and British group of white abolitionist women supported both abolition and racial justice.

In an effort to boycott the sale of sugar made from slave labor, Lydia Maria Child and her husband raised beets for sugar production. Some white women expressed their abolitionist sentiments by helping fugitive slaves escape on the Underground Railroad, although it was a federal crime to harbor fugitives and the penalties were severe. Abolitionist journalist Julia Louisa Lovejoy left New Hampshire for Kansas and provided New England newspapers with reports of the escalating violence between pro-slavery proponents and abolitionists. The 1830s were a peak time for the formation of female antislavery societies and activities. African American Frances Watkins Harper wrote antislavery poems in addition to speeches. Other abolitionist women organized boycotts of slave-made cotton goods and went on house-to-house antislavery petition drives. Petition activity actually gained momentum in 1836 as a reaction to the Gag Rule, the congressional decision to table all antislavery petitions. Believing that the South was suppressing civil liberties in the North, women flooded Congress with antislavery petitions and in the process strengthened their claim to full citizenship rights. Abolitionist strategies also included antislavery fairs that became more elaborate over time and proved to be successful fund-raisers. Political parties of the forties and fifties drew support from abolitionist women. Women could not vote, but some identified with the Free Soil Party and became actively engaged in the nation's most pressing issue of deciding the future of slavery.

From the time women first began lecturing in public, gender issues threatened to overwhelm the entire abolitionist movement. The familiar allegation of such women being out of their "place" had gained prominence with the New England clergy's *Pastoral Letter*. Reacting to the Grimké sisters' public lecture tour in 1838, the clergy claimed women were behaving unnaturally and acting in defiance of Scripture and God. Ironically Protestant ministers had helped construct the belief that white Protestant women possessed special gender-based piety and moral authority. Women internalized this belief in their own moral authority and benevolence, and it empowered them to address a wide range of moral and humanitarian concerns, including abolitionism. Sarah Grimké's reply to the Pastoral Letter is a pivotal document in the history of women's rights and vividly demonstrates the link between abolitionism and women's rights.

William Lloyd Garrison, the most radical of the white male abolitionists, worked for both racial equality and women's rights. He welcomed white and black women into the cause and encouraged them to lecture and publish articles in *The Liberator,* the official newspaper of Garrison's American Anti-Slavery Society (AASS). Abolitionist women such as Elizabeth Emery and Mary Abbot wrote letters to *The Liberator* expressing their abhorrence of slavery. With Garrison's sponsorship and financial support, not only the Grimké sisters but also African American and white women abolitionists went on extensive lecture tours as representatives of the AASS. Garrison's decision in 1840 to allow Abby Kelley and other women to play active roles within the AASS caused the organization to splinter into two groups. Many abolitionist men believed women should not be allowed to join male organizations, let alone assume positions of responsibility.

Garrison's belief in gender and racial equality was not widely shared. Opposition to women's activist participation was more indicative of public opinion. The abolitionist movement did not enjoy wide spread support and anti-abolitionist riots proliferated. Hostility over women speaking in public made female abolitionists the target of verbal and physical attacks. Pelted with rocks and refuse, surrounded by hostile mobs, they placed their lives at risk. Sentiments reached a fever pitch in the burning of Pennsylvania Hall in Philadelphia in 1838 shortly after a meeting of the Anti-Slavery Convention of American Women. Angelina Grimké was one of the speakers. A new building, Pennsylvania Hall had been designed specifically to provide a place for abolitionist events. Abolitionism aroused passionate opposition not only because it was an unpopular cause, but also because white and free women of color who participated in it were viewed as being "out of their place," threatening both gender and racial norms.

For women such as Sarah Grimké, abolitionist activism served as a precursor for the fight for women's rights. New England ministers, who tried to silence Grimké, encountered her militant defiance based on Scripture and women's rights. Amidst male efforts to deprive women of their right to speak, women defended their growing public involvement in the antislavery crusade. They struggled for self-definition and against prescribed roles. Some came to view their restricted rights and legal nonexistence as wives as analogous to the conditions of slavery. For these women, the formation of a women's rights crusade offered the promise of ending gender-based oppression. In contrast, other abolitionist women retreated from public activism. The ordeal of speaking in public or attending meetings amidst virulent hostility and mob riots proved too overwhelming.

MARIA M. STEWART, *Address Delivered at the African Masonic Hall, Boston* (February 27, 1833)

Free born, African American, Maria Stewart (1803–1879) was the nation's first woman to lecture against slavery in a public forum. Also precedent breaking, she addressed a racially mixed audience of men and women. Her lectures took place in Boston during the early 1830s, and three of the four speeches also were published in *The Liberator*, the nation's leading antislavery newspaper. Massachusetts abolished slavery in 1783 and compared to other Northern cities, abolitionist activism flourished there. Although

Stewart worked as a domestic and had little formal education, she addressed complex and controversial issues of slavery, racism, and women's rights. Her public speaking and assumption of authority included her outspoken criticism of African American men whom she alleged needed self improvement, challenged gender roles. Not surprisingly, she encountered widespread opposition. In addition to racism, Stewart and other African American women also confronted the gendered beliefs of black men who preferred that women not assume public roles but uphold norms of public silence, a belief they shared with white men.

Although Stewart did not continue her public speaking career and left Boston for New York City, she continued to support antislavery activities and women's rights. What are the major points of her anti-slavery argument? What particular aspects of African American male behavior did she criticize? How did she link her allegations against African American men with her role of public critic and speaker?*

African rights and liberty is a subject that ought to fire the breast of every free man of color in these United States, and excite in his bosom a lively, deep, decided and heart-felt interest. When I cast my eyes on the long list of illustrious names that are enrolled on the bright annals of fame among the whites, I turn my eyes within, and ask my thoughts, "Where are the names of *our* illustrious ones?" It must certainly have been for the want of energy on the part of the free people of color, that they have been long willing to bear the yoke of oppression. It must have been the want of ambition and force that has given the whites occasion to say, that our natural abilities are not as good, and our capacities by nature inferior to theirs. They boldly assert, that, did we possess a natural independence of soul, and feel a love for liberty within our breasts, some one of our sable race, long before this, would have testified it, notwithstanding the disadvantages under which we labor. We have made ourselves appear altogether unqualified to speak in our own defence, and are therefore looked upon as objects of pity and commiseration. We have been imposed upon, insulted and derided on every side; and now, if we complain, it is considered as the height of impertinence. We have suffered ourselves to be considered as Bastards, cowards, mean, faint-hearted wretches; and on this account, (not because of our complexion) many

despise us, and would gladly spurn us from their presence.

These things have fired my soul with a holy indignation, and compelled me thus to come forward; and endeavor to turn their attention to knowledge and improvement; for knowledge is power. I would ask, is it blindness of mind, or stupidity of soul, or the want of education, that has caused our men who are 60 to 70 years of age, never to let their voices be heard, or their hands be raised in behalf of their color? Or has it been for the fear of offending the whites? If it has, O ye fearful ones, throw off your fearfulness, and come forth in the name of the Lord, and in the strength of the God of Justice, and make yourselves useful and active members in society; for they admire a noble and patriotic spirit in others; and should they not admire it in us? If you are men, convince them that you possess the spirit of men; and as your day, so shall your strength be. Have the sons of Africa no souls? feel they no ambitious desires? shall the chains of ignorance forever confine them? shall the insipid appellation of "clever negroes," or "good creatures," any longer content them? Where can we find among ourselves the man of science, or a philosopher, or an able statesman, or a counsellor at law? Show me our fearless and brave, our noble and gallant ones. Where are our lecturers on natural history, and our critics in useful

---

* In the public domain.

knowledge? There may be a few such men among us, but they are rare. It is true, our fathers bled and died in the revolutionary war, and others fought bravely under the command of Jackson, in defence of liberty. But where is the man that has distinguished himself in these modern days by acting wholly in the defence of African rights and liberty? There was one, although he sleeps, his memory lives.

I am sensible that there are many highly intelligent gentlemen of color in those United States. . . .

White Americans, by their prudence, economy and exertions, have sprung up and become one of the most flourishing nations in the world, distinguished for their knowledge of the arts and sciences, for their polite literature. While our minds are vacant, and starving for want of knowledge, theirs are filled to overflowing. Most of our color have been taught to stand in fear of the white man, from their earliest infancy, to work as soon as they could walk, and call "master," before they scarce could lisp the name of *mother.* Continual fear and laborious servitude have in some degree lessened in us that natural force and energy which belong to man; or else, in defiance of opposition, our men, before this, would have nobly and boldly contended for their rights. But give the man of color an equal opportunity with the white from the cradle to manhood, and from manhood to the grave, and you would discover the dignified statesman, the man of science, and the philosopher. But there is no such opportunity for the sons of Africa, and I fear that our powerful ones are fully determined that there never shall be. Forbid, ye Powers on high, that it should any longer be said that our men possess no force. O ye sons of Africa, when will your voices be heard in our legislative halls, in defiance of your enemies, contending for equal rights and liberty? How can you, when you reflect from what you have fallen, refrain from crying mightily unto God, to turn away from

us the fierceness of his anger, and remember our transgressions against us no more forever. But a God of infinite purity will not regard the prayers of those who hold religion in one hand, and prejudice, sin and pollution in the other; he will not regard the prayers of self-righteousness and hypocrisy. Is it possible, I exclaim, that for the want of knowledge, we have labored for hundreds of years to support others, and been content to receive what they chose to give us in return? Cast your eyes about, look as far as you can see; all, all is owned by the lordly white, except here and there a lowly dwelling which the man of color, midst deprivations, fraud and opposition, has been scarce able to procure. Like king Solomon, who put neither nail nor hammer to the temple, yet received the praise; so also have the white Americans gained themselves a name, like the names of the great men that are in the earth, while in reality we have been their principal foundation and support. We have pursued the shadow, they have obtained the substance; we have performed the labor they have received the profits; we have planted the vines, they have eaten the fruits of them.

I would implore our men, and especially our rising youth, to flee from the gambling board and the dance-hall; for we are poor, and have no money to throw away. I do not consider dancing as criminal in itself, but it is astonishing to me that our young men are so blind to their own interest and the future welfare of their children, as to spend their hard earnings for this frivolous amusement; for it has been carried on among us to such an unbecoming extent, that it has became absolutely disgusting. "Faithful are the wounds of a friend, but the kisses of an enemy are deceitful." Had those men among us, who have had an opportunity, turned their attention as assiduously to mental and moral improvement as they have to gambling and dancing, I might have remained quietly at home, and they stood contending in my place. . . .

ELIZABETH EMERY AND MARY P. ABBOTT, *Letter to The Liberator* (1836)

Women wrote letters to William Lloyd Garrison's abolitionist newspaper, *The Liberator,* that reflected their antislavery commitment. The following letter by Elizabeth Emery and Mary P. Abbot, of Andover, Massachusetts, expressed the intensity of their moral outrage against slavery. What justification did they provide for women's abolitionist activism? What is the significance of the phrase "her oppressed sister cries aloud for help"? In what ways does the letter express biracial sisterhood?*

Andover, Massachusetts, August 22, 1836

Mr. Editor:

In these days of women's doings, it may not be amiss to report the proceedings of some ladies in Andover. The story is now and then told of a new thing done here, as the opening of a railroad, or the building of a factory, but we have news better than all— it is the formation of a "Female Antislavery Society."

The call of our female friends across the waters—the energetic appeal of those untiring sisters in the work of emancipation in Boston—above all, the sighs, the groans, the deathlike struggles of scourged sisters in the South—these have moved our hearts, our hands. We feel that woman has a place in this Godlike work, for women's woes, and women's wrongs, are borne to us on every breeze that flows from the South; woman has a place, for she forms a part in God's created intelligent instrumentality to reform the world. God never made her to be inactive nor in all cases to follow in the wake of man. When man proves recreant to his duty and faithless to his Maker, woman, with her feeling heart, should rouse him—should start his sympathies—should cry in his ear, and raise such a storm of generous sentiment, as shall never let him sleep again. We believe God gave woman a heart to feel—an eye to weep—a hand to work—a tongue to speak. Now let her use that tongue to speak on slavery. Is it not a curse—a heaven-daring abomination? Let her employ that hand, to labor for the slave. Does not her sister in bonds, labor night and day without reward? Let her heart grieve, and her eye fill with tears, in view of a female's body dishonored—a female's mind debased—a female's soul forever ruined! Woman [had] nothing to do with slavery! Abhorred the thought!! We will pray to abhor it more and more. Is not woman abused—woman trampled upon— woman spoiled of her virtue, her probity, her influence, her joy! And this, not in India—not in China—not in Turkey—not in Africa but in America—in the United States of America, in the birthplace of Washington, the father of freedom, the protector of woman, the friend of equality and human rights!

Woman out of her place, in feeling, playing, and acting for the slave! Impious idea! Her oppressed sister cries aloud for help. She tries to lift her manacled hand—to turn her bruised face—to raise her tearful eye, and by all these, to plead a remembrance in our prayers—an interest in our labors. . . . Woman then may not be dumb. Christian sisters of Boston! We gladly respond to your call. We will "leave no energy unemployed— no righteous means untried. We will grudge no expense—yield to no opposition—forget fatigue, till by the strength of prayer and sacrifice, the spirit of love shall have overcome sectional jealousy—political rivalry— prejudice against color—cowardly concession of principle—wicked compromise with sin— devotion to gain, and spiritual despotism,

---

* From Elizabeth Emery and Mary P. Abbott, "Letter to *The Liberator*," *The Liberator,* August 27, 1836, 6: 138.

which now bear with a mountain's weight upon the slave." As Christian women, we will do a Christian woman's duty.

The Constitution of our Society is so similar to that of other Antislavery Societies, it may not be necessary to give a copy of it. Our preamble gives our creed:

"We believe American Slavery is a sin against God—at war with the dictates of humanity, and subversive of the principles of freedom, because it regards rational beings as goods and chattel; robs them of compensation for their toil—denies to them the protection of law—disregards the relation of husband and wife, brother and sister, parent and child; shuts out from the intellect the light of knowledge; overwhelms hope in despair and ruins the soul—thus sinking to the level of brutes, more than one million of American females, who are created in God's image, a little lower than the angels', and consigns them over to degradation, physical, social, intellectual and moral: consequently, every slaveholder is bound instantly to cease from all participation in such a system. We believe that we should have no fellowship with these works of darkness, but rather reprove them—and that the truth spoken in love, is mighty to the removal of slavery, as of all other sins."

On such a creed, we base the constitution, which binds us together, and which we omit. . . .

[M]ay fearful foreboding lead the slave holder to timely repentance.

Elizabeth Emery, President
Mary P. Abbott, Rec. Secretary

Sarah Mapps Douglass, *Letter to William Basset, a Lynn, Massachusetts, Abolitionist* (Dec. 1837)

Sarah Mapps Douglass's (1806–1882) family was prominent in the free African American community of Philadelphia. Two of her closest friends were the Grimké sisters, with whom she shared her Quaker faith and with whom she discussed the restrictive policy that prevented her from freely choosing a place to sit at religious meetings. She found it demeaning to have to sit on the back bench assigned only to black people. Douglass publicized the policy in an antislavery newspaper. As a religious group, the Society of Friends or Quakers tended to be more sympathetic to abolitionism than other Protestant denominations. Nonetheless white Quakers also practiced patterns of institutional segregation and racist behavior. Despite protest, neither Douglass nor the Grimké sisters were able to get the discriminatory seating policy changed.

Why might Douglass have experienced this manifestation of racism in a religious setting as particularly hurtful? What reasons does she give for white prejudice against African Americans?*

Phila [Penn.] December, 1837.

Esteemed Friend.

Your favor of the 7th came safe to hand. It needed no apology. The fact of your being an abolitionist; the friend of my beloved sisters Sarah and Angelina Grimké, the friend of my poor and oppressed bretheren and sisters enti[t]les you to my warmest gratitude and esteem. I thank God that he has enabled you to renounce error and strengthened you to come up to the help of the Lord against the mighty. I pray that you may run the race set before you without halting, keeping your eye ste[a]dfastly fixed on the great Captain of our salvation.

---

* Weld-Grimké Collection, Clements Library, University of Michigan, Ann Arbor.

The questions you ask me, make me feel my weakness, and in view of the great responsibility that rests upon me in answering them, my flesh trembles; yet will I cast my burden on Him, who is strength in weakness and resolve to do my duty; to tell the truth and leave the consequences to God. I thank you for the "Letter to a member of the Society of Friends". I can set my seal to the truth of the following paragraph, extracted from it. "It will be allowed that the Negro Pew or its equivalent may be found in some of our meeting houses where men and women bretheren and sisters by creat[i]on and heirs of the same glorious immortality are seated by themselves on a back bench for no other reason but because it has pleased God to give them a complexion darker than our own." And as you request to know particularly about Arch Street Meeting, I may say that the experience of years has made me wise in this fact, that there is a bench set apart at that meeting for our people, whether *officially* appointed or not I cannot say; but this I am free to say that my mother and myself were told to sit there, and that a friends sat at each end of the bench to prevent white persons from sitting there. And even when a child my soul was made sad with hearing five or six times during the course of one meeting this language of remonstrance addressed to those who were willing to sit by us. "This bench is for the black people." "This bench is for the people of color." And oftentimes I wept, at other times I felt indignant and queried in my own mind are these people Christians. Now it seems clear to me that had not this bench been set apart for oppressed Americans, there would have been no necessity for the oft-repeated and galling remonstrance, galling indeed, because *I believe they despise us for our color.* I have not been in Arch Street meeting for four years; but my mother goes once a week and frequently she has a *whole long bench* to herself. The assertion that our people who attend their meetings prefer sitting by themselves, is not true. A very near

friend of ours, that fears God and who has been a constant attender of Friends meeting from his childhood, says "Thou mayest tell William Basset, that I know that 'Friends' appointed a seat for our people at the meeting which I attend. Several years ago a friend came to me and told me that 'Friends' had appointed a back bench for us. I told him with some warmth that I had just as lief sit on the floor as sit there. I do not care about it, Friends do not do the thing that is right." Judge now, I pray you, whether this man preferred sitting by himself. Two sons of the person I have just mentioned, have left attending Friends meetings within the last few months, because they could no longer endure the "scorning of those that are at ease, and the contempt of the proud." Conversing with one of them today, I asked, why did you leave Friends. "Because they do not know how to treat me, I do not like to sit on a back bench and be treated with contempt, so I go where I am better treated." Do you not like their principles and their mode of worship? "Yes, I like their principles, but not their practice. They make the *highest* profession of any sect of Christians, and are the most deficient in practice." In reply to your question "whether there appears to be a diminution of prejudice towards you among Friends," I unhesitatingly answer, no. I have heard it frequently remarked and have observed it myself, that in proportion as we become intellectual and respectable, so in proportion does their disgust and prejudice increase.

Yet while I speak this of Friends as a body, I am happy to say that there is in this city a "noble few", who have cleansed their garments from the foul stain of prejudice, and are doing all their hands find to do in promoting the moral and mental elevation of oppressed Americans.

Some of these are members of Anti-Slavery Societies and others belong to the old abolition School.

While I have been penning this letter living desires have sprung up in my soul that

I might "nothing extenuate nor set down ought in malice". Doubtless you know that our beloved A. E. G[rimké] is convalescent. Did all the members of Friends society feel for us, as the sisters Grimké do, how soon, how very soon would the fetters be stricken from the captive and cruel prejudice be driven from the bosoms of the professed followers of Christ. We were lying wounded and bleeding, trampled to the very dust by the heel of our bretheren and our sisters, when Sarah and Angelina Grimké passed by; they saw our low estate and their hearts melted within them; with the tenderness of ministering angels they lifted us from the dust and poured the oil of consolation, the balm of sympathy into our lacerated bosoms; they identified themselves with us, took our wrongs upon them, and made our oppression and woe theirs. Is it any marvel then that we call them blessed among women? We value them not because they belong to the great and the mighty of our land, but because they love Christ and our afflicted bretheren. Most cordially do we approve every step they have taken since they left us, believing that the unerring spirit of truth is their leader [and] friend. I hope this letter may be satisfactory to you; use it, and the account of my brother in any way you may think proper, but do not give my name unless it is absolutely necessary. Please tell our beloved A. E. G. that her friends entreat her not to exert herself until she is quite strong. May the Lord bless you, and may you anchor your little bark on the rock, Christ Jesus; that so, when the storm of persecution arises, You may suffer no loss.

Prays fervently
Sarah M. Douglass

LYDIA MARIA CHILD, Excerpt from the Appeal: *"Prejudices Against People of Color, and our Duties in Relation to this Subject"* (1833)

An amazingly prolific writer, Lydia Maria Child (1802–1880) wrote novels, children's books, manuals containing advice to housewives, and antislavery tracts. She had the rare ability to move easily from light-hearted literature to writing about the most serious national issues. She also sponsored and served as editor of Harriet Jacobs's *Incidents in the Life of a Slave Girl*. Public anger accompanied her publication of *An Appeal of That Class of Americans Called Africans* in 1833. The book was comprehensive and well researched and offered tightly structured arguments refuting not only slavery but also racial prejudice. Northern readers did not want to acknowledge either their complicity in slavery or their own racist beliefs. As a result, Child's popularity as an author suffered and her book sales declined. She was, however, more than welcome in abolitionist circles, and her book became a "must read" sensation. Many future abolitionists credited her book with convincing them of the justice of the cause.

   Which of Child's views might be considered radical even by abolitionist standards? How would you evaluate Child's arguments?*

Chapter VIII

Prejudices Against People of Color, and Our Duties in Relation to This Subject

WHILE we bestow our earnest disapprobation on the system of slavery, let us not flatter ourselves that we are in reality any better than our brethren of the South. Thanks to our soil and climate, and the early exertions of the Quakers, the *form* of slavery does not exist among us; but the very *spirit* of the hateful and mischievous thing is here in all its strength. The manner in which we use

---

* Lydia Maria Child, *An Appeal of That Class of Americans Called Africans* (Boston: Allen & Ticknor, 1833).

what power we have, gives us ample reason to be grateful that the nature of our institutions does not intrust us with more. Our prejudice against colored people is even more inveterate than it is at the South. The planter is often attached to his negroes, and lavishes caresses and kind words upon them, as he would on a favorite hound: but our coldhearted, ignoble prejudice admits of no exception—no intermission.

The Southerners have long continued habit, apparent interest and dreaded danger, to palliate the wrong they do; but we stand without excuse. They tell us that Northern ships and Northern capital have been engaged in this wicked business; and the reproach is true. Several fortunes in this city have been made by the sale of negro blood. If these criminal transactions are still carried on, they are done in silence and secrecy, because public opinion has made them disgraceful. But if the free States wished to cherish the system of slavery forever, they could not take a more direct course than they now do. Those who are kind and liberal on all other subjects, unite with the selfish and the proud in their unrelenting efforts to keep the colored population in the lowest state of degradation; and the influence they unconsciously exert over children early infuses into their innocent minds the same strong feelings of contempt.

The intelligent and well informed have the least share of this prejudice; and when their minds can be brought to reflect upon it, I have generally observed that they soon cease to have any at all. But such a general apathy prevails and the subject is so seldom brought into view, that few are really aware how oppressively the influence of society is made to bear upon this injured class of the community. When I have related facts, that came under my own observation, I have often been listened to with surprise, which gradually increased to indignation. In order that my readers may not be ignorant of the extent of this tyrannical prejudice, I will as briefly as possible state the evidence, and leave them to judge of it, as their hearts and consciences may dictate. In the first place, an unjust law exists in this Commonwealth, by which marriages between persons of different color is pronounced illegal. I am perfectly aware of the gross ridicule to which I may subject myself by alluding to this particular; but I have lived too long, and observed too much, to be disturbed by the world's mockery. In the first place, the government ought not to be invested with power to control the affections, any more than the consciences of citizens. A man has at least as good a right to choose his wife, as he has to choose his religion. His taste may not suit his neighbors; but so long as his deportment is correct, they have no right to interfere with his concerns. In the second place, this law is a *useless* disgrace to Massachusetts. Under existing circumstances, none but those whose condition in life is too low to be much affected by public opinion, will form such alliances; and they, when they choose to do so, *will* make such marriages, in spite of the law. I know two or three instances where women of the laboring class have been united to reputable, industrious colored men. These husbands regularly bring home their wages, and are kind to their families. If by some of the odd chances, which not unfrequently occur in the world, their wives should become heirs to any property, the children may be wronged out of it, because the law pronounces them illegitimate. And while this injustice exists with regard to *honest,* industrious individuals, who are merely guilty of differing from us in a matter of taste, neither the legislation nor customs of slave-holding States exert their influence against *immoral* connexions.

In one portion of our country this fact is shown in a very peculiar and striking manner. There is a numerous class at New Orleans, called Quateroons, or Quadroons, because their colored blood has for several successive generations been intermingled with the white.

The women are much distinguished for personal beauty and gracefulness of motion; and their parents frequently send them to France for the advantages of an elegant education. White gentlemen of the first rank are desirous of being invited to their parties, and often become seriously in love with these fascinating but unfortunate beings. Prejudice forbids matrimony, but universal custom sanctions temporary connexions, to which a certain degree of respectability is allowed, on account of the peculiar situation of the parties. These attachments often continue for years—sometimes for life—and instances are not unfrequent of exemplary constancy and great propriety of deportment.

Pastoral Letter to New England Churches (1837)

The Congregational clergy denounced outspoken women abolitionists in this pastoral letter. The Grimké sisters were the particular targets of their wrath. The letter spelled out in detail why the "obtrusive and ostentatious" behavior of these women was "unnatural" and defied Christian precepts. The clergy urged women to remain strictly within their God-ordained female sphere. Ministers reminded women that their essential character was like a vine that needed to cling to men for protection and support. What other arguments did the clergy provide to support female subordination and passivity? What role did they assign to women? When do women forfeit male protection?*

We invite your attention to the dangers which at present seem to threaten the female character with widespread and permanent injury.

The appropriate duties and influence of woman are clearly stated in the New Testament. Those duties and that influence are unobtrusive and private, but the source of mighty power. When the mild, dependent, softening influence of woman upon the sternness of man's opinions is fully exercised, society feels the effects of it in a thousand forms. The power of woman is in her dependence, flowing from the consciousness of that weakness which God has given her for her protection, and which keeps her in those departments of life that form the character of individuals and of the nation. There are social influences which females use in promoting piety, and the great objects of Christian benevolence which we cannot too highly commend. We appreciate the unostentatious prayers and efforts of woman in advancing the cause of religion at home and abroad; in Sabbath-schools; in leading religious inquirers to the pastors for instruction; and in all such associated effort as becomes the modesty of her sex; and earnestly hope that she may abound more and more in these labors of piety and love.

But when she assumes the place and tone of man as a public reformer, our care and protection of her seem unnecessary; we put ourselves in self-defense against her; she yields the power which God has given her for protection, and her character becomes unnatural. If the vine, whose strength and beauty is to lean upon the trellis-work and half conceal its clusters, thinks to assume the independence and the overshadowing nature of the elm, it will not only cease to bear fruit, but fall in shame and dishonor into the dust. We cannot, therefore, but regret the mistaken conduct of those who encourage females to bear an obtrusive and ostentatious part in measures of reform, and countenance any of that sex who so far forget themself as to incinerate in the character of public lecturers and teachers.

---

* From "Pastoral Letter of the General Association of Massachusetts to the Congregational Churches Under Their Care," reprinted in *The Liberator,* August 11, 1837.

SARAH GRIMKÉ, *Reply to Pastoral Letter* (1837)

Women who were opposed to slavery, such as the Grimké sisters, dramatically departed from what many men and women considered appropriate female behavior. The daughters of a Southern slave owner, both Sarah and Angelina Grimké became Quakers and joined the abolitionist crusade. The sisters lectured on behalf of William Lloyd Garrison's American Anti-Slavery Society. In her reply to the *Pastoral Letter,* Sarah Grimké (1792–1873) directly addressed the question of women speaking in public. Lashing out against the "self-styled lords of creation," she demanded equality and moral accountability for women. Grimké's reply was a pioneer feminist's argument for women's power. What evidence did she offer to support her defense for women's equality with men? Why did she equate women's submission with hypocrisy?*

[The Pastoral Letter] says, "We invite your attention to the dangers which at present seem to threaten the FEMALE CHARACTER with widespread and permanent injury." I rejoice that they have called the attention of my sex to this subject, because I believe if woman investigates it, she will soon discover that danger is impending, though from a totally different source from that which the Association apprehends—danger from those who, having long held the reins of *usurped* authority, are unwilling to permit us to fill that sphere which God created us to move in, and who have entered into league to crush the immortal mind of woman. I rejoice, because I am persuaded that the rights of woman, like the rights of slaves, need only be examined, to be understood and asserted, even by some of those who are now endeavoring to smother the irrepressible desire for mental and spiritual freedom which glows in the breast of many who hardly dare to speak their sentiments.

"The appropriate duties and influence of woman are clearly stated in the New Testament. Those duties are unobtrusive and private, but the sources of *mighty power.* When the mild, *dependent,* softening influence of woman upon the sternness of man's opinions, is fully exercised, society feels the effects of it in a thousand ways." No one can desire more earnestly than I do, that woman may move exactly in the sphere which her Creator has assigned her; and I believe her having been

displaced from that sphere, has introduced confusion into the world. It is therefore of vast importance to herself, and to all the rational creation, that she should ascertain what are her duties and privileges as a responsible and immortal being. The New Testament has been referred to, and I am willing to abide by its decision, and must enter my protest against the false translations of some passages by the MEN who did that work, and against the perverted interpretations by the MEN who undertook to write commentaries thereon. I am inclined to think, when we are admitted to the honor of studying Greek and Hebrew, we shall produce some various readings of the Bible, a little different from those we now have.

I find the Lord Jesus defining the duties of his followers in his sermon on the Mount, laying down grant principles by which they should be governed, without any preference to sect or condition:—"Ye are the light of the world. A city that is set on a hill cannot be hid. Neither do men light a candle and put it under a bushel, but on a candlestick, and it giveth light unto all that are in the house. Let your light so shine before men, that they may see your good works, and glorify your Father which is in heaven." I follow him through all his precepts, and find him giving the same directions to women as to men, never even referring to the distinction now so strenuously insisted upon between masculine and feminine virtues: this is one of the anti-Christian "traditions of men"

---

* From Sarah Grimké, "Province of Women: The Pastoral Letter," *The Liberator,* October 6, 1837.

which are taught instead of the "commandments of God." Men and women were CREATED EQUAL; they are both moral and accountable beings, and whatever is right for man to do, is right for woman to do.

But the influence of woman, says the Association, is to be private and unobtrusive; her light is not to shine before man like that of her brethren; but she is passively to let the lords of the creation, as they call themselves, put the bushel over it, lest peradventure it might appear that the world has been benefited by the rays of her candle. Then her quenched light is of more use than if it were set on the candlestick:—"Her influence is the source of mighty power." This has ever been the language of man since he laid aside the whip as a means to keep woman in subjection. He spares her body, but the war he has waged against her mind, her heart, and her soul, has been no less destructive to her as a moral being. How monstrous is the doctrine that the woman is to be dependent on man! Where in all the sacred scriptures is this taught? But, alas, she has too well learned the lesson which he has labored to teach her. She has surrendered her dearest RIGHTS, and has been satisfied with the privileges which man has assumed to grant her, whilst he has amused her with the show of power, and absorbed all the reality into himself. He has adorned the creature, whom God gave him as companion, with baubles and gewgaws, turned her attention to personal attractions, offered incense to her vanity, and made her the instrument of his selfish gratification, a plaything to please his eye, and amuse his hours of leisure.—"Rule by obedience, and by submission sway," or in other words, study to be a hypocrite, pretend to submit, but gain your point, has been the code of household morality which woman has been taught. The poet has sung in sickly strains the loveliness of woman's dependence upon man, and now we find it re-echoed by those who profess to teach the religion of the Bible. God says, "Cease ye from man whose breath is in his nostrils, for wherein is he to be accounted of?" Man says, depend upon me. God says, "He will

teach us of his ways." May says, believe it or not; I am to be your teacher. This doctrine of dependence upon man is utterly at variance with the doctrine of the Bible. In that book I find nothing like the softness of woman, nor the sternness of man; but both are equally commanded to bring forth the fruits of the Spirit—Love, meekness, gentleness.

But we are told, "the power of woman is in her dependence, flowing from a consciousness of that weakness which God has given her for her protection." If physical weakness is alluded to. I cheerfully concede the superiority; if brute force is what my brethren are claiming, I am willing to let them have all the honor they desire; but if they mean to intimate that mental or moral weakness belongs to woman more than to man. I utterly disclaim the charge; our powers of mind have been crushed, as far as man could do it; our sense of morality has been impaired by his interpretation of our duties, but nowhere does God say that he has made any distinction between us as moral and intelligent beings.

Sarah Grimké (Courtesy of the Library of Congress)

ANGELINA GRIMKÉ, *An Appeal to the Woman of the Nominally Free States* (1838)

Angelina Grimké (1805–1879) joined her elder sister, Sarah in opposing efforts to silence abolitionist women. Fervent abolitionists, both Angelina and Sarah also upheld a deep commitment to biracial sisterhood across the lines of racial division.

In the following excerpt from her "Appeal," Angelina Grimké made a passionate plea for sisterhood: for white women in the North to treat free African American women with equality and respect. She provided a wide range of examples that demonstrated that freedom for women of color was diminished by racist restrictions and demeaning treatment. Her words vividly articulate how the Grimké sisters upheld racial equality as well as abolitionism. What examples of Northern racism does she cite? Why did she believe that the "degradation of slavery" fostered the oppression of free African American women?*

The Colored Women of the North Are Oppressed

[Another] reason we would urge for the interference of northern women with the system of slavery is, that in consequence of the odium which the degradation of slavery has attached to *color* even in the free States, our *colored sisters* are dreadfully oppressed here. Our seminaries of learning are closed to them, they are almost entirely banished from our lecture rooms, and even in the house of God they are separated from their white brethren and sisters as though we were afraid to come in contact with a colored skin. . . .

Here, then, are some of the bitter fruits of that inveterate prejudice which the vast proportion of northern women are cherishing towards their colored sisters; and let us remember that every one of us who denies the influence of this prejudice, . . . is awfully guilty in the sight of Him who is no respecter of persons. . . .

But our colored sisters are oppressed in other ways. As they walk the streets of our cities, they are continually liable to be insulted with the vulgar epithet of "nigger"; no matter how respectable or wealthy, they cannot visit the Zoological Institute of New York except in the capacity of nurses or servants—no matter how worthy, they cannot gain admittance into or receive assistance from any of the charities of this city. In Philadelphia, they are cast out of the Widow's Asylum, and their children are refused admittance to the House of Refuge, the Orphan's House and the Infant School connected with the Almshouse, though into these are gathered the very offscouring of our population. These are only specimens of that soul-crushing influence from which the colored women of the north are daily suffering. Then, again, some of them have been robbed of their husbands and children by the heartless kidnapper, and others have themselves been dragged into slavery. If they attempt to travel, they are exposed to great indignities and great inconveniences. Instances have been known of their actually dying in consequence of the exposure to which they were subjected on board of our steamboats. No money could purchase the use of a berth for a delicate female because she had a colored skin. Prejudice, then, degrades and fetters the minds, persecutes and murders the bodies of our free colored sisters. Shall *we* be silent at such a time as this? . . .

Much may be done, too, by sympathizing with our oppressed colored sisters, who are suffering in our very midst. Extend to

---

* From Angelina Grimké, *An Appeal to the Woman of the Nominally Free States.* Issued by an Anti-Slavery Convention of American Women, 2nd ed. (Boston: Isaac Knapp, 1838), 13–16, 19–23, 49–53, 60–61.

them the right hand of fellowship on the broad principles of humanity and Christianity, treat them as *equals,* visit them as *equals,* invite them to cooperate with you in the Anti-Slavery and Temperance and Moral Reform Societies—in Maternal Associations and Prayer Meetings and Reading Companies. . . .

Multitudes of instances will continually occur in which you will have the opportunity of *identifying yourselves with this injured class* of our fellow-beings: embrace these opportunities at all times and in all places, in the true nobility of our great Exemplar, who was ever found among the *poor and the despised,* elevating and blessing them with his counsels and presence. In this way, and this alone, will you be enabled to subdue that deep-rooted prejudice which is doing the work of oppression in the free States to a most dreadful extent.

When this demon has been cast out of your hearts, when *you* can recognize the colored woman as a WOMAN—*then* will you be prepared to send out an appeal to our Southern sisters, entreating them to "go and do likewise."

ANGELINA GRIMKÉ, *Speech at Pennsylvania Hall* (1838)

This was the last public speech that Angelina Grimké (1805–1879) gave. She and her sister Sarah had spent the year giving antislavery lectures. They endured virulent criticism and, as in the case of this meeting of the Anti-Slavery Convention of American Women, mob violence. Shortly after this speech, Angelina married the abolitionist Theodore Dwight Weld. She remained an ardent abolitionist and also a supporter of women's rights but did not engage in a second public lecture tour. While Grimké spoke at Pennsylvania Hall in Philadilphia, the mob's screams outside the hall grew louder and its behavior more menacing, including the throwing of rocks through the windows. The anger over the biracial membership of the convention added to the frenzy. The next day anti-abolitionist fury continued and the rioters set Pennsylvania Hall on fire. The newly constructed building was completely destroyed.

How did Grimké respond to mob violence while she was trying to speak? With reference to the slavery issue, what reaction did she expect to find in Pennsylvania? What special appeal did she make to the women of Philadelphia?*

Men, brethren and fathers—mothers, daughters and sisters, what came ye out for to see? A reed shaken with the wind? Is it curiosity merely, or a deep sympathy with the perishing slave, that has brought this large audience together? [A yell from the mob without the building.] Those voices without ought to awaken and call out our warmest sympathies. Deluded beings! "they know not what they do." They know not that they are undermining their own rights and their own happiness, temporal and eternal. Do you ask, "what has the North to do with slavery?" Hear it—hear it. Those voices without tell us that the spirit of slavery is *here,* and has been roused to wrath by our abolition speeches and conventions: for surely liberty would not foam and tear herself with rage, because her friends are multiplied daily, and meetings are held in quick succession to set forth her virtues and extend her peaceful kingdom. This opposition shows that slavery has done its deadliest work in the hearts of our citizens. Do you ask, then, "what has the North to do?" I answer, cast out first the spirit of slavery from your own hearts, and then lend your aid to convert the South. Each one present has a work to do, be his or her situation what it may, however limited their means, or insignificant their

---

* In the public domain.

supposed influence. The great men of this country will not do this work; the church will never do it. A desire to please the world, to keep the favor of all parties and of all conditions, makes them dumb on this and every other unpopular subject. They have become worldly-wise, and therefore God, in his wisdom, employs them not to carry on his plans of reformation and salvation. He hath chosen the foolish things of the world to confound the wise, and the weak to overcome the mighty.

As a Southerner I feel it is my duty to stand up here to-night and bear testimony against slavery. I have seen it—I have seen it. I know it has horrors that can never be described. I was brought up under its wing: I witnessed for many years its demoralizing influences, and its destructiveness to human happiness. It is admitted by some that the slave is not happy under the *worst* forms of slavery. But I have *never* seen a happy slave. I have seen him dance in his chains, it is true; but he was not happy. There is a wide difference between happiness and mirth. Man cannot enjoy the former while his manhood is destroyed, and that part of the being which is necessary to the making, and to the enjoyment of happiness, is completely blotted out. The slaves, however, may be, and sometimes are, mirthful. When hope is extinguished, they say, "let us eat and drink, for tomorrow we die." [Just then stones were thrown at the windows,—a great noise without, and commotion within.] What is a mob? What would the breaking of every window be? What would the levelling of this Hall be? Any evidence that we are wrong, or that slavery is a good and wholesome institution? What if the mob should now burst in upon us, break up our meeting and commit violence upon our persons— would this be any thing compared with what the slaves endure? No, no: and we do not remember them "as bound with them," if we shrink in the time of peril, or feel unwilling to sacrifice ourselves, if need be, for their sake. [Great noise.] I thank the Lord that there is yet life left enough to feel the truth, even though it

rages at it—that conscience is not so completely seared as to be unmoved by the truth of the living God.

Many persons go to the South for a season, and are hospitably entertained in the parlor and at the table of the slave-holder. They never enter the huts of the slaves; they know nothing of the dark side of the picture, and they return home with praises on their lips of the generous character of those with whom they had tarried: Or if they have witnessed the cruelties of slavery, by remaining silent spectators they have naturally become callous—an insensibility has ensued which prepares them to apologize even for barbarity. Nothing but the corrupting influence of slavery on the hearts of the Northern people can induce them to apologize for it; and much will have been done for the destruction of Southern slavery when we have so reformed the North that no one here will be willing to risk his reputation by advocating or even excusing the holding of men as property. The South know it, and acknowledge that as fast as our principles prevail, the hold of the master must be relaxed. [Another outbreak of mobocratic spirit, and some confusion in the house.]

Many times have I wept in the land of my birth, over the system of slavery. I knew of none who sympathized in my feelings—I was unaware that any efforts were made to deliver the oppressed—no voice in the wilderness was heard calling on the people to repent and do works meet for repentance—and my heart sickened within me. Oh, how should I have rejoiced to know that such efforts as these were being made. I only wonder that I had such feelings. I wonder when I reflect under what influence I was brought up that my heart is not harder than the nether millstone. But in the midst of temptation I was preserved, and my sympathy grew warmer, and my hatred of slavery more inveterate, until at last I have exiled myself from my native land because I could no longer endure to hear the wailing of the slave. I fled to the land of Penn; for here, thought I, sympathy for the slave will surely be found. But I found it not. The people were kind and hospitable, but the slave had no place in their thoughts. Whenever questions were put to me as to his condition, I felt that they were dictated by an idle curiosity, rather than by that deep feeling which would lead to effort for his rescue. I therefore shut up my grief in my own heart. I remembered that I was a Carolinian, from a state which framed this iniquity by law. . . . My heart sunk within me at the abominations in the midst of which I had been born and educated. What will it avail, cried I in bitterness of spirit, to expose to the gaze of strangers the horrors and pollutions of slavery, when there is no ear to hear nor heart to feel and pray for the slave. The language of my soul was, "Oh tell it not in Gath, publish it not in the streets of Askelon." But how different do I feel now! Animated with hope, nay, with an assurance of the triumph of liberty and good will to man, I will lift up my voice like a trumpet, and show this people their transgression, their sins of omission towards the slave, and what they can do towards affecting Southern mind, and overthrowing Southern oppression.

We may talk of occupying neutral ground, but on this subject, in its present attitude, there is no such thing as neutral ground. He that is not for us is against us, and he that gathereth not with us, scattereth abroad. If you are on what you suppose to be neutral ground, the South look upon you as on the side of the oppressor. And is there one who loves his country willing to give his influence, even indirectly, in favor of slavery—that curse of nations? God swept Egypt with the besom of destruction, and punished Judea also with a sore punishment, because of slavery. And have we any reason to believe that he is less just now?—or that he will be more favorable to us than to his own "peculiar people?" [Shoutings, stones thrown against the windows, &c.]

There is nothing to be feared from those who would stop our mouths, but they themselves should fear and tremble. The current is even now setting fast against them. If the arm of the North had not caused the Bastile of slavery to totter to its foundation, you would not hear those cries. A few years ago, and the South felt secure, and with a contemptuous sneer asked, "Who are the abolitionists? The abolitionists are nothing?"—Ay, in one sense they were nothing, and they are nothing still. But in this we rejoice, that "God has chosen things that are not to bring to nought things that are." [Mob again disturbed the meeting.]

We often hear the question asked, "What shall we do?" Here is an opportunity for doing something now. Every man and every woman present may do something by showing that we fear not a mob, and, in the midst of threatenings and revilings, by opening our mouths for the dumb and pleading the cause of those who are ready to perish.

To work as we should in this cause, we must know what Slavery is. Let me urge you then to buy the books which have been written on this subject and read them, and then lend them to your neighbors. Give your money no longer for things which pander to pride and lust, but aid in scattering "the living coals of truth" upon the naked heart of this nation,—in circulating appeals to the sympathies of Christians in behalf of the outraged and suffering slave. But, it is said by some, our "books and papers do not speak the truth." Why, then, do they not contradict what we say? They cannot. Moreover the South has entreated, nay commanded us to be silent; and what greater evidence of the truth of our publications could be desired?

Women of Philadelphia! allow me as a Southern woman, with much attachment to the land of my birth, to entreat you to come up to this work. Especially let me urge you to petition. *Men* may settle this and other questions at the ballot-box, but you have no such right; it is only through petitions that you can reach the Legislature. It is therefore peculiarly *your* duty to petition. Do you say, "It does no good?" The South already turns pale at the number sent. They have read the reports of the proceedings of Congress, and there have seen that among other petitions were very many from the women of the North on the subject of slavery. This fact has called the attention of the South to the subject. How could we expect to have done more as yet? Men who hold the rod over slaves, rule in the councils of the nation: and they deny our right to petition and to remonstrate against abuses of our sex and of our kind. We have these rights, however, from our God. Only let us exercise them: and though often turned away unanswered, let us remember the influence of importunity upon the unjust judge, and act accordingly. The fact that the South look with jealousy upon our measures shows that they are effectual. There is, therefore, no cause for doubting or despair, but rather for rejoicing.

It was remarked in England that women did much to abolish Slavery in her colonies. Nor are they now idle. Numerous petitions from them have recently been presented to the Queen, to abolish the apprenticeship with its cruelties nearly equal to those of the system whose place it supplies. One petition two miles and a quarter long has been presented. And do you think these labors will be in vain? Let the history of the past answer. When the women of these States send up to Congress such a petition, our legislators will arise as did those of England, and say, "When all the maids and matrons of the land are knocking at our doors we must legislate." Let the zeal and love, the faith and works of our English sisters quicken ours—that while the slaves continue to suffer, and when they shout deliverance, we may feel the satisfaction of *having done what we could.*

JULIA HARDY LOVEJOY, *Letter to* **The Independent Democrat,** *Concord, New Hampshire* **(Aug. 1, 1855)**

Julia Hardy Lovejoy (1812–1882), a passionate abolitionist, left New Hampshire with her husband and children and journeyed to the newly opened Kansas territory. The decision to move to Kansas expressed their commitment to abolitionism and the struggle to make Kansas a free state.

The Lovejoys were part of a group of abolitionists sent to Kansas by the New England Emigrant Aid Society. Julia sent reports of the escalating violence between abolitionists and pro-slavery settlers to New England newspapers. She provided a detailed description of the hardships of daily life on the Kansas frontier, as well as information about the unremitting violence that shaped events in the five years prior to the Civil War. The major objective of her reports was to keep New England abolitionists aware of pro-slavery activities and violence and to promote migration to Kansas to counteract pro-slavery population growth. The violent events she witnessed made her even more convinced of the righteousness of the abolitionist cause. How does Lovejoy describe this objective in the excerpt from this 1855 letter to the press?*

Provisions are falling rapidly, so that the greatest trouble in this part of the Territory, now is about our Missourian neighbors, whose "hearts are set on mischief." We were apprehending trouble if not "hard fighting" in our quiet community at the opening of the Legislature, in Pawnee, a few miles above here, as some of the "viler sort," had threatened to "exterminate every abolitionist here, and demolish their houses"; and I can assure you, every man, not excepting our good peace-loving minister, WAS PREPARED FOR THEM! The people in this Territory have suffered until "forbearance is no longer a virtue" and now if help is afforded from no other source, they are resolved individually to defend their "rights" and their homes. Mr. L. was present at Pawnee, at the opening of our Guasi legislature, and

---

* In the public domain.

notwithstanding the blustering and threats of the half-drunk pro-slavery party, not one solitary revolver was fired at any free-soil man or one bowie-knife aimed at one defenceless head. Though a more reckless set, stirred up to deeds of daring by the fumes of the brandy bottle, never probably met for like purposes; and Stringfellow, when elected speaker of the House of Representatives, invited his "cronies" to a certain Hotel, "to discuss together the merits of a bottle of champaigne." They made a mere cypher of Gov. Reeder, taking every thing out of his hands, and finally adjourned to the "Shawnee Mission," more than a hundred miles south [east]—a miserable pro-slavery "sink," leaving the Governor "alone in his glory" to follow, or remain behind, as he should choose. He and Judge Johnson came leisurely along a few days afterward, stopping for the night, with our next door neighbor—the Governor looking unscathed, notwithstanding the fiery ordeal he had just passed thro'. True, he retained a few slight scratches on his face, the effects of being unceremoniously knocked down by the notorious Stringfellow, editor of the "Squatter Sovereign," one of the vilest pro-slavery sheets that ever disgraced the American press! Ah! Mr. Editor: scenes have been enacted in the Territory, within a few months past, and lawless ruffianism, perpetrated on peaceable, unoffending citizens, sufficient to rouse the spirit of '76, in the breast of every freeman; and it is aroused. Military companies are forming, and though we may be accounted feeble in regard to numerical strength, compared with the hordes that may flock here from Missouri, the "battle is not always to the strong," and truth

and justice, will eventually triumph. "Kanzas must be free" though blood is shed, and hundreds fall victims to the bloody moloch of slavery. Jehovah is on the side of the oppressed, and He will yet arise in His strength, and His enemies will be scattered.

There is work enough for every minister, or free-soil man that can be spared from the old Granite State, or any part of New England. Mr. L. has preached every Sabbath since he left the East, and in June entered on his duties as a missionary, on "Fort Riley Mission," officially appointed. His field of labor extends from Pottawatomie Mission, 30 miles on the South [east], to 70 or 80 miles West from here beyond the Fort, and finds 12 places where they need constant Sabbath preaching. Drones that cannot work hard or live on coarse fare, or sleep in cabins, with or without a bed, or on the open prairie need not come here—they are not wanted, for they will be going back the second week, telling a doleful story of "Kanzas fare." But those who can endure and be willing to "rough" it for the sake of doing good in the cause of liberty and religion, let them come, and God speed them in their glorious work! A great work is to be done, and Kanzas is the great battlefield where a mighty conflict is to be waged with the monster slavery, and he will be routed and slain.

Amen and Amen.

JULIA LOUISA LOVEJOY.

LAWRENCE, KANSAS TERRITORY

**ELIZABETH JENNINGS GRAHAM, *"A Wholesome Verdict,"*
New York Tribune (Feb. 23, 1855)**

During the pre–Civil War era, African Americans in New York City were the targets of racial attacks. Discrimination was pervasive, and people of color were expected to obey segregationist policies that restricted their access to public accommodations and urban amenities. On her way to church, on a Sunday in 1854, Elizabeth Jennings Graham (1830–1901), then a twenty-four-year-old unmarried schoolteacher, boarded a horse-drawn omnibus in New York City that was reserved for white passengers. Refusing to get off the bus, she was physically dragged along the floor and forcibly ejected by the bus conductor and driver with the help of a policeman. Her bonnet ripped, her dress soiled, and her body bruised, a defiant Elizabeth Jennings sued the bus company. This was a century before Rosa Parks contested racial segregation.

Like many African American women of the nineteenth and twentieth centuries, Jennings was a civil rights activist. The following document from the *New York Tribune* describes the court decision that ruled in her favor. In what ways is the news account supportive of the verdict in favor of Jennings? What reasons might account for Jennings not having greater historical recognition?*

The case of Elizabeth Jennings vs. the Third Ave. Railroad Company, was tried yesterday in the Brooklyn circuit, before Judge Rockwell. The plaintiff is a colored lady, a teacher in one of the public schools, and the organist in one of the churches in this City. She got upon one of the Company's cars last summer, on the Sabbath, to ride to church. The conductor finally undertook to get her off, first alleging the car was full, and when that was shown to be false, he pretended the other passengers were displeased at her presence.

She saw nothing of that, and insisted on her rights. He took hold of her by force to expel her. She resisted, they got her down on the platform, jammed her bonnet, soiled her dress, and injured her person. Quite a crowd gathered around, but she effectually (effectively) resisted, and they were not able to get her off. Finally, after the car had gone on further, they got the aid of a policeman, and succeeded in getting her from the car.

Judge Rockwell gave a very clear and able charge, instructing the Jury that the Company were liable for the acts of their agents, whether committed carelessly and negligently, or willfully and maliciously. That they were common carriers, and as such bound to carry all respectable persons; that colored person, if sober, well-behaved, and free from disease, had the same rights as others; and could neither be excluded by any rules of the Company, nor by force or violence; and in case of such expulsion or exclusion, the Company was liable.

The plaintiff claimed $500 in her complaint, and a majority of the Jury were for giving her the full amount; but others maintained some peculiar notions as to colored people's rights, and they finally agreed on $225, on which the Court added ten per cent, besides the costs.

FRANCES WATKINS HARPER, Excerpt from *Speech* (1857)

Born to free African American parents in the slave city of Baltimore, Maryland, Frances Watkins Harper (1825–1911) was a leading abolitionist writer and lecturer. She also won acclaim for her novels and poetry. Active in women's rights as well as abolitionism, later in the nineteenth century, Harper participated in the founding of the National Association of Colored Women. In this speech, Harper addresses the abusive Fugitive Slave Act and Northern reaction to it. The act made it a federal offense if Northerners did not help return fugitive slaves to their owners.

How does Harper illuminate the contradiction between the Fugitive Slave Act and America's revolutionary heritage? With reference to the issue of fugitive slaves, what purpose do Harper's references to different areas of the world serve?**

---

* "A Wholesome Verdict," *New York Tribune*, February 23, 1855, 7:4.
** In the public domain.

But a few months since, a man escaped from bondage and found a temporary shelter almost beneath the shadow of Bunker Hill. Had that man stood upon the deck of an Austrian ship, beneath the shadow of the house of the Hapsburgs, he would have protection. Had he been wrecked upon an island or colony of Great Britain, the waves of the tempest-lashed ocean would have washed him to deliverance. Had he landed on the territory of vine-encircled France, and a Frenchman had reduced him to a thing, and brought him here under the protections of our institutions and our laws, for such a nefarious deed, that Frenchman would have lost his citizenship in France. Beneath the feebler light, which glimmers from the Koran, the Bay of Tunis would have granted him freedom in his own dominions. Beneath the ancient pyramids of Egypt he would have found liberty for the soil by the glorious Nile—is now consecrated to freedom. But from Boston Harbor, made memorable by three-penny tax tea— Boston in its proximity to the plains of Lexington and Concord, Boston, beneath the shadow of Bunker Hill and almost in sight in Plymouth Rock, he is thrust back from liberty and manhood and reconverted into a chattel. You have heard that down south they keep bloodhounds to hunt slaves, yea bloodhounds go back to your kennels. When you have failed to catch the flying fugitive, when his stealthy tread is heard in the place where the bones of the revolutionary sires repose, the ready North is base enough to do your shameful service. But when I come here to ask justice, we have no higher law than the Constitution.

Frances Watkins Harper (Courtesy of the Library of Congress)

SARAH REMOND, Excerpt from her *Autobiography* (1861)

Sarah Remond (1826–1894) was a member of a well-known, affluent, free-black family that resided in Salem, Massachusetts. Abolitionist activists, Sarah and her family were also pioneers in the fight for civil rights. Her autobiographical excerpt recounts her personal experiences with racism. She was denied entry into Salem High School despite her academic excellence because of racial exclusion. The second incident involved her forcible removal by police from a theater because of her refusal to sit in the segregated balcony. As a paid lecturer for Garrison's American Anti-Slavery Society, she was sent on a lecture tour to Britain. In speeches and her writing, she described how prejudice encircled her life. She encountered racism as a constant shadow and felt free from its oppression only in Europe, where she experienced social acceptance and racial equality. Remond ultimately chose to live in Europe. In her early forties, she gained admission to an Italian medical school and became a doctor. She described her second-rate treatment and her denial of civil rights in America as "a public branding with degradation."

What action did Remond's father take over the segregationist school policy? How would you describe her civil rights activism?*

My eldest brother had been admitted to one of the public schools in Salem, and at a much later period the three youngest children, including myself, were admitted to one of the public primary schools. All went on well for a time and the children generally treated us kindly, although we were very frequently made to feel that prejudice had taken root in their hearts. My sister and I remained in this school a very short time, passed the examination, and entered the high school for girls. . . . We had been in this school a very short time, when we were informed that the school committee contemplated founding a school exclusively for colored children.

They intended to found a school for young and old, advanced pupils and those less advanced: boys and girls were all to occupy but one room. The many disadvantages can be seen at a glance. It did not matter to this committee, who merely reflected the public sentiment of the community, in what district a colored child might live; it must walk in the heat of the summer, and the cold of winter, to this one school. But more than all this, it was publicly branding us with degradation. The child of every foreigner could enter any public school, while the children of native-born parents were to be thus insulted and robbed of their personal rights.

My father waited upon the school committee, and most earnestly protested against their proposed plan. We still continued to attend the school, but felt much anxiety. One morning, about an hour before the usual time for dismissing pupils, the teacher informed us that we would no longer be permitted to attend the school, that he had received orders from the committee to give us this information, and added, "I wish to accompany you home, as I wish to converse with your parents upon the matter." Some of the pupils seemed indignant, and two expressed much sympathy. I had no words for any one; I only wept bitter tears, then, in a few minutes, I thought of the great injustice practised upon me, and longed for some power to help me to crush those who thus robbed me of my personal rights.

Years have elapsed since this occurred, but the memory of it is as fresh as ever in my mind. We had been expelled from the school on the sole ground of our complexion. The teacher walked home with us, held a long conversation with our parents, said he was pained by the course taken by the school committee, but added it was owing to the prejudice against color which existed in the community. He also said we were among his best pupils, for good lessons, punctuality, etc. Add to this the fact that my father was a tax-payer for years before I was born, and it will need no extra clear vision to perceive that American prejudice against free-born men and women is as deep-rooted as it is hateful and cruel.

CHAPTER 7

Women's Rights and the Contest over Woman's "Place"

Female abolitionist societies enabled women to strengthen their organizational and public speaking skills. By entering the public debate over the issue of slavery, outspoken women directly challenged the constraints of the domestic sphere. The debate over women's rights versus women's restricted gendered sphere or "place" gained momentum with the entry of women as abolitionist lecturers. The Grimke sisters, Lucretia Mott, Lucy Stone, and other women who engaged in public speaking violated a deeply entrenched social custom and provoked widespread outrage. Despite criticism and even violence, these women would not be silenced. Not even the mob violence that resulted in the burning of their meeting place in 1838 deflected women from their antislavery commitment. In fact, among some women, attempts at suppression produced a contradictory result: the demand for female empowerment. From a historical perspective, it is clear that antislavery activism heightened women's awareness of their own political, social, cultural, and legal subordination. Women's rights arguments coexisted with those for abolitionism and gained momentum between the 1830s and the Seneca Falls Convention in 1848. White middle-class women who supported women's rights retained their commitment to the abolitionist cause, and some, including Lucy Stone, divided their time between the two movements.

The Seneca Falls Convention held in New York State in 1848 on behalf of women's rights brought the issue into the public arena and officially launched the organization, recruitment, and mobilization for women's rights ultimately on a national basis. The Seneca Falls Convention initiated a struggle to end men's exclusive claim to leadership of religious, political, legal, educational, and professional institutions. Numerous precursors and multiple influences paved the way for the Seneca Falls Convention. The natural rights discourse expressed in the convention's Declaration of Sentiments reflected eighteenth-century American and European enlightenment thinking and used the Declaration of Independence as a frame of reference. The equation of women's rights with natural rights transcended cultural and national borders and helped cement alliances of reform-minded women that stretched across the Atlantic Ocean to Britain, France, and Germany, creating transnational feminist networks that allowed for an exchange of information and ideas as well as mutual support. Within the United States, racist thinking made it difficult to expand the same concept of natural rights to include African American women's quest for racial equality.

White working-class women also used rights arguments to assert their agency and their objective of workplace justice, including higher wages and better conditions. They linked the rhetoric of republican rights for liberty to their outcries against factory oppression. Although middle-class women's rights advocates focused more on political and legal inequality, in the period after Seneca Falls, pioneer feminists Betsy Cowles (see Chapter 3) and Caroline Healy Dall (Chapter 4) made gender-based workplace inequity the major focus of their investigations. At a time when moral reformers approached the subject of prostitution in terms of the "fallen" women, Dall linked workplace discrimination and extremely low wages as causes of prostitution. Although female moral reformers did not mount a comprehensive women's rights argument, they challenged sexual standards that upheld male entitlement to the female body.

Women rights activists of the pre–Civil War era grew to maturity at a time of democratic growth and economic expansion. As more white men gained the vote, voting rights crossed class lines and became a white male preserve. The male claim to political participation caused men to object when women addressed public issues, particularly when they did so in a public forum and even worse if they spoke to a mixed audience of men and women. As the Grimke sisters found, that included speaking out against slavery. In fact, the more women joined the ferment of reform that characterized the pre–Civil War era, the more they encountered a chorus of male outrage. They were out of their place or sphere, behaving in ways that were "unnatural," "unsexed," and "unwomanly." The contest over a woman's proper place molded the public discourse. Yet, even women such as Catherine Beecher and Sarah Hale, editor of *Godey's Lady's Magazine,* who advocated women's private, family-oriented role, expanded the definition of women's roles to include elementary school teaching, the public exercise of female moral authority, and writing and missionary work. Hale even promoted a feminized version of medical practice (see Chapter 3).

The gendered belief that woman's place was in the home was based on the assumption that men and women were polar opposites, so sharply differentiated that each needed a separate identity and role in society to fulfill either masculine or feminine destinies. Advocates of this binary gendered view stressed women's essential inborn characteristics that developed independently of historical context. They emphasized maternal and domestic qualities, as well as dependency and need for male protection. Unlike rational, purposeful, and intelligent men, women were considered sentimental and emotional, endowed with a superior degree of piety and benevolence. Articles and books proclaimed women's unique domestic gifts and their responsibility as Caroline Gilman noted to create marital harmony through self-sacrifice and denial.

Women's rights activists shared the reform optimism of the pre–Civil War period, as well as the belief that the collective action of ordinary women could transform society. Women flocked to religious revivals and, filled with moral purpose, joined abolitionist and temperance crusades that took them beyond the confines of their homes and increased their confidence and empowerment. Beginning in the early 1830s, women also organized petition drives to both the federal and state governments on behalf of diverse causes, including abolitionism. The extensive use of petitions demonstrated women's political activism even without their having political rights. In New York State, women petitioned the state government on behalf of married women's property rights prior to the Seneca Falls Convention. In an 1848 petition to the New York State Assembly, sent shortly before the Seneca Falls Convention, women petitioners objected to their loss of property and legal identity when they married.

In the years before the Civil War, women reformers found their activism blocked by men. Lucretia Mott and Elizabeth Cady Stanton were forced to sit in the gallery behind a screen at an antislavery conference in London in 1840. Silenced and rendered invisible, their loss of agency served as a catalyst for the key roles they played in organizing the first women's rights conference at Seneca Falls. Lucy Stone's commitment to women's rights intensified as a result of men's efforts—including drenching her with cold water—to end her public speaking on behalf of abolition. Some years later, both the mainstream abolitionist and temperance movements splintered over the issue of women's subordinate place within male-dominated reform organizations. Women's temperance advocates, including Antoinette Brown Blackwell, the nation's first ordained minister, revised the temperance agenda and in the face of male opposition linked the cause directly to women's rights. Within male-dominated reform organizations, women increasingly refused to comply with second-class status.

Although most men rejected the effort at social transformation, female rights advocates received support from some men, including Frederick Douglass, the nation's leading African American abolitionist, and a number of prominent white male abolitionists, including William Lloyd Garrison. Male supporters who were present at Seneca Falls witnessed the Declaration of Sentiments' lengthy indictment against the male usurpation of power. Women's rights embraced the fundamental American belief that the exercise of political power must rest on the consent of the governed. With this in mind, proponents demanded that women be given the right to vote. Voting would give women direct access to the public sphere and political power. Suffrage for women was a direct challenge to male power and met with extreme resistance, not only from men but also from women such as Catharine Beecher who were intent on preserving women's non-political and private, family oriented identity. Women's rights crusaders championed the right of women to determine their own identity because much of what they found intolerable—denial of educational and professional opportunities—depended on tying women from birth to exclusive domestic roles. They combated gender inequities that sustained male power and privilege and at the same time fostered female dependence by limiting economic opportunity and erasing married women's legal identity. They lashed out against all assumptions that limited women's educational achievement and undermined their self-confidence.

Female reformers also challenged the husband's power over his wife. Suffragist Emily Collins addressed the lingering custom of husbands' physical chastisement of their wives. Of major concern to all female reformers was the legal tradition that resulted in the loss of the wife's legal identity and the husband's right to her property, wages, and guardianship of children. The tradition of the wife losing her maiden name was symbolic of the loss of personal identity. To combat this, Elizabeth Cady Stanton added her married name (Stanton) to her maiden name, and Lucy Stone kept her maiden name after her marriage to Henry Blackwell. Stanton, Ernestine Rose, and Susan B. Anthony played central roles in the reform of married women's legal status in New York State. Their demand for women's autonomy and married women's legal rights was built on American ideals of inalienable rights, individual conscience, and personal liberty. They acknowledged that males and females were different in terms of women's maternal role and perceived moral authority. Equality of rights did not mean that women were the same as men. However, they believed that many of the differences between men and women were not innate, but the result of divergent gender expectations, education, and social roles.

Rebellion against prescribed and restricted gender roles also extended to dress reform. The voices of health reform and women's rights advocates challenged women to exchange their corsets, layers of petticoats, hoops, and long skirts for a short dress worn over loose trousers that would provide greater comfort and would not drag along the ground. Known as the "bloomer" outfit after Amelia Bloomer's promotion of dress reform in her newspaper, *The Lily,* similar costumes were worn by women who followed health reform advice and went for the water cure. Women who dared to appear in public in the bloomer costume provoked outrage. Wearing pants symbolized male authority. Clothing was more than a fashion statement or bodily covering. It delineated gender. In an era of polarized gender distinctions, clothing clarified distinctions between femininity and masculinity. Even the modified pants and shorter skirts of the bloomer outfit subverted gendered clothing regulations and provoked male anxiety that women in pants placed their own manhood at risk. Concerned that clothing reform deflected attention from more significant issues, women's rights advocates abandoned shorter skirts and bloomers and returned to corsets, petticoats, and long skirts, uncomfortable clothing that compromised mobility and health. Elizabeth Smith Miller, the first to return to the older style in public, admitted that in her case, it was not public pressure but her own wish to return to more fashionable clothing that led her to abandon dress reform.

By the late nineteenth century, the popularity of bike riding among women reinvigorated dress reform. As Frances Willard, the nation's leading temperance advocate noted, not only was bicycle riding liberating, it promoted clothing reform.

ELIZABETH CADY STANTON, *Declaration of Sentiments* (1848)

Elizabeth Cady Stanton (1815–1902) played a major role in drafting the Declaration of Sentiments that was presented at the convention at Seneca Falls, New York, in 1848. The Declaration is possibly the most significant document for women in the history of the United States. It summarized the way in which women's rights advocates believed men usurped power and tyrannized women. The document paralleled the Declaration of Independence—the abusive power of men was substituted for that of England. The inclusion of the demand for women's suffrage proved to be the most controversial aspect of the argument for women's rights.

What is meant by the Declaration's allegation that men have assigned to women "a sphere of action"? Did the Declaration deny or uphold the view of women's moral superiority? In what ways did the Declaration speak for all women? In what ways did it reflect the particular experience of white middle-class women?*

---

* From "Declaration of Sentiments," in Elizabeth Cady Stanton, Susan B. Anthony, and Matilda J. Gage, eds., *History of Woman Suffrage* (Rochester: Charles Mann, 1881), I: 67–94.

When, in the course of human events, it becomes necessary for one portion of the family of man to assume among the people of the earth a position different from that which they have hitherto occupied, but one to which the laws of nature and of nature's God entitle them, a decent respect to the opinions of mankind requires that they should declare the causes that impel them to such a course.

We hold these truths to be self-evident: that all men and women are created equal; that they are endowed by their Creator with certain inalienable rights; that among these are life, liberty and the pursuit of happiness; that to secure these rights governments are instituted, deriving their just powers from the consent of the governed. Whenever any form of government becomes destructive of these ends, it is the right of those who suffer from it to refuse allegiance to it, and to insist upon the institution of a new government, laying its foundation on such principles, and organizing its powers in such form, as to them shall seem most likely to effect their safety and happiness. Prudence, indeed, will dictate that governments long established should not be changed for light and transient causes; and accordingly all experience has shown that mankind are more disposed to suffer, while evils are sufferable, than to right themselves by abolishing the forms to which they are accustomed. But when a long train of abuses and usurpations, pursuing invariably the same object, evinces a design to reduce them under absolute despotism, it is their duty to throw off such government, and to provide new guards for their future security. Such has been the patient sufferance of the women under this government, and such is now the necessity which constrains them to demand the equal station to which they are entitled.

The history of mankind is a history of repeated injuries and usurpations on the part of man toward woman, having in direct object the establishment of an absolute tyranny over her. To prove this, let facts be submitted to a candid word.

He has never permitted her to exercise her inalienable right to the elective franchise.

He has compelled her to submit to laws, in the formation of which she had no voice.

He has withheld from her rights which are given to the most ignorant and degraded men—both natives and foreigners.

Having deprived her of this first right of a citizen, the elective franchise, thereby leaving her without representation in the halls of legislation, he has oppressed her on all sides.

He has made her, if married, in the eye of the law, civilly dead.

He has taken from her all right in property, even to the wages she earns.

He has made her, morally, an irresponsible being, as she can commit many crimes with impunity, provided they be done in the presence of her husband. In the covenant of marriage, she is compelled to promise obedience to her husband, he becoming, to all intents and purposes, her master, the law giving him power to deprive her of her liberty, and to administer chastisement.

He has so framed the laws of divorce, as to what shall be the proper causes, and in case of separation, to whom the guardianship of the children shall be given, as to be wholly regardless of the happiness of women—the law, in all cases, going upon a false supposition of the supremacy of man, and giving all power into his hands.

After depriving her of all rights as a married woman, if single, and the owner of property, he has taxed her to support a government which recognizes her only when her property can be made profitable to it.

He has monopolized nearly all the profitable employments, and from those she is permitted to follow, she receives but a scanty remuneration. He closes against her all the avenues to wealth and distinction which he considers most honorable to himself. As a teacher of theology, medicine, or law, she is not known.

He has denied her the facilities for obtaining a thorough education, all colleges being closed against her.

He allows her in Church, as well as in State, but a subordinate position, claiming Apostolic authority for her exclusion from the ministry, and, with some exceptions, from any public participation in the affairs of the Church.

He has created a false public sentiment by giving to the world a different code of morals for men and women, by which the moral delinquencies which exclude women from society are not only tolerated, but deemed of little account in man.

He has usurped the prerogative of Jehovah himself, claiming it as his right to assign for her a sphere of action, when that belongs to her conscience and to her God.

He has endeavored, in every way he could, to destroy her confidence in her own powers, to lessen her self-respect, and to make her willing to lead a dependent and abject life.

Now, in the view of this entire disfranchisement of one-half of the people of this country, their social and religious degradation, in view of the unjust laws above mentioned, and because women do feel themselves aggrieved, oppressed, and fraudulently deprived of their most sacred rights, we insist that they have immediate admission to all the rights and privileges which belong to them as citizens of the United States.

In entering upon the great work before us, we anticipate no small amount of misconception, misrepresentation, and ridicule; but we shall use every instrumentality within our power to effect our object. We shall employ agents, circulate tracts, petition the State and National legislatures, and endeavor to enlist the pulpit and the press on our behalf. We hope this Convention will be followed by a series of Conventions embracing every part of the country.

CATHARINE BEECHER, *An Essay on Slavery and Abolitionism in Reference to the Duty of American Females* (1837)

Catharine Beecher (1800–1878) was a member of the prominent Beecher family, sister of both the famous author Harriet Beecher Stowe and the renowned minister Henry Ward Beecher. In contrast to women's rights activists who challenged preassigned roles and believed women should choose their own sphere or place, Beecher promoted prescribed domestic and family roles. She wrote the following essay to combat the growing political activism of women in the abolitionist movement.

What basic assumptions guided Beecher's argument about women's "place" and "duties"? Why did she counsel women to remain uninvolved in abolitionist protest? How does she justify women accepting permanent subordinate status? In what ways does Beecher's depiction of women's duties dramatically differ from the arguments presented in the Declaration of Sentiments?*

My Dear Friend . . .

It has of late become quite fashionable in all benevolent efforts, to shower upon our sex an abundance of compliments, not only for what they have done, but also for what they can do; and so injudicious and so frequent, are these oblations, that while I feel an increasing respect for my countrywomen, that their good sense has not been decoyed by these appeals to their vanity and ambition, I cannot but apprehend that there is some need of inquiry as to the just bounds of female influence, and the times, places, and manner in which it can be appropriately exerted.

---

* In the public domain.

It is the grand feature of the Divine economy, that there should be different stations of superiority and subordination, and it is impossible to annihilate this beneficent and immutable law. . . . In this arrangement of the duties of life, Heaven has appointed to one sex the superior, and to the other the subordinate station, and this without any reference to the character or conduct of either. It is therefore as much for the dignity as it is for the interest of females, in all respects to conform to the duties of this relation. And it is as much a duty as it is for the child to fulfil similar relations to parents, or subjects to rulers. But while woman holds a subordinate relation in society to the other sex, it is not because it was designed that her duties or her influence should be any the less important, or all-pervading. But it was designed that the mode of gaining influence and of exercising power should be altogether different and peculiar. . . .

Woman is to win every thing by peace and love; by making herself so much respected, esteemed and loved, that to yield to her opinions and to gratify her wishes will be the free-will offering of the heart. But this is to be all accomplished in the domestic and social circle. . . . Then, the fathers, the husbands, and the sons will find an influence thrown around them to which they will yield not only willingly but proudly. . . .

Whatever, in any measure, throws a woman into the attitude of a combatant, either for herself or others . . . throws her out of her appropriate sphere. If these general principles are correct, they are entirely opposed to the plan of arraying females in any Abolition movement: because it enlists them in an effort to coerce the South by the public sentiment of the North; because it brings them forward as partisans in a conflict that has been begun and carried forward by measures that are any thing rather than peaceful in their tendencies; because it draws them forth from their appropriate retirement, to expose themselves to the ungoverned violence of mobs, and to sneers and ridicule in public places; because it leads them into the arena of political collision, not as peaceful mediators to hush the opposing elements, but as combatants to cheer up and carry forward the measures of strife.

If it is asked, "May not woman appropriately come forward as a suppliant for a portion of her sex who are bound in cruel bondage?" It is replied, that, the rectitude and propriety of any such measure, depend entirely on its probable results. If petitions from females will operate to exasperate; if they will be deemed obtrusive, indecorous, and unwise, by those to whom they are addressed; if they will increase, rather than diminish the evil which it is wished to remove; if they will be the opening wedge, that will tend eventually to bring females as petitioners and partisans into every political measure that may tend to injure and oppress their sex . . . then it is neither appropriate nor wise, nor right, for a woman to petition for the relief of oppressed females. . . .

In this country, petitions to congress, in reference to the official duties of legislators, seem, IN ALL CASES, to fall entirely without the sphere of female duty. Men are the proper persons to make appeals to the rulers whom they appoint, and if their female friends, by arguments and persuasions, can induce them to petition, all the good that can be done by such measures will be secured. But if females cannot influence their nearest friends, to urge forward a public measure in this way, they surely are out of their place, in attempting to do it themselves.

There are some other considerations, which should make the American females peculiarly sensitive in reference to any measure, which should even *seem* to draw them from their appropriate relations in society. . . .

For the more intelligent a woman becomes, the more she can appreciate the wisdom of that ordinance that appointed her subordinate station, and the more her taste will conform to the graceful and dignified retirement and submission it involves.

CAROLINE GILMAN, *Recollections of a Southern Matron* (1838)

Male authority flourished on Southern plantations. The following excerpt is from a novel written by a Northern woman who moved with her husband to Charleston, South Carolina. Caroline Gilman (1794–1888) intended the book to be a guide for the creation of marital harmony. She recommended that women sacrifice independent thought and action. Note how the wife denies her own wishes in order to please her husband.

Why do you suppose the author considered it so vital for women to remain submissive to their husbands? Would her advice have equal or less relevance for women in the North? What does she mean by the remark that a good wife's "first study must be self-control, almost to hypocrisy"?*

The planter's bride, who leaves a numerous and cheerful family in her paternal home, little imagines the change which awaits her in her own retired residence. She dreams of an independent sway over her household, devoted love and unbroken intercourse with her husband, and indeed longs to be released from the eyes of others, that she may dwell only beneath the sunbeam of his. And so it was with me. After our bustling wedding and protracted journey, I looked forward to the retirement at Bellevue as a quiet port in which I should rest with Arthur, after drifting so long on general society. The romance of our love was still in its glow, as might be inferred by the infallible sign of his springing to pick up my pocket-handkerchief whenever it fell. . . .

For several weeks all kinds of droll associations were conjured up, and we laughed at anything and nothing. What cared we for fashion and pretension? There we were together, asking for nothing but each other's presence and love. At length it was necessary for him to tear himself away to superintend his interests. I remember when his horse was brought to the door for his first absence of two hours; an observer would have thought that he was going on a far journey, had he witnessed that parting; and so it continued for some days, and his return at each time was like the sun shooting through a three days' cloud.

But the period of absence was gradually protracted; then a friend sometimes came home with him, and their talk was of crops and politics, draining the fields and draining the revenue, until I (country ladies will believe me) fell off into a state as nearly approaching sleep as a straight-backed chair would allow. . . .

Arthur was a member of a social club— but he had allowed several citations to pass unnoticed, until it occurred to him that he was slighting his friends; I thought so too, and said so, without permitting the sigh to escape that lay at the bottom of my heart, at the idea of his passing an evening away from me.

"They shall not keep me long from you, my love," he said, as we parted; "I have little joy without you." . . .

This club engagement, however, brought on others. I was not selfish, and even encouraged Arthur to go to hunt and to dinner parties, although hoping that he would resist my urging. He went frequently, and a growing discomfort began to work upon my mind. I had undefined forebodings; I mused about past days; my views of life became slowly disorganized; my physical powers enfeebled; a nervous excitement followed; I nursed a moody discontent, and ceased a while to reason clearly. Woe to me had I yielded to this irritable temperament! I began immediately, on principle, to busy myself about my household. The location of Bellevue was picturesque—the dwelling airy and commodious; I had, therefore, only to exercise taste in external and internal

---

* From Caroline Howard Gilman, *Recollections of a Southern Matron* (New York: Harper & Brothers, 1838), 250–57.

arrangements to make it beautiful through-out. I was careful to consult my husband in those points which interested him, without annoying him with mere trifles. If the reign of romance was really waning, I resolved not to chill his noble confidence, but to make a steadier light rise on his affections. If he was absorbed in reading, I sat quietly waiting the pause when I should be rewarded by the communication of ripe ideas; if I saw that he prized a tree which interfered with my flowers, I sacrificed my preference to a more sacred feeling; if any habit of his annoyed me, I spoke of it once or twice calmly, and then bore it quietly if unreformed; I wel-comed his friends with cordiality, entered into their family interests, and stopped my yawns, which, to say the truth, was some-times an almost desperate effort, before they reached eye or ear.

This task of self-government was not easy. To repress a harsh answer, to confess a fault, and to stop (right or wrong) in the midst of self-defense, in gentle submission, some-times requires a struggle like life and death; but these *three* efforts are the golden threads with which domestic happiness is woven; once being the fabric with this woof, and trials shall not break nor sorrow tarnish it.

Men are not often unreasonable; their difficulties lie in not understanding the moral and physical structure of our sex. They often wound through ignorance, and are surprised at having offended. How clear it is, then, that woman loses by petulance and recrimination! Her first study must be self-control, almost to hypocrisy. A good wife must smile amid a thousand perplexities, and clear her voice to tones of cheerfulness when her frame is drooping with disease, or else languish alone. Man, on the contrary, when trials beset him, expects to find her ear and heart a ready receptacle; and, when sickness assails him, her soft hand must nurse and sustain him. . . .

LUCRETIA MOTT, *Discourse on Women* (1849)

One of the best-known advocates of abolition and women's rights, Lucretia Mott (1793–1880) lectured extensively. Her background and experience as a Quaker woman who was allowed to speak at religious meetings prepared her for public speaking. Her husband shared her views and also attended the Seneca Falls Convention with her. Mott was one of the conveners of the convention. As was the case with pioneer feminists, Mott encountered other women's refusal to support equal rights. To what did she attribute women's resistance to their own independence? What does the remark "she hugs her chains" mean? How do Mott's views contradict the wife described by Gilman in the previous document?*

The question is often asked, "What does woman want, more than she enjoys? What is she seeking to obtain? Of what rights is she deprived? What privileges are withheld from her?" I answer, she asks nothing as a favor, but as a right, she wants to be acknowledged a moral, responsible being. She is seeking not to be governed by laws, in the making of which she has no voice. She is deprived of almost every right in civil society, and is a cipher in the nation, except in the right of presenting a petition. In religious society her disabilities, as already pointed out, have greatly retarded her progress. Her exclusion from the pulpit or ministry—her duties marked out for her by her equal brother, man, subject to creeds, rules, and disciplines made for her by him—this is unworthy of her true

* From Lucretia Mott, *Discourse on Women*, December 1849, 12–20.

dignity. In marriage, there is assumed superiority, on the part of the husband, and admitted inferiority, with a promise of obedience, on the part of the wife. This subject calls loudly for examination, in order that the wrong may be redressed. Customs suited to darker ages in Eastern countries are not binding upon enlightened society. The solemn covenant of marriage may be entered into without these lordly assumptions, and humiliating concessions and promises. . . .

So with woman. She has so long been subject to the disabilities and restrictions, with which her progress has been embarrassed, that she has become enervated, her mind to some extent paralyzed; and, like those still more degraded by personal bondage, she hugs her chains. Liberty is often presented in its true light, but it is liberty for man. . . .

Liberty is not less a blessing, because oppression has so long darkened the mind that it cannot appreciate it. I would therefore urge, that woman be placed in such a situation in society, by the yielding of her rights, and have such opportunities for growth and development, as shall raise her from this low, enervated and paralyzed condition, to a full appreciation of the blessing of entire freedom of mind. . . .

The law of husband and wife, as you gather it from the books, is a disgrace to any civilized nation. The theory of the law degrades the wife almost to the level of slaves. When a woman marries, we call her condition coverture, and speak of her as a *femme covert*. The old writers call the husband baron, and sometimes, in plain English, lord. . . . The merging of her name in that of her husband is emblematic of the fate of all her legal rights. The torch of Hymen serves but to light the pile on which these rights are offered up. The legal theory is, that marriage makes the husband and wife one person, and that person is the *husband*. On this subject, reform is loudly called for. There is no foundation in reason or expediency, for the absolute and slavish subjection of the wife to the husband, which forms the foundation of the present legal relations. Were woman, in point of fact, the abject thing which the law, in theory, considers her to be when married, she would not be worthy of the companionship of man.

EMILY COLLINS, *Reminiscences of the Suffrage Trail* (c. 1881)

Emily Collins's (1814-1909) recollections were included in Elizabeth Cady Stanton, Susan B. Anthony, and Matilda Joselyn Gage's *History of Woman Suffrage*. Collins was a lifelong advocate for women's suffrage. Countless women connected the antislavery struggle to the need for women's rights. The parallel between the wrongs against the slave and the wrongs against women is shown by Collins's descriptions of wife beating. Collins argued that the husband's "supremacy" over his wife provided the basis for physical abuse. What other reasons did Collins provide for husband's physical abuse of their wives?*

I was born and lived almost forty years in South Bristol, Ontario County—one of the most secluded spots in Western New York; but from the earliest dawn of reason I pined for that freedom of thought and action that was then denied to all womankind. I revolted in spirit against the customs of society and the laws of the State that crushed my aspirations, and debarred me from the pursuit of almost any object worthy of an intelligent, rational

---

* From Emily Collins, "Reminiscences of the Suffrage Trail," in Elizabeth Cady Stanton, Susan B. Anthony, and Matilda J. Gage, eds., *History of Woman Suffrage* (Rochester: Charles Mann, 1881), I: 67–94.

mind. But not until that meeting at Seneca Falls in 1848, of the pioneers in the cause, which gave this feeling of unrest form and voice, did I take action. Then I summoned a few women in our neighborhood together, and formed an Equal Suffrage Society, and sent petitions to our Legislature; but our efforts were little known beyond our circle, as we were in communication with no person or newspaper. Yet there was enough of wrong in our narrow horizon to rouse some thought in the minds of all.

In those early days a husband's supremacy was often enforced in the rural districts by corporeal chastisement, and it was considered by most people as quite right and proper—as much so as the correction of refractory children in like manner. I remember in my own neighborhood a man who was a Methodist class leader and exhorted, and one who was esteemed a worthy citizen, who, every few weeks, gave his wife a beating with a horsewhip. He said it was necessary, in order to keep her in subjection, and because she scolded so much. Now this wife, surrounded by six or seven little children, whom she must wash, dress, feed, and attend to day and night, was obliged to spin and weave cloth for all the garments of the family. She had to milk the cows, make butter and cheese, do all the cooking, washing, baking, and mending for the family, and, with the pains of maternity forced upon her every eighteen months, was whipped by her pious husband, "because she scolded." And pray, why should he not have chastised her? The laws made it his privilege—and the Bible, as interpreted, made it his duty. It is true, women repined at their hard lot; but it was thought to be fixed by a divine decree, for "The man shall rule over these," and "Wives, be subject to your husbands," and "Wives, submit yourselves unto your husbands as unto the Lord," caused them to consider their fate inevitable, and to feel that it would be contravening God's law to resist it. It is ever

thus; where Theology enchains the soul, the Tyrant enslaves the body. But can anyone, who has any knowledge of the laws that govern our being of heredity and pre-natal influences—be astonished that our jails and prisons are filled with criminals, and our hospitals with sickly specimens of humanity? As long as the mothers of the race are subject to such unhappy conditions, it can never be materially improved. Men exhibit some common sense in breeding all animals except those of their own species.

All through the Anti-Slavery struggle, every word of denunciation of the wrongs of the Southern slave, was, I felt, equally applicable to the wrongs of my own sex. Every argument for the emancipation of the colored man, was equally one for that of woman, and I was surprised that all abolitionists did not see the similarity in the condition of the two classes. I read, with intense interest, everything that indicated an awakening of public or private thought to the idea that woman did not occupy her rightful position in the organization of society; and, when I read the lectures of Ernestine L. Rose and the writings of Margaret Fuller, and found that other women entertained the same thoughts that had been seething in my own brain, and realized that I stood not alone, how my heart bounded with joy! The arguments of that distinguished jurist, Judge Hurlburt, encouraged me to hope that men would ultimately see the justice of our cause, and concede to women their natural rights.

I hailed with gladness any aspiration of women toward an enlargement of their sphere of action. . . .

But, it was the proceedings of the Convention, in 1848, at Seneca Falls, that first gave a direction to the efforts of the many women, who began to feel the degradation of their subject condition, and its baneful effects upon the human race. They then saw the necessity for associated action, in order to obtain the elective franchise, the only key that would unlock the doors of their prison. . . .

Would to heaven that women could be persuaded to use the funds they acquire by their sewing-circles and fairs, in trying to raise their own condition above that of "infants, idiots, and lunatics," with whom our statutes class them, instead of spending the money in decorating their churches, or sustaining a clergy, most of whom are striving to rivet the chains still closer that bind, not only our own sex, but the oppressed of every class and color.

The elective franchise is now the one object for which we must labor; that once attained, all the rest will be easily acquired. Moral Reform and Temperance Societies may be multiplied *ad infinitum,* but they have about the same effect upon the evils they seek to cure, as clipping the top of a hedge would have toward extirpating it. Please forward me a copy of the petition for suffrage. We will engage to do all we can, not only in our own town, but in the adjoining ones of Richmond, East Bloomfield, Canandaigua, and Naples. I have promises of aid from people of influence in obtaining signatures. In the meantime we wish to disseminate some able work upon the enfranchisement of women. We wished to represent our Assemblyman elect, whoever he may be, with some work of this kind, and solicit his candid attention to the subject. People are more willing to be convinced by the calm perusal of an argument, than in a personal discussion.

SOJOURNER TRUTH, *A'n't I a Woman?* (1851)

Frances Gage, a suffrage advocate, recorded this speech by Sojourner Truth (c. 1797–1883) at the women's rights convention in Akron, Ohio (1851). Although Gage added rhetorical flourishes and dramatic embellishments, the speech expressed Truth's sentiments. An example of the exaggeration surrounding Truth was the claim that she was 110 years old. An ex-slave with a dual commitment to abolitionism and women's rights, Truth galvanized audiences and became an icon in her own lifetime. In the following speech, Truth responded to clergymen's anti-suffrage arguments that God had given men "superior intellect" and limited women to motherhood and domesticity. Using her own experiences as a former slave who had survived physical and emotional oppression, Truth challenged the assumption that women were physically weak. In establishing an image of women's strength, what particular qualities did Truth emphasize? How does her speech relate to women's rights?*

Sojourner Truth, Mrs. Stowe's "Lybian Sibyl," was present at this Convention. Some of our younger readers may not know that Sojourner Truth was once a slave in the State of New York, and carries today as many marks of the diabolism of slavery, as ever scarred the back of a victim in Mississippi. Though she can neither read nor write, she is a woman of rare intelligence and commonsense on all subjects. She is still living, at Battle Creek, Michigan, though now 110 years old. Although the exalted character and personal appearance of this noble woman have been often portrayed, and her brave deeds and words many times rehearsed, yet we give the following graphic picture of Sojourner's appearance in one of the most stormy sessions of the Convention, from reminiscences by Frances D. Gage.

Sojourner Truth. The leaders of the movement trembled on seeing a tall, gaunt black woman in a gray dress and white turban, surmounted with an uncouth sunbonnet, march deliberately into the church, walk with the air of a queen up the aisle, and take her seat upon the pulpit steps. A buzz of disapprobation was heard all over the house,

---

* From Sojourner Truth, "Ain't I a Woman?" in *History of Woman Suffrage,* Elizabeth Cady Stanton, Susan B. Anthony, and Matilda J. Gage, eds. (Rochester: Charles Mann, 1881), I: 403–4.

and there fell on the listening ear, "An abolition affair!" "Woman's rights and niggers!" "I told you so!" "Go to it, darkey!"

I chanced on that occasion to wear my first laurels in public life as president of the meeting. At my request order was restored, and the business of the Convention went on. Through all these sessions old Sojourner, quiet and reticent as the "Lybian Statue," sat crouched against the wall on the corner of the pulpit stairs, her sunbonnet shading her eyes, her elbows on her knees, her chin resting upon her broad, hard palms. At intermission she was busy selling the "Life of Sojourner Truth," a narrative of her own strange and adventurous life. Again and again, timorous and trembling ones came to me and said, with earnestness, "Don't let her speak, Mrs. Gage, it will ruin us. Every newspaper in the land will have our cause mixed up with abolition and niggers, and we shall be utterly denounced." My only answer was, "We shall see when the time comes."

The second day the work waxed warm. Methodist, Baptist, Episcopal, Presbyterian and Universalist ministers came in to hear and discuss the resolutions presented. One claimed superior rights and privileges for man, on the ground of "superior intellect"; another, because of the "manhood of Christ; if God had desired the equality of woman, He would have given some token of His will through the birth, life and death of the Saviour." Another gave us a theological view of the "sin of our first mother."

There were very few women in those days who dared to "speak in meeting"; and the august teachers of the people were seemingly getting the better of us, while the boys in the galleries, and the sneers among the pews, were hugely enjoying the discomfiture, as they supposed, of the "strong-minded." Some of the tender-skinned friends were on the point of losing dignity, and the atmosphere betokened a storm. When, slowly from her seat in the corner rose Sojourner Truth, who, till now, had scarcely lifted her head. "Don't let her speak!" gasped half a dozen in my ear. She moved slowly and solemnly to the front, laid her old bonnet at her feet, and turned her great speaking eyes to me. There was a hissing sound of disapprobation above and below. I rose and announced "Sojourner Truth," and begged the audience to keep silence for a few moments.

The tumult subsided at once, and every eye was fixed on this almost Amazon form, which stood nearly six feet high, head erect, and eyes piercing the upper air like one in a dream. At her first word there was a profound hush. She spoke in deep tones, which, though not loud, reached every ear in the house, and away through the throng at the doors and windows.

"Wall, chilren, whar dar is so much racket dar must be somethin' out o' kilter. I tink dat 'twixt de niggers of de Sof and de womin at de Noft, all talkin' 'bout rights, de white men will be in a fix pretty soon. But what's all dis here talkin' 'bout?

"Dat man ober dar say dat womin needs to be helped into carriages, and lifted ober ditches, and to hab de best place everywhar. Nobody eber helps me into carriages, or ober mud-puddles, or gibs me any best place!" And raising herself to her full height, and her voice to a pitch like rolling thunder, she asked, "And a'n't I a woman? Look at me! Look at my arm! (and she bared her right arm to the shoulder, showing her tremendous muscular power). I have ploughed, and planted, and gathered into barns, and no man could head me! And a'n't I a woman? I could work as much and eat as much as a man—when I could get it—and bear de lash as well! And a'n't I a woman? I have borne thirteen chilren, and seen 'em mos' all sold off to slavery, and when I cried out with my mother's grief, none but Jesus heard me! And a'n't I a woman?

"Den dey talks 'bout dis ting in de head; what dis dey call it?" ("Intellect," whispered some one near.) "Dat's it, honey. What's dat got to do wid womin's rights or nigger's rights? If my cup won't hold but a pint, and yours holds a quart, wouldn't ye be mean not to let me half my little half-measure full?" And she pointed her significant finger, and sent a keen glance at the minister who had made the argument. The cheering was long and loud.

"Den dat little man in black dar, he say women can't have as much rights as men 'cause Christ wan't a woman! Whar did your Christ come from?" Rolling thunder couldn't have stilled that crowd, as did those deep, wonderful tones, as she stood there with out-stretched arms and eyes of fire. Raising her voice still louder, she repeated, "Whar did your Christ come from? From God and a woman! Man had nothin' to do wid Him." Oh, what a rebuke that was to that little man.

Turning again to another objector, she took up the defense of Mother Eve. I cannot follow her through it all. It was pointed, and witty, and solemn; eliciting at almost every sentence deafening applause, and she ended by asserting: "If de fust woman God ever made was strong enough to turn the world upside down all alone, dese women togedder (and she glanced her eyes over the platform) ought to be able to turn in back, and get it right side up again! And now dey is asking to do it, de men better let 'em." Long-continued cheering greeted this. "'Bleeged to ye for hearin' on me, and now ole Sojourner han't got nothin' more to say."

Amid roars of applause, she returned to her corner, leaving more than one of us with streaming eyes, and hearts beating with grat-itude. She had taken us up in her strong arms and carried us safely over the slough of difficulty by turning the whole tide in our favor. I have never in my life seen anything like the magical influence that subdued the mobbish spirit of the day, and turned the sneers and jeers of an excited crowd into notes of respect and admiration. Hundreds rushed up to shake hands with her, and con-gratulate the glorious old mother, and bid her Godspeed on her mission of "testifyin' again concerning the wickedness of this 'ere people."

ERNESTINE ROSE, *This Is the Law but Where Is the Justice of It?* (1852)

Ernestine Rose (1810–1892) was a pioneer in the struggle to give married women legal rights. She played a key role in agitating for legal reform that led to New York State's Married Women's Property Act. A Polish Jewish immigrant, Rose joined the mainly native-born Protestant women's rights crusade and frequently gave public lectures. In this speech to a women's rights convention, she presented a vehement argument against a husband's ownership of his wife, and the denial of freedom and equality that ran counter to the promise of republican life. Rose also claimed that the duties of married women were as "indispensable" and more "arduous" than those of husbands. In what ways would this be an accurate description of married women's roles?*

Here, in this far-famed land of freedom, under a Republic that has inscribed on its banner the great truth that "all men are created free and equal, and endowed with inalienable rights to life, liberty, and the pursuit of happi-ness" . . . even here, in the very face of this eternal truth, woman, the mockingly so-called "better half" of man, has yet to plead for her rights, nay, for her life. For what is life without liberty, and what is liberty without equality of rights? And so for the pursuit of happiness, she is not allowed to choose any line of action that

---

* From Ernestine Rose, "This Is the Law but Where Is the Justice of It?" in *History of Woman Suffrage,* Elizabeth Cady Stanton, Susan B. Anthony, and Matilda J. Gage, eds. (Rochester: Charles Mann, 1881), I: 237–41.

might promote it; she has only thankfully to accept what man in his magnanimity decides is best for her to do, and this is what he does not choose to do himself.

Is she then not included in that declaration? Answer, ye wise men of the nation, and answer truly; add not hypocrisy to oppression! Say that she is not created free and equal, and therefore (for the sequence follows on the premise) that she is not entitled to life, liberty, and the pursuit of happiness. But with all the audacity arising from an assumed superiority, you dare not so libel and insult humanity as to say, that she is not included in that declaration; and if she is, then what right has man, except that of might, to deprive woman of the rights and privileges he claims for himself? And why, in the name of reason and justice, why should she not have the same rights? Because she is woman? Humanity recognizes no sex; virtue recognizes no sex; mind recognizes no sex; life and death, pleasure and pain, happiness and misery, recognize no sex. . . . Like him she enjoys or suffers with her country. Yet she is not recognized as his equal!

In the laws of the land she has no rights; in government she has no voice. And in spite of another principle, recognized in this Republic, namely, that "taxation without representation is tyranny," she is taxed to defray the expenses of that unholy, unrighteous custom called war, yet she has no power to give her vote against it. From the cradle to the grave she is subject to the power and control of man. Father, guardian, or husband—one conveys her like some piece of merchandise over to the other.

At marriage she loses her entire identity, and her being is said to have become merged in her husband. Has nature thus merged it? Has she ceased to exist and feel pleasure and pain? . . . And when at his nightly orgies, in the grog-shop and the oyster-cellar, or at the gaming table, he squanders the means she helped, by her co-operation and economy, to accumulate, and she awakens to penury and destitution; will it supply the wants of her children to tell them that, owing to the superiority

of man she had no redress by law, and that as her being was merged in his, so also ought theirs to be? What an inconsistency, that from the moment she enters that compact, in which she assumes the high responsibility of wife and mother, she ceases legally to exist, and become a purely submissive being. Blind submission in woman is considered a virtue, while submission is itself wrong, and resistance to wrong is virtue, alike in woman as in man.

But it will be said that the husband provides for the wife, or in other words, he feeds, clothes, and shelters her! I wish I had the power to make everyone before me fully realize the degradation contained in that idea. Yes! He *keeps* her, and so he does a favorite horse: by law they are both considered his property. Both may, when the cruelty of the owner compels them to run away, be brought back by the strong arm of the law. . . .

Carry out the republican principle of universal suffrage, or strike it from your banners and substitute "Freedom and Power to one half of society, and Submission and Slavery to the other." Give woman the elective franchise. Let married women have the same right to property that their husbands have; for whatever the difference in their respective occupations, the duties of the wife are as indispensable and far more arduous than the husband's. Why then should the wife, at the death of her husband, not be his heir to the same extent that he is heir to her? In this inequality there is involved another wrong. When the wife dies, the husband is left in the undisturbed possession of all there is, and the children are left with him; no change is made, no stranger intrudes on his home and his affliction. But when the husband dies, the widow, at best receives but a mere pittance, while strangers assume authority denied to the wife. The sanctuary of affection must be desecrated by executors; everything must be ransacked and assessed, lest she should steal something out of her own house; and to cap the climax, the children must be placed under guardians. When the husband dies poor, to be sure, no guardian is required, and the children are left for the mother to care and toil for, as best she may. But when anything is left for their maintenance, then it must be placed in the hands of strangers for safekeeping!

According to a late act, the wife has a right to the property she brings at marriage, or receives in any way after marriage. Here is some provision for the favored few; but for the laboring many, there is none. The mass of the people commence life with no other capital than the union of heads, hearts, and hands. To the benefit of this best of capital, the wife has no right. If they are unsuccessful in married life, who suffers more the bitter consequences of poverty than the wife? But if successful, she cannot call a dollar her own. The husband may will away every dollar of the personal property, and leave her destitute and penniless, and she has no redress. . . . This is law, but where is the justice of it?

LUCY STONE AND HENRY B. BLACKWELL, *Marriage Contract* (1855)

Like many women's rights advocates, Lucy Stone's (1818–1893) initial reform commitment was abolition-ism. In 1855, she married Henry Blackwell, a leading abolitionist and women's rights advocate. Stone's marriage contract went beyond that of Elizabeth Cady Stanton's, who merely omitted the word *obey* from her 1840 marriage contract. Not only did Stone's contract include that she would keep her maiden name, but it also addressed property and guardianship rights. Why was the issue of property rights so important for pre–Civil War feminists? Would poorer women be equally concerned?*

While acknowledging our mutual affection by publicly assuming the relationship of husband and wife, yet in justice to ourselves and a great principle, we deem it a duty to declare that this act on our part implies no sanction of, nor promise of voluntary obedience to such of the present laws of marriage, as refuse to recognize the wife as an independent, rational being, while they confer upon the husband an injurious and unnatural superiority, investing him with legal powers which no honorable man would exercise, and which no man should possess. We protest especially against the laws which give to the husband:

1. The custody of the wife's person.
2. The exclusive control and guardianship of their children.
3. The sole ownership of her personal, and use of her real estate, unless previously settled upon her, or placed in the hands of trustees, as in the case of minors, lunatics, and idiots.
4. The absolute right to the product of her industry.
5. Also against laws which give to the widower so much larger and more permanent an interest in the property of his deceased wife, than they give to the widow in that of the deceased husband.
6. Finally, against the whole system by which "the legal existence of the wife is suspended during marriage," so that in most States, she neither has a legal part in the choice of her residence, nor can she make a will, nor sue or be sued in her own name, nor inherit property.

We believe that personal independence and equal human rights can never be forfeited, except for crime; that marriage should be an equal and permanent partnership and so recognized by law; that until it is so recognized, married partners should provide against the radical injustice of present laws, by every means in their power.

---

* From Lucy Stone and Henry B. Blackwell, "Marriage Contract," in *History of Woman Suffrage,* Elizabeth Cady Stanton, Susan B. Anthony, and Matilda J. Gage, eds. (Rochester: Charles Mann, 1881), I: 260–61.

We believe that where domestic difficulties arise, no appeal should be made to legal tribunals under existing laws, but that all difficulties should be submitted to the equitable adjustment of arbitrators mutually chosen.

Thus reverencing law, we enter our protest against rules and customs which are unworthy of the name, since they violate justice, the essence of law.

Henry B. Blackwell
Lucy Stone

ELIZABETH SMITH MILLER, *"Reflections on Woman's Dress and the Record of a Personal Experience"* (1892)

In the following document, Elizabeth Smith Miller (1822–1909) cited her reasons for wearing and then abandoning the short skirt and trousers bloomer outfit. Even though the outfit was named for Amelia Bloomer, who popularized the dress reform in her newspaper *The Lilly*, Miller was the first to appear in public in the outfit. A daughter of the abolitionist Gerrit Smith and a cousin of Elizabeth Cady Stanton, Miller was an abolitionist and a suffragist who enjoyed membership in a family of reformers. Her father encouraged her effort to promote dress reform through the wearing the bloomer outfit. Dress reform was tied to hygiene, comfort, and health and was a component of the wider women's reform agenda for greater liberation.

Since the clothing attracted inordinate amounts of negative press coverage and public ridicule, women reformers abandoned the comfortable outfit in an effort to have the more important aspects of their agenda addressed. According to the negative arguments against dress reform, women wearing pants turned gender norms upside down and subverted male roles. Stripped of male authority, men would assume feminine roles of home and baby care. Miller did not, however, abandon bloomers because of public outrage. What reasons does she give for abandoning the wearing of shorter skirts and bloomers? In what ways do women today continue to compromise comfort and possibly health for the sake of appearance?*

I am asked to give a statement of my experience in adopting wearing, and abandoning the short skirt.

In the spring of 1851, while spending many hours at work in the garden, I became so thoroughly disgusted with the long skirt, that the dissatisfaction—the growth of years—suddenly ripened into the decision that this shackle should no longer be endured. The resolution was at once put into practice. Turkish trousers to the ankle with a skirt reaching some four inches below the knee, were substituted for the heavy, untidy and exasperating old garment.

Soon after making this change, I went to Seneca Falls to visit my cousin Mrs. Stanton. She had so long deplored with me our common misery in the toils of this crippling fashion, that this means of escape was hailed with joy and she at once joined me in wearing the new costume. Mrs. Bloomer, a friend and neighbor of Mrs. Stanton, then adopted the dress, and as she was editing a paper in which she advocated it, the dress was christened with her name. Mrs. Stanton and I often exchanged visits and sometimes travelled together. We endured, in various places, much gaping curiosity and the harmless jeering of street boys. In the winter of 1852 and 1853, when my father was in congress, I was also in the cosmopolitan city of Washington, where I found my peculiar costume much less conspicuous. My street dress was a dark brown corded silk, short skirt and straight trousers, a short but graceful and richly trimmed French cloak of

---

black velvet with drooping sleeves, called a "cantatrice"—a sable tippet and a low-crowned beaver hat with a long plume.

I wore the short dress and trousers for many years, my husband, being at all times and in all places, my staunch supporter. My father, also gave the dress his full approval, and I was also blessed by the tonic of Mrs. Stanton's inspiring words: "The question is no longer [rags], how do you look, but woman, how do you feel?"

The dress looked tolerably well in walking standing and walking, but in sitting, a more awkward, uncouth effect, could hardly be produced imagined—it was a perpetual violation of my love of the beautiful. So, by degrees, as my aesthetic senses gained claimed the ascendancy, I lost sight of the great advantages of my dress—its lightness and cleanliness on the streets, its allowing me to carry my babies up and down stairs with perfect ease and safety, and its beautiful

harmony with sanitary laws—, consequently the skirt was lengthened several inches and the trousers abandoned. As months passed, I proceeded in this retrograde movement, until, after a period of some seven years, I quite "fell from grace" and found myself again in the bonds of the old swaddling clothes—a victim to my love of beauty.

In consideration of what I have previously said in regard to fashion, I feel at liberty to add that I do not wear a heavy, trailing skirt, nor have I ever worn a corset; my bonnet shades my face; my spine was preserved from the bustle, my feet from high heels; my shoulders are not turreted, nor has fashion clasped my neck with her choking collar.

All hail to the day when we shall have a reasonable and beautiful dress that shall encourage exercises on the road and in the field—that shall leave us the free use of our limbs—that shall help and not hinder, our perfect development.

Women in Hoop Skirts. 1859 (© Bettmann/CORBIS All Rights Reserved)

The Bloomer Costume (Courtesy of the Library of Congress)

Bathing Dresses 1868 (The New York Public Library)

FRANCES WILLARD, *"A Wheel within a Wheel; How I Learned to Ride a Bicycle"* (1895)

In the late nineteenth century, bike riding served as a catalyst for dress reform. Women embraced the newly invented two-wheel bicycle that imparted a sense of mobility that opposed middle-class gender norms that restricted female outdoor activity. For safety and comfort, women adopted controversial bloomers and some even wore trousers. As Frances Willard (1839–1898) described the experience, bike riding could be liberating and transformative. The president of the national Woman's Christian Temperance Union and a suffragist (Chapter 10), Willard took up bike riding at age fifty-three when she had health problems. Willard's enthusiasm and delight in bike riding resonate across the barrier of time. What particular aspects of bike riding did Willard regard as most liberating? How did she contrast the freedom of her girlhood with the gendered restrictions of her maturity?*

From my earliest recollections, and up to the ripe age of fifty-three, I had been an active and diligent worker in the world. This sounds absurd; but having almost no toys except such as I could manufacture, my first plays were but the outdoor work of active men and women on a small scale. Born with an inveterate opposition to staying in the house, I very early learned to use a carpenter's kit and a gardener's tools, and followed in my mimic way the occupations of the poulterer and the farmer, working my little field with a wooden plow of my own making, and felling saplings with an ax rigged up from the old iron of the wagon-shop. Living in the country, far from the artificial restraints and conventions by which most girls are hedged from the activities that would develop a good physique, and endowed with the companionship of a mother who let me have my own sweet will, I "ran wild" until my sixteenth birthday, when the hampering long skirts were brought, with their accompanying corset and high heels; my hair was clubbed up with pins, and I remember writing in my journal, in the first heartbreak of a young human colt taken from its pleasant pasture, "Altogether, I recognize that my occupation is gone."

From that time on I always realized and was obedient to the limitations thus imposed, though in my heart of hearts I felt their unwisdom even more than their injustice. My work then changed from my beloved and breezy outdoor world to the indoor realm of study, teaching, writing, speaking, and went on almost without a break or pain until my fifty-third year, when the loss of my mother accentuated the strain of this long period in which mental and physical life were out of balance, and I fell into a mild form of what is called nerve-wear by the patient and nervous prostration by the lookers-on. Thus ruthlessly thrown out of the usual lines of reaction on my environment, and sighing for new worlds to conquer, I determined that I would learn the bicycle. . . .

Let me remark to any young woman who reads this page that for her to tumble off her bike is inexcusable. The lightsome elasticity of every muscle, the quickness of the eye, the agility of motion, ought to preserve her from such a catastrophe. I have had [only one] fall. . . . I have proceeded on a basis of the utmost caution, and aside from . . . one pitiful performance the bicycle has cost me hardly a single bruise. . . .

---

* Frances Willard, *A Wheel Within a Wheel: How I Learned to Ride the Bicycle* (1895). Reprinted in Stephanie Twin, *Out of the Bleachers* (Old Westbury, NY: Feminist Press, 1979), 104–5, 112–14.

If I am asked to explain why I learned the bicycle I should say I did it as an act of grace, if not of actual religion. The cardinal doctrine laid down by my physician was, "Live out of doors and take congenial exercise"; but from the day when, at sixteen years of age, I was enwrapped in the long skirts that impeded every footstep, I have detested walking and felt with a certain noble disdain that the conventions of life had cut me off from what in the freedom of my prairie home had been one of life's sweetest joys. Driving is not real exercise; it does not renovate the river of blood that flows so sluggishly in the veins of those who from any cause have lost the natural adjustment of brain to brawn. Horseback-riding, which does promise vigorous exercise, is expensive. The bicycle meets all the conditions and will ere long come within the reach of all.

Therefore, in obedience to the laws of health, I learned to ride. I also wanted to help women to a wider world, for I hold that the more interests women and men can have in common, in thought, word, and deed, the happier will it be for the home. Besides, there was a special value to women in the conquest of the bicycle by a woman in her fifty-third year, and one who had so many comrades in the white-ribbon army that her action would be widely influential. . . .

It is needless to say that a bicycling costume was a prerequisite. This consisted of a skirt and blouse of tweed, with belt, rolling collar, and loose cravat, the skirt three inches from the ground; a round straw hat; and walking-shoes with gaiters. It was a simple, modest suit, to which no person of common sense could take exception.

Women with Bicycles (Stuhr Museum of the Prairie Pioneer)

CHAPTER 8

Western Expansion:
Different Viewpoints, Diverse Stories

For decades, American historians following the path of the late-nineteenth-century historian Fredrick Jackson Turner, who celebrated Western expansion as pivotal to national development and the establishment of democratic institutions. Turner essentially upheld the nineteenth-century American consensus that the expanding Anglo-American nation represented the heroic progress of civilization and wilderness conquest. In the contemporary period, historians have completely overhauled Turner's interpretive framework. Among other criticisms, revisionists allege that Turner was ethnocentric failed to include women in his analysis and was dismissive of the death and displacement of American Indians.

In recent years, women's historians have viewed the American settlement of the West from a multicultural lens and provided a corrective to the distortions of an Anglo-centric narrative. From the perspective of women's history, white women were important in the story of Western expansion, but their experience was not universal. Spanish and Mexican women living in areas subsequently incorporated into the United States experienced the tidal wave of American settlement in terms of loss of property and social status. Although white women and their families freely settled in the territories and states of the trans-Mississippi West, free African American women and their families encountered racial hostility, segregation, and even exclusion. Following the exclusion laws passed in Illinois and Indiana, Oregon excluded free blacks in its new state constitution in 1857. The California gold rush and subsequent years of massive American settlement brought opportunity to whites but habitat destruction, displacement, and death to large numbers of California's indigenous tribes. In an interview years after Americans took control of California, Isadora Filomea expressed her resentment of American conquest and bitterness over habitat loss.

Long before the California gold rush and the lure of the Oregon Territory, Anglo-Americans constantly were on the move. Many residents from New York migrated to Michigan during the 1820s and a continuing exodus of people from New England and New York journeyed to the Ohio Valley. Encroachment on Indian land was continual.

During the early 1820s, while Texas was still part of Mexico, thousands of English-speaking American settlers arrived there.

Nancy Ward and other Cherokee women led a resistance movement, pleading with their tribal leaders not to cede any more land to whites. Some white women also organized petition drives, such as those in Steubenville, Ohio, opposing the federal government's effort to remove the Cherokee nation from Georgia to the trans-Mississippi West. Unfortunately for the Cherokees and other Southern tribes, the pressure for removal overwhelmed restraint. President Andrew Jackson's decision led to the forcible relocation of the Cherokee and other "civilized" Southern tribes to the Oklahoma Territory. Once the federal government, real estate interests, or settlers wanted land occupied by Indians, power, not justice, determined the outcome. From efforts at coexistence and accommodation, to attacks on settlements, to all-out war, Indian tribes defended their homelands with every means available to them.

Leaving New York State for the West in 1843, Narcissa Whitman was one of the first of two white women to journey on the Overland Trail and cross the Rocky Mountains into the Oregon Territory. Her journal describes her missionary zeal and how she and her husband attempted to bring Christianity to the local Cayuse Indians. Thousands of other settlers would soon follow and build farms in the midst of Indian lands. A survey of women's journals and letters demonstrates little if any concern about the toll of expansion in terms of the disruption of American Indians' lives, as well as their displacement. From the gold rush experiences of Luzena Wilson and Mary Ballou, we learn of the hardships of adjusting to a new and demanding environment combined with the unending domestic toil and family care that consumed women's time and energy. Many white women also shared the American belief in Manifest Destiny, an American form of imperialism that assumed that God ordained westward expansion as part of a larger struggle between civilization and savagery.

Land hunger also took other American settlers to the newly opened, Indian lands of Kansas and Nebraska. Westward migration was linked to the explosive issue of whether slavery would be allowed in the newly opened territories such as Kansas. Julia Lovejoy and her family arrived in Kansas from New Hampshire in 1855, as abolitionists determined to keep Kansas free (see Chapter 6).

Continual loss of land, coercive relocation to reservations, and failure of the government to make promised payments provided some of the reasons for the Sioux Uprising in 1862 and the tragic loss of lives on the Minnesota frontier described by Norwegian immigrant Guri Olsdtatter.

Scandinavian and German farming families were part of an exodus from Western and Northern Europe that settled in the upper Midwest, Ohio Valley, and the Great Plains. Immigrant families added to the displacement of indigenous people and the transfer of tribal land to white settlers. The 1862 Homestead Act furthered the process of agricultural development and the U.S. government's displacement of American Indians.

Decades before the mass migration to the West of Anglo-American women on the overland trails, Juan Bautista de Anza led an expedition from the Sonora area of Mexico/Arizona to the northern frontier of California that was home to indigenous tribes but had almost no Spanish colonists. In the effort to populate Alta California and secure Spanish control of the northern Mexican frontier, women and their families accompanied priests, servants, and soldiers on the journey north. Known as *Californios,* the descendants of these families subsequently were incorporated into the United States.

Interviews conducted with Spanish descendants of these families, as well as descendants of Mexicans and Indians, are now being published, making it possible to reclaim the voices of forgotten women. In her recollection of her experience as a house-keeper in the San Gabriel, California, mission, Eulalia Perez recalled her successful domestic and administrative responsibilities during the period of Spanish colonial con-trol. Mexico achieved independence from Spain in 1822, but under the treaty of Guadalupe Hidalgo in 1848, the United States conquest was recognized, and a vast por-tion of Mexican territory, including California and Arizona, was incorporated into the United States. Rosalia Vallejo Leese, a member of an elite Mexican family who witnessed John Fremont's declaration of California's independence, revealed in an interview her enduring hostility to the American conquest. The U.S. government did not honor Mexican land ownership, and the arrival of Anglo settlers and real estate speculators interfered with the Spanish and Mexican land use patterns and ranchero culture. Wives lost property rights they had enjoyed under Spanish law, but they gained greater access to divorce.

For some Euro-American women, relocation to the "far" West was a welcome opportunity and for others a sorrowful departure; they were torn away from all that was familiar and dear. Distinctive in their religious view of polygamy but very much part of the white settlement process in the West, Mormons arrived in Utah in 1846. For Luzena Wilson, the California gold rush economy presented a once-in-a-lifetime oppor-tunity to get rich. Her entrepreneurial gifts emerged while still on the Overland Trail when she realized that her path to wealth meant the sale of home-cooked meals. Mary Ballou, who journeyed with her husband to California through the Isthmus of Panama, also put her entrepreneurial skills to economic advantage. Although California entered the Union as a free state, Biddy Mason arrived as one of the slaves of Robert Smith, a Mormon settler headed for San Bernardino. After several years of enslavement, Mason successfully sued for her freedom and subsequently became wealthy through real estate transactions.

On the trail and during settlement, gender roles proved fluid in women's work. In addition to their customary domestic tasks, women assumed a greater amount of physical labor; however, men did not readily share female work roles. Pregnancy and childbirth added to the hardship of women on the Overland Trail. Epidemics, complications from childbirth, and infant mortality added to the death toll. In addition to loss of lives, fear of Indian attack also pervaded women's accounts of their overland journeys. Nevertheless, peaceful interactions, as in the case of Luzena Wilson, rather than violence characterized most pre–Civil War encounters.

The overwhelming ratio of men to women on the gold rush mining frontier and in the rapidly developing San Francisco urban hub served as a magnet for prostitutes. A few prospered and managed their own bordellos. But the odds for success were not favorable: Many prostitutes died young. Most Chinese prostitutes arrived as indentured laborers, sold by their families or coerced by contractors to serve as sex workers for Chinese men. Contracts such as the one included in this chapter document the prostitutes' terms of coercive sexual labor. Prostitution proliferated in part because the extreme demographic imbalance of Chinese males to Chinese females fostered demand. By 1875, racial and gender-based immigration policies excluded not only prostitutes but also poorer Chinese women from entering the country. Congress eventually passed a discriminatory, Chinese Exclusion Act in 1882.

NANCY WARD, *Cherokee Women Petition their Tribal Leaders* (1817)

Nancy Ward (c. 1738–c.1824) is remembered as the last "Beloved Woman" of the Cherokee people. She was the head of the Cherokee Women's Council and, as a Beloved Woman, had the right to attend the male council of chiefs. Although her larger objective was peaceful coexistence with whites, she did not advocate capitulation. Ward led Cherokee women in their opposition to the sale of land to whites. Despite variations among tribes, gender norms of American Indians diverged from those of Anglo-Americans. Cherokee women had political influence that survived their partial acculturation. From the Euro-American perspective, Indian women had too much political power and in their farming responsibilities also failed to conform to women's place and prescribed domestic roles. What are the major reasons cited by the Cherokee women about the need to preserve the Cherokee land?*

Cherokee Women Resist Removal

Petitions of the Women's Councils, 1817, 1818
Petition
May 2, 1817

The Cherokee ladys now being present at the meeting of the chiefs and warriors in council have thought it their duty as mothers to address their beloved chiefs and warriors now assembled.

Our beloved children and head men of the Cherokee Nation, we address you warriors in council. We have raised all of you on the land which we now have, which God gave us to inhabit and raise provisions. We know that our country has once been extensive, but by repeated sales [it] has become circumscribed to a small track, and [we] never have thought it our duty to interfere in the disposition of it till now. If a father or mother was to sell all their lands which they had to depend on, which their children had to raise their living on, which would be indeed bad & to be removed to another country. We do not wish to go to an unknown country [to] which we have understood some of our children wish to go over the Mississippi, but this act of our children would be like destroying your mothers.

Your mothers, your sisters ask and beg of you not to part with any more of our land.

We say ours. You are our descendants; take pity on our request. But keep it for our growing children, for it was the good will of our creator to place us here, and you know our father, the great president, will not allow his white children to take our country away. Only keep your hands off of paper talks for it's our own country. For [if] it was not, they would not ask you to put your hands to paper, for it would be impossible to remove us all. For as soon as one child is raised, we have others in our arms, for such is our situation & will consider our circumstance.

Therefore, children, don't part with any more of our lands but continue on it & enlarge your farms. Cultivate and raise corn & cotton and your mothers and sisters will make clothing for you which our father the president has recommended to us all. We don't charge any body for selling any lands, but we have heard such intentions of our children. But your talks become true at last; it was our desire to forwarn you all not to part with our lands.

Nancy Ward to her children: Warriors to take pity and listen to the talks of your sisters. Although I am very old yet cannot but pity the situation in which you will hear of their minds. I have great many grand children which [I] wish them to do well on our land.

---

* In the public domain.

LADIES OF STEUBENVILLE, OHIO, *Petition Against Indian Removal* (Feb. 15, 1830)

Petitions from women against Indian removal were a significant step to claiming a political role in defiance of efforts to eliminate women from political participation. Despite the cautious tone of the Steubenville petition, it serves as an example of women entering the political debate about national issues The Steubenville petitioners believed that women's moral authority and religious benevolence justified the extension of their participation in national issues.

Women had earlier petitioned government, but their requests were personal, not political. In the case of previous temperance petitions, they had relied on male leadership. How would you account for the women's apologetic tone? What role does female sentiment play? In what ways does the Steubenville Petition express both Protestant women's assumption of moral as well as political authority?*

FEBRUARY 15, 1830

Read:—ordered that it lie upon the table.

To the Honorable the Senate and House of Representatives of the United States.

The memorial of the undersigned, residents of the state of Ohio, and town of Steubenville,

RESPECTFULLY SHEWETH:

That your memorialists are deeply impressed with the belief, that the present crisis in the affairs of the Indian nations, calls loudly on *all* who can feel for the woes of humanity, to solicit, with earnestness, your honorable body to bestow on this subject, involving, as it does, the prosperity and happiness of more than fifty thousand of our fellow Christians, the immediate consideration demanded by its interesting nature and pressing importance.

It is readily acknowledged, that the wise and venerated founders of our country's free institutions have committed the powers of Government to those whom nature and reason declare the best fitted to exercise them; and your memorialists would sincerely deprecate any presumptuous interference on the part of their own sex with the ordinary political affairs of the country, as wholly unbecoming the character of the American females. Even in private life, we may not presume to direct the general conduct, or control the acts of those

who stand in the near and guardian relations of husbands and brothers; yet all admit that *there are times* when duty and affection call on us to *advise* and *persuade*, as well as to cheer or console. And if we approach the public Representatives of our husbands and brothers, only in the humble character of suppliants in the cause of mercy and humanity, may we not hope that even the small voice of *female* sympathy will be heard?

Compared with the estimate placed on woman, and the attention paid to her on other nations, the generous and defined deference shown by all ranks and classes of men, in this country, to our sex, forms a striking contrast; and as an honorable and distinguishing trait in the American Character, has often excited the admiration of intelligent foreigners. Nor is this general kindness lightly regarded or coldly appreciated; but, with warm feelings of affection and pride, and hearts swelling with gratitude, the mothers and daughters of America bear testimony to the generous nature of their countrymen.

When, therefore, injury and oppression threaten to crush a hapless people within our borders, we, the feeblest of the feeble, appeal with confidence to those who should be representatives of national virtues as they are the depositaries of national powers, and implore them to succor the weak and unfortunate. In despite of the *undoubted national right*

---

* In the public domain.

which the Indians have to the land of their forefathers, and in the face of solemn treaties, pledging the faith of the nation for their secure possession of those lands, it is intended, we are told, to force them from their native soil, to compel them to seek new homes in a distant and dreary wilderness. To you, then, as the constitutional protectors of the Indians within our territory, and as the peculiar guardians of our national character, and our counter's welfare, we solemnly and honestly appeal, to save this remnant of a much injured people from annihilation, to shield our country from the curses denounced on the cruel and ungrateful, and to shelter the American character from lasting dishonor.

And your petitioners will ever pray.

JOURNAL OF NARCISSA WHITMAN, *Letter to her Mother* (May 2, 1840)

Between 1836 and 1847, Narcissa Whitman (1808–1847) and her husband Marcus were missionaries to the Cayuse Indians in the Oregon Territory, near what is now Walla Walla, Washington. Whitman gave up the comforts of home to journey on the Overland Trail and become one of the first white women to cross the Rocky Mountains. She was a missionary, not merely a missionary's wife. She was born and grew up a devout Presbyterian in upstate New York at a time when Protestant benevolence encouraged women in their missionary work. Whitman's objective to convert Indians to Christianity expressed her core beliefs, and she married Marcus in order to receive the official missionary designation that was denied to the unmarried. Over time, hostility displaced the good will the Cayuse initially had shown the Whitmans. Language barriers increased her inability to transcend cultural differences. Whitman kept a detailed journal and wrote numerous letters that describe some of the discomfort she experienced with the Cayuses' disregard for her domestic standards of cleanliness and need for privacy. The Whitmans' efforts at religious conversion also met with little success. In 1847, the Indians, devastated by a measles epidemic, upset over the increasing numbers of white settlers, and suspicious of white behavior, murdered Whitman, her husband, and other males living in the mission.

What role would the gendered belief in women's moral authority play in Whitman's choice to be a missionary? What evidence does she provide of her difficulty in making cultural accommodations to Indian lifestyles?*

Rev. Mrs. H.K.W. Perkins, Wascopum

WIELETPOO

May 2, 1840

My Dear Mother:

I cannot describe how much I have longed to see you of late. I have felt the want of your sympathy, your presence and counsel more than ever. One reason doubtless is it has been so long since I have received a single letter from any one of the dear friends at home. Could they know how I feel and how much good their letters do me, they would all of them write a great deal and write often, too, at least every month or two, and sent to Boston and to Westport, to the care of Rev. Joseph McCoy; they would surely reach us. Our associates receive them in great numbers, which does not make us feel any better for ourselves. We are daily expecting the arrival of Mr. Lee's ship, laden with associates for that mission, and we have the encouragement from the board to expect four or five families for our own mission. By them we hope to receive letters in abundance. It is a

---

* In the public domain.

consoling thought to us that we are permitted the prospect of having other fellow laborers to join us again so soon. We feel that we cannot do our work too fast to save the Indian—the hunted, despised and unprotected Indian—from entire extinction.

A tide of immigration appears to be moving this way rapidly. What a few years will bring forth we know not. A great change has taken place even since we first entered the country, and we have a reason to believe it will stop here. Instead of two lonely American females we now number fourteen, and soon may twenty or—more, if reports are true. We are emphatically situated on the highway between the states and the Columbia River, and are a testing place for the weary travelers, consequently a greater burden rests upon us than upon any of our associates—to be always ready. And doubtless many of those who are coming to this mission their resting place will be with us until they seek and find homes of their own among the solitary wilds of Oregon.

Could dear mother know how I have been situated the two winters past, especially winter before last, I know she would pity me. I often think how disagreeable it used to be to her feelings to do her cooking in the presence of men—sitting about the room. This I have had to bear ever since I have been here—at times it has seemed as if I could not endure it any longer. It has been the more trying because our house has been so miserable and cold—small and inconvenient for us—many people as have lived in it. But the greatest trial to a woman's feelings is to have her cooking and eating room always filled with four or five or more Indians—men—especially at meal time, but we hope this trial is nearly done, for when we get into our other house we have a room there we devote to them especially, and shall not permit them to go into the other part of the house at all. They are so filthy they make a great deal of cleaning wherever they go, and this wears out a woman very fast. We must clean after them, for we have come to elevate them and not to suffer ourselves to sink down to their standard. I hardly know how to describe my feelings at the prospect of a clean, comfortable house, and one large enough so that I can find a closet to pray in.

As a specimen I will relate a circumstance that occurred this spring. When the people began to return from their winter quarters, we told them it would be good for them to build a large house (which they often do by putting several lodges together) where it would be convenient for all to attend worship and not meet in the open air. They said they should not do it, but would worship in our new house and asked us if there were not houses in heaven to worship in. We told them our house was to live in and we could not have them worship there for they would make it so dirty and fill it so full of fleas that we could not live in it. We said to them further, that they did not help us build it and that people in other places build their houses of worship and did not let one man do it all alone, and urged them to join together by and by and build one for themselves of adobe. But it was of no avail to them; they murmured still and said we must pay them for their land we lived on. Something of this kind is occurring almost all the time when certain individuals are here; such as complaining because we do not feed them more, or that we will not let them run all over the house, etc., etc.

They are an exceedingly proud, haughty and insolent people, and keep us constantly upon the stretch after patience and forbearance. We feed them far more than any of our associates do their people, yet they will not be satisfied. Notwithstanding all this, there are many redeeming qualities in them, else we should have been discouraged long ago. We are more and more encouraged the longer we stay among them.

They are becoming quite independent in cultivation and make all their ground look as clean and mellow as a garden. Great numbers of them cultivate, and with but a single horse will take any plow we have, however large, and do their own ploughing. They have a great thirst for hogs, hens and cattle, and several of them have obtained them already.

Our greatest desire and anxiety is to see them becoming true Christians. For this we labor and pray, and trust in God for the blessing on our labors. But the labor is great and we are weak and feeble, and sometimes are ready to faint. We need the prayers of our Christian friends at home and I trust we have them. Could they know just how we are situated and all our discouragement I know they would pray more ardently for us and more importunately for us.

GURI OLSDATTER, *Letter to her Family* (1866)

Minnesota frontier settlers experienced a horrifying ordeal: the Sioux Uprising in 1862 and the death of several hundred people. Guri Olsdatter lost her husband and her son and did not write her family in Norway about the tragedy until four years later. For the vast majority of immigrants who settled in the American West, land ownership and opportunity for a new start in life outweighed the risks. Caught in the negative underside of American Indian retaliation over dispossession, Minnesota frontier families paid the ultimate price.

How would you describe the tone of this letter? What does the passage of four years between the tragedy and the writing of the letter suggest?*

dear daughter and your husband and children, and my beloved mother: I have received your letter of April fourteenth, this year, and I send you herewith my heartiest thanks for it, for it gives me great happiness to hear from you and to know that you are alive, well, and in general thriving. I must also report briefly to you how things have been going with me recently, though I must ask you to forgive me for not having told you earlier about my fate. I do not seem to have been able to do so much as to write to you, because during the time when the savages raged so fearfuly here I was not able to think about anything except being murdered, with my whole family, by these terrible heathen. But God be praised, I escaped with my life, unharmed by them, and my four daughters also came through the danger unscathed. Guri and Britha were carried off by the wild Indians, but they got a chance the next day to make their escape; when the savages gave them permission to go home to get some food, these young girls made use of the opportunity to flee and thus they got away alive, and on the third day after they had been taken, some Americans came along who found them on a large plain or prairie and brought them to people. I myself wandered aimlessly around on my land with my youngest daughter and I had to look on while they shot my precious husband dead, and in my sight my dear son Ole was shot through the shoulder. But he got well again from this wound and lived a little more than a year and then was taken sick and died. We also found my oldest son Endre shot dead, but I did not see the firing of this death shot. For two days and nights I hovered about here with my little daughter, between fear and hope and almost crazy, before I found my wounded son and a couple of other persons, unhurt, who helped us to get away to a place of greater security. To be an eyewitness to

---

* In the public domain.

these things and to see many others wounded and killed was almost too much for a poor woman; but, God be thanked, I kept my life and my sanity, though all my movable property was torn away and stolen. But this would have been nothing if only I could have had my loved husband and children—but what shall I say? God permitted it to happen thus, and I had to accept my heavy fate and thank Him for having spared my life and those of some of my dear children.

I must also let you know that my daughter Gjasrtru has land, which they received from the government under a law that has been passed, called in our language "the Homestead law," and for a quarter section of land they have to pay sixteen dollars, and after they have lived there five years they receive a deed and complete possession of the property and can sell it if they want to or keep it if they want to. She lives about twenty-four American miles from here and is doing well. My daughter Guri is away in house service for an American about a hundred miles from here; she has been there working for the same man for four years; she is in good health and is doing well; I visited her recently, but for a long time I knew nothing about her, whether she was alive or not.

My other two daughter, Britha and Anna, are at home with me, are in health, and are thriving here. I must also remark that it was four years on the twenty-first of last August since I had to flee from my dear home, and since that time I have not been on my land, as it is only a sad sight because at the spot where I had a happy home, there are now only ruins and remains left as reminders of the terrible Indians. Still I moved up here to the neighborhood again this summer. A number of families have moved back here again so that we hope after a while to make conditions pleasant once more. Yet the atrocities of the Indians are and will be fresh in memory; they have now been driven beyond the boundaries of the state and we hope that they never will be allowed to come here again. I am now staying at the home of Sjur Anderson, two and a half miles from my home. I must also tell you how much I had before I was ruined in this way. I had seventeen head of cattle, eight sheep, eight pigs, and a number of chickens; now I have six head of cattle, four sheep, one pig; five of my cattle stayed on my land until February, 1863, and lived on some hay and stacks of wheat on the land; and I received compensation from the government for my cattle and other movable property that I lost. Of the six cattle that I now have three are milk cows and of these I have sold butter, the summer's product, a little over two hundred and thirty pounds; I sold this last month and got sixty-six dollars for it. In general I may say that one or another has advised me to sell my land, but I would rather keep it for a time yet, in the hope that some of my people might come and use it; it is difficult to get such good land again, and if you, my dear daughter, would come here, you could buy it and use it and then it would not be necessary to let it fall into the hands of strangers. And now in closing I must send my very warm greetings to my unforgetable dear mother, my dearest daughter and her husband and children, and in general to all my relatives, acquaintances, and friends. And may the Lord by his grace bend, direct, and govern our hearts so that we sometime with gladness may assemble with God in the eternal mansions where there will be no more partings, no sorrows, no more trials, but everlasting joy and gladness, and contentment in beholding God's face. If this be the goal for all our endeavors through the sorrows and cares of this life, then through his grace we may hope for a blessed life hereafter, for Jesus sake.

Always your devoted

GURI OLSDATTER

Write to me soon.

EULALIA PEREZ, *Reminiscences* (1877)

Eulalia Perez (c. 1768–c. 1878) provides a detailed account of her responsibilities and daily tasks within the Spanish Mission of San Gabriel during the early 1820s. At the time of the interview, she claimed to be 140 years old, and historians believe that she may have been born as early as 1768, although her birthdate remains uncertain. The following excerpt from her testimony was transcribed in 1877.

The missions were institutions of religious and social control and exemplified Spain's major means of Christianizing and controlling California's indigenous population. In her work for the mission, Perez played a role in upholding patriarchal Spanish control and even consented to remarriage against her own personal wishes. She became chief cook and keeper of the mission keys shortly after she joined the mission. Her work combined significant administrative functions as well as domestic tasks. Perez's duties also placed her in control of San Gabriel's Indian women laborers, who were forced to live within or nearby the mission. Perez recalled how the Indian girls and unmarried women were locked in their rooms at night. She also described their daily work schedules. What purposes would be served by this strict discipline and work assignments for Indian women? How would you describe Perez's responsibilities as the mission's chief housekeeper?*

I, EULALIA PÉREZ, was born at the presidio of Loreto, in Baja California.

My father's name was Diego Pérez and he worked in the naval department at the presidio. My mother's name was Antonia Rosalía Cota. They both were white people through and through.

I do not remember the date of my birth, but I do know that I was fifteen years old when I married Miguel Antonio Guillén, a soldier of the presidio company of Loreto. When I was living in Loreto, I had three sons and one daughter. Two of the boys died in Loreto at a young age and another boy, . . .

The last time I came to San Gabriel, there were only two women in this whole part of California who really knew how to cook. One was Maró Luisa Cota, the wife of Claudio Líapez, the *mayordomo* at the mission. The other woman was María Ignacia Amador, the wife of Francisco Javier Alvarado. She knew how to cook, sew, read, and write, and she could take care of the sick. She was a fine *curandera*. Her job was to sew and take care of the church garments. In her home, she

taught some children how to read and write, but she did not have a formal school.

On important feast days, such as that of the patron saint and Easter, the two women would be called upon to prepare the large meal, the meat dishes, sweets, and other things. The Fathers wanted to help me because I was a widow supporting a family. They looked for ways to give me work without upsetting the other women. Father Sánchez and Father Zalvidea discussed the matter and decided to see who was the best cook. One woman would cook first, followed by the next one, and I would be the last one to cook. The woman who surpassed the others would be assigned to teach the Indian cooks how to cook.

The next day, I went to cook. I made several soups, a variety of meat dishes, and anything else that came to mind that I knew how to make. Tomás, the Indian cook, paid close attention to what I was doing, as the Father had told him to do.

The men I mentioned came at dinnertime. After they finished the meal, Father Sánchez asked them what they thought of the food, beginning with the oldest man, Don

* Eulalia Perez, Reminiscences transcribed in Testimonios translated by Rose Marie Beebe and Robert M. Senkewicz. copyright © 2006 Heyday Books. Reprinted by permission.

Ignacio Tenorio. This señor pondered for quite some time. He said that it had been many years since he had eaten as well as he had that day. He doubted that a person would eat better food at the king's table. The other men also praised the meal highly.

The Father then asked Tomás which of the three señoras he liked best and which one knew the most. He said it was me.

Based on this, I was given a job at the mission. First, two Indians were assigned to me so I could teach them how to cook. One was named Tomás and the other was "El Gentil." I taught them so well that I had the pleasure of seeing them turn out to be very fine cooks. They were, perhaps, the best cooks in this whole part of the country.

The Fathers were very happy and this helped me earn more of their respect. I spent about a year teaching those two Indians. I did not have to work; I just supervised them because they now had some basic knowledge of cooking.

The Fathers then talked among themselves and agreed to hand over the mission keys to me. This was in 1821, if I remember correctly. I remember that my daughter María Rosario was seven years old at the time and was gravely ill. Father José Sánchez administered the last rites to her. He attended to her with the greatest care and we were finally able to rejoice because we did not lose her. At that time, I was already the *llavera*.

The *llavera* had various responsibilities. First, she would distribute the daily rations for the *pozolera*. To do this, she had to count the number of single women and men, field workers, and vaqueros—those who rode with saddles and those who rode bareback. Besides that, she had to give daily rations to the people who were married. In short, she was in charge of the distribution of the rations for the Indians and she was also in charge of the Fathers' kitchen. She was in charge of the key to the clothing storehouse, from where material would be taken to make dresses for single and married women, as well as children. She also had to supervise the cutting of clothes for men.

She was also in charge of cutting and making clothes and other items, from head to toe, for the vaqueros who used saddles. Those who rode bareback received nothing more than their shirt, blanket, and loincloth. Those who rode with saddles received the same clothing as the *gente de razón*. They were given a shirt, a vest, pants, a hat, boots, shoes, and spurs. And they were given a saddle, a bridle, and a *reata* for their horse. Each vaquero would also receive a large kerchief made of silk or cotton, and a sash of Chinese silk or red crepe cloth or whatever other material might be in the storehouse.

All work having to do with clothing was done by my daughters under my supervision. I would cut and arrange the pieces of material and my five daughters would do the sewing. When they could not keep up with the workload, I would let the Father know. He would then hire women from the pueblo of Los Angeles and pay them.

In addition, I had to supervise the area where soap was made, which was very large, and also the wine presses. I supervised and

Eulalia Perez (Courtesy of The Bancroft Library. University of California, Berkeley)

worked in the crushing of olives to make olive oil. Domingo Romero would drain off the liquid, but I would supervise him as he did this.

Luis, the soap maker, was in charge of the actual soap production, but I supervised everything.

I supervised the distribution of leather, calfskin, chamois, sheepskin, *tafilete,* red cloth, tacks, thread, silk, etc.—everything related to the making of saddles and shoes, as well as everything that is needed in a saddle workshop and a shoe workshop.

ISADORA FILOMENA, *Testimony of the Widow of Prince Solano* (1874)

A member of the Churucto tribe of California Indians, Isadora Filomena was taken captive as a child by Solano, chief of the Sessions. Little is known about her life, other than this interview. Taking women captive was not uncommon. Filomena was subsequently baptized and married to Solano. In this excerpt from an interview recorded many years later, she recalled her prestige as wife of a powerful chieftain. In addition, because of her husband's close tie to the Mexican general Vallejo, she also enjoyed certain material comforts. Her lifestyle ended with the American conquest of California. She blamed "the Blond men who stole everything" for her own decline and remained resistant to American domination. Although Filomena's Indian background diverged in most respects from that of Rosalia Vallejo Leese's elite Spanish position, both women remained hostile to U.S. control of their lands. The lifestyle of the Churucto tribe was essentially that of hunter-gatherers. How does Filomena describe the customs of the Churucto tribe? How would you compare the evidence of her resistance to American rule to that of Rosalia Leese in the following document?*

MY NAME IS ISIDORA. I am ninety years old. The Indians who knew me when I was the wife of Chief Solano called me "Princess" and they still treat me like a princess. And even some of the white men, such as Remigio Berreyesa, Gonzalo Ramírez, Captain Salvador Vallejo, and many others who from time to time come to Lacryma Montis to visit us still call me Princess. They remember that whenever my husband would get angry, I would do everything possible to calm him down.

Although I was young, I, like the other Indians of my tribe, worshiped the god named Puis, who was a mortal being like myself. He dressed all in white feathers but wore black feathers on his head. My people worshiped him as if he were a real god.

Later, I married the great Solano, prince of the Suysunes, Topaytos, Yoloitos, and Chuructas. He became prince of the Topaytos

after he conquered them. During his lifetime he inspired fear in everyone, white men and Indians, with the exception of his friend General Guadalupe Vallejo. Solano always refused offers of friendship from Sutter, Yount, and many other blonde men who wanted to be his friends.

The priest Guias (Prince Solano always called Reverend Fray Lorenzo de la Concepción Quijas by the name Guias), who baptized me and gave me the name Isidora Filomena, taught me how to be very charitable toward the poor, very gentle with my husband, and very compassionate toward the prisoners.** This is why I prevented my husband from killing enemy prisoners after he had conquered all of his enemies with the eight thousand men he led. Back then, it was customary to tie the prisoners to trees and shoot arrows at them. I told him, "Leave them with Vallejo. He will make them

---

* Isadora Filomena, testimony of the widow of Prince Solano in Testimonios translated by Rose Marie Beebe and Robert M. Senkewicz. copyright © 2006 Heyday Books. Reprinted by permission.
** This footnote was appended to the interview: "He would take communion with brandy and would take a swig to do Mass. hie was always drunk."

work the land." Fr. Guias advised the same thing. Solano followed our advice and many poor souls were spared.

I belonged to Solano before I married him and even before I was baptized. I am not a Suysun like he is. I belong to the Churucto tribe. My father's tribe lived near Cache Creek. I do not know the name of the county to which it belongs today. On a trip Solano took there to do some negotiating, he stole me. My father and many Satiyomi went after him, but they could not catch him.

I have already gone downhill. I drink a lot of liquor because I do not have very much land filled with cattle. The blonde men stole everything. They left nothing for poor Isidora, who married Bill after Solano died. Bill is not a very loving man. I did not give birth again. With Solano I gave birth to eight little ones. They all died except for one son named Joaquín, who works the land to make a living. He usually gives me twenty pesos. Commander Vallejo lets me live in a house with some land for free. . . .

We would use our fingers to count, and that is how we counted up to ten. Ten in the Suysun language is pronounced *papa cien.* We did not have enough fingers to count from ten on up, so we would make piles of sticks. That way we could count up to one hundred.

Before the white men arrived in Soscol, we had lots of food and it was very good and easy to obtain without much work. There were lots of animals to hunt, and the country-side provided lots of wild onions. We called the wild onions *ur.* We also had wild soap that we called *amoles.* It still grows abundantly near San Rafael. I sometimes send Bill there to look for it. That soap cleans better than any soap made by man. It removes all stains and does not burn your body or make your skin hurt.

In my land, everyone of my race had very red skin like mine. All the women were very tall. I was perhaps one of the shortest. Many of us live to be more than one hundred years old. The women's hair never turns

white. Men's hair changes color. Our Indians do not have large feet or large hands like the white Germans or the Mexicans. They are tall and their feet and hands are small. They always go barefoot. My tribe and many others would eat quite a bit of fish. One could find many varieties of fish in our rivers. But the fish that was most abundant was the type called salmon. We did not always catch fish with nets. Many times, when the river would be low, we would place poles in the middle of the river and we could catch lots of fish that way. Some of the fish would be eaten fresh and the rest would be dried and put away for the winter.

When the white man arrived, I did not know what liquor was. But Sutter, who was a *gente de razón,* would send *Joaquinero* Indians to trade liquor for hides, pelts, and dried fish. Sutter had an Indian wife. She was not from California. She was a Kanaka Indian who arrived with him on a ship. I do not like the white man very much because he is very tricky and a thief. My *compadre* Peralta and friend Bernales had many cattle. Sutter tricked them and took everything but paid for nothing.

We would have very nice dances. The men would dance with men. The women would dance with women. The men danced naked. After the *gente de razón* came, the women wore a skirt. But before, when there were only Indians here, the women only wore a necklace like this one, around their necks. (She showed me the necklace and sold it to me.) They wore a crown of feathers on their heads and a string of beads we call *abalorios.* They wrapped their body from the chest all the way up to the neck with little beads. The larger beads were made into a sash and tied with a shell at the waist. They wore earrings made of feathers and bills from geese and ducks. They would hang the earrings from their ears with a duck bone that had been filed down with flint until it was very thin.

The food we like the most is *topoc* and *huraja.*

Some Suysun women had sashes with feathers. Many wore nothing more than a pelt that hung in front but did not go around their waist. Churucto Indians would paint their bodies with charcoal and red ochre. This paint was not permanent. We all had houses made of tule and we lived comfortably. We liked to bathe very much because cleanliness makes you strong. We would teach little boys how to hunt. Women did the cooking and took care of the little children.

ROSALIA VALLEJO LEESE, *Testimony "Hoisting of the Bear Flag"* (1877)

Rosalie Vallejo Leese (1811–1889) intentionally refused to learn English as an expression of her enduring opposition against the American takeover of California in 1846.

Her recollections described John Fremont's declaration of California as an independent republic, a short-lived one, once the Treaty of Guadalupe Hidalgo was signed and the republic became a territory of the United States. Leese was from a prominent Mexican California family whose fortunes and status declined with the American assumption of power. Her brother, Mariano Vallejo, an important Mexican army officer, and her husband were briefly imprisoned by John Fremont after the Bear State Revolt.

How does Rosalia describe the Bear State Revolt? Why does she refer to the American overthrow of Mexican control as "the robbery of California"?*

Q: *Mrs. Leese, could you please tell me what you know about the raising of the Bear Flag in Sonoma?*

A: On June 14, 1846, at about 5:30 in the morning, an old man named Don Pepe de la Rosa came to my home and told me that a group of seventy-two ragged desperados had surrounded General Vallejo's house. Many of those men were sailors from whaling ships who had jumped ship. They arrested General Vallejo, Captain Salvador Vallejo, and Víctor Prudón. When I heard this alarming news, I quickly got dressed and rushed out to the street to see if there was any truth to what the old man had said. The first thing I saw was Colonel Prudón running off to try and rescue Captain Salvador Vallejo—a ruffian named Benjamin Kelsey was trying to murder Captain Vallejo in cold blood. What other word would you use to describe the killing of an unarmed prisoner by a strong brute who had seventy men just like himself right behind him? Kelsey's comrades had dragged Captain Vallejo off to where Doctor Semple and his group were located, but Prudón arrived in the nick of time to save his life.

From appearances, Doctor Semple seemed to be more humane than the rest of that godforsaken bunch. I also saw ex-Commander General Vallejo, who was dressed in the uniform of a Mexican army general. A large group of rough-looking men were holding him prisoner. Some of the men were wearing caps made from the skins of coyotes or wolves. Others were wearing slouch hats full of holes or straw hats as black as charcoal. Most of these marauders had on buckskin pants, but some were wearing blue pants that reached only to the knee. Several of the men were not wearing shirts, and only fifteen or twenty of the whole bunch were wearing shoes.

---

* Rosalia Vallejo Leese, "Hoisting of the Bear Flag" in Testimonios translated by Rose Marie Beebe and Robert M. Senkewicz. copyright © 2006 Heyday Books. Reprinted by permission.

After talking among themselves for a while, a good number of the men mounted their horses and rode off with the prisoners. General Vallejo, Captain Salvador Vallejo, Colonel Víctor Prudón, and my husband, Jacob Leese, were taken to Sacramento and were left to the tender mercies of that demon John A. Sutter. Although he had married in Europe and had several children, he had left his wife and children behind and was living openly with two black mistresses. These women were from the Sandwich Islands. Sutter had brought them to California on his ship.

After General Vallejo was hurriedly taken away, the marauders who had stayed behind in Sonoma raised a piece of linen cloth on the flagpole located in the corner of the plaza near the old mission church. The cloth was about the size of a large towel, and they had painted a red bear and one star on it. John C. Frémont was the man who had planned this all-out robbery of California. Even though he was an officer in the U.S. army, it is fair to assume that Frémont was afraid to compromise the honor of his government. He was not about to let his thieves steal California while waving the flag that lovers of liberty throughout the world hold dear. This was why he adopted a flag unknown to civilized nations.

As soon as the Bear Flag was raised, I was told by the thieves' interpreter that I was now a prisoner. This interpreter's name was Solís. He was a former servant of my husband's. Solís pointed to four ragged desperados who were standing close to me with their pistols drawn. I surrendered because it would have been useless to resist. They demanded the key to my husband's storehouse and I gave it to them. No sooner had I given them the key than they called their friends over and began ransacking the storehouse. There

were enough provisions and liquor there to feed two hundred men for two years. A few days after my husband was taken away, John C. Frémont arrived in Sonoma. He said that his sole purpose for coming was to arrange matters to everyone's satisfaction and protect everyone from extortion or oppression. Many paid writers have characterized Frémont with a great number of endearing epithets, but he was a tremendous coward. Listen to me! I have good reason to say this. On June 20, we received news that Captain Padilla was on his way to Sonoma with a squad of one hundred men to rescue us. As soon as Frémont heard about this, he sent for me. He ordered me to write Padilla a letter and tell him to return to San José and not come near Sonoma. I flatly refused to do that, but Frémont was bent on having his own way. He told me that if I refused to tell Padilla exactly what he told me to say, and if Padilla approached Sonoma, he would order his men to burn down our houses with us inside. I agreed to his demands, not because I wanted to save my own life, but because I was pregnant and did not have the right to endanger the life of my unborn child. Moreover, I judged that a man who had already gone this far would stop at nothing to attain his goals. I also wanted to spare the Californio women from more trouble, so I wrote that ominous letter which forced Captain Padilla to retrace his steps. While on alert for Padilla's possible attack, Frémont changed out of his fancy uniform into a blue shirt. He put away his hat and wrapped an ordinary handkerchief around his head. He decided to dress like this so he would not be recognized. Is this the way a brave man behaves?

During the whole time that Frémont and his ring of thieves were in Sonoma, robberies were very common. The women did not dare go out for a walk unless they were escorted by their husband or their brothers. One of my servants was a young Indian girl who was about seventeen years old. I swear that John C. Frémont ordered me to send that girl to the officers' barracks many times. However, by resorting to tricks, I was able to save that poor girl from falling into the hands of that lawless band of thugs who had imprisoned my husband.

During the two months that my husband was held prisoner, I sent him exquisite food and gold, but that despicable Sutter arranged it so my husband never received one dollar. On more than one occasion Sutter had been forced to acknowledge the superiority of Mr. Leese. For an entire week, Sutter made my husband sleep on the bare floor and assigned an uncouth man from Missouri to guard his room. Whenever that guard opened the door, he would insult the

prisoners. This band of ungrateful horse thieves, trappers, and runaway sailors had deprived these prisoners of their liberty.

I could tell you about the many crimes committed by the Bear Flag mob, but since I do not wish to detain you any longer, I will end this conversation with this those hateful men instilled so much hate in me for the people of their race that, even though twenty-eight years have gone by since then, I still cannot forget the insults they heaped upon me. Since I have not wanted to have anything to do with them, I have refused to learn their language.

Monterey
June 27, 1874

By Rosalía de Leese

LUZENA STANLEY WILSON, *Memories recalled years later for her daughter, Correnah Wilson Wright* **(1881)**

Luzena Stanley Wilson (1820–1902) recounted her recollections of her pioneer experience in California to her daughter Correnah Wilson Wright in 1881. The memoir was published in 1934, and Wright claimed she had followed her mother's words as closely as possible. The Wilson family had prospered, and Wright graduated from Mills College in 1875. Even in the small community of Vacaville, California, where the Wilsons lived, cultural diversity proliferated.

Wilson, her husband, and their two children migrated from Missouri to California in 1849 in response to the excitement of the discovery of gold. She had a gift for seizing the opportunity to make money in the gold rush economy and for years operated a successful boarding house and restaurant. The Wilson family was among the first to buy land from Emanuel Vaca, a Mexican landowner for whom the community was named. Cross-cultural contacts with her Mexican neighbors became part of Wilson's everyday life. Despite cultural bias, her views about her Mexican neighbors provide a glimpse into lifestyles that were rapidly disappearing. Her evaluations of Mexicans were not too different from her negative observations of the families from the American South that also occupied nearby farms.

How does Wilson describe her Mexican neighbors? What faults does she perceive the farmers from the American South to possess? How would you evaluate Wilson's views of her neighbors?*

Our nearest neighbors were the members of the Spanish colony, who lived only three-quarters of a mile away, in the little Laguna Valley. The lord of the soil, the original

owner of all the land included in the grant on which we lived, was Manuel Vaca, and around him clustered the Spanish population of great or lesser note. Some of their adobe houses still

---

* In the public domain.

remain, in unpleasing, barren, squalid desolation, a rude and fast-decaying monument to the vanished grandeur of Spanish California, and a shelter to American settlers of even less energy and enterprise than the "greasers". About us in all directions roamed herds of cattle and droves of mustangs, which constituted the wealth of the settlement and a whole day's hard riding about the grant would not reveal half the extent of their four-footed possessions. Even at that early day some portions of the original grant had already passed from Vaca to American owners. Today of all that great body of fertile valley and leagues of pasture land scarcely more than two or three hundred acres can be found in the possession of his heirs.

The Mexican character of slothfulness and procrastination assisted materially to undermine their financial stability, and they succumbed to the strategy and acuteness of the American trader. It was but a few years till the proud rulers of the valley were the humblest subjects of the new monarchs, reduced from affluence almost to beggary by too greatly trusted Yankees. . . . All the accompaniments of Spanish happiness were to be found in the small precinct occupied by their dwellings. An army of vaqueros congregated every day about the settlement, smoked cigarettes, ran races, played cards for high stakes, and drank bad whisky in unlimited quantities. The man of position felt proud of his patrician blood, and condescended when he addressed his surrounding inferiors. He wore a broad sombrero, gold-laced jacket and wide bell-decked pantaloons, girt his waist with a flaming sash, wore jangling at his heels, large, clanking, silver spurs, swung a lariat with unerring aim, and in the saddle looked a centaur. The belles of the valley coquetted with the brave riders, threw at them melting glances from their eyes, and whispered sweet nothings in the melodious Spanish tongue. I was always treated with extreme consideration by the Spanish people, and they quite frequently invited me to participate in their

dances and feasts, which they gave to celebrate their great occasions. We had been in the valley only about two months, when Seor Vaca came riding over one morning to ask me, by the aid of an interpreter, to attend a ball to be given that night at his house. I was quite unfamiliar with the manner and customs of the Spanish people, and my acceptance of the cordial and pressing invitation was prompted quite as much by curiosity as by my friendly feelings for my neighbors.

When we arrived at the adobe house the light streamed through open windows and doors far out into the night and revealed, tethered all about, the saddle-horses of the guests and lit up many black-eyed, smiling faces, looking to see how the Americans would be received. Don Manuel with his daughter, greeted us with all the ceremony and courtesy of a Spanish grandee and showed us to the place of honor. We were ushered into a long room illuminated with tallow dips, destitute of furniture, with the exception of the two or three chairs reserved exclusively for the use of the American visitors. On either side were many mats, on which reclined with careless grace and ease the flirting belle and beau and the wrinkled duennas of the fiesta. The musical accompaniment to the dancing, which had already begun, was played upon guitar and tambourine, and the laughing, chattering, happy crowd swayed and turned in wave-like undulation to the rhythm of a seductive waltz. They fluttered their silken vari-colored scarfs, and bent their lithe bodies in graceful dances which charmed my cotillion and quadrille-accustomed eyes. The young ladies were dressed in true Mexican costume; snowy chemises of soft fine linen, cut low, displayed the plump necks, leaving bare the dimpled arms; bright hued silk petticoats in great plaid patterns and shawls and scarfs of brilliant scarlet, set off in contrast their glossy, jet hair, their red lips, and their sparkling, tigerish, changing eyes. The men in holiday attire of velvet jackets of royal purple and emerald green, profusely trimmed with gold and silver braids, were as gaudy in color and picturesque in appearance as the feminine portion of the assembly. The refreshments comprised strangely compounded but savory Spanish stews, hot with chilies, great piles of tortillas, and gallons of only tolerable whisky. Near midnight they were served informally. Some of the guests ate reclining on their mats, some standing about the long, low table, some lounging in door-ways and window-seats—all laughing, talking, coquetting and thoroughly enjoying the passing minutes, forgetful of yesterday, heedless of tomorrow, living only in the happy present. Among the prominent and honored guests were members of the most wealthy and influential Spanish families of the country. I remember well the pretty faces and manly figures of the Armijos, Picos, Penas, and Berryessas, who have long since been gathered in peace to their fathers, or are still living, holding prominent places in various California communities. . . .

The Spanish population gradually vanished before the coming immigration. The thick-walled adobe houses, which sheltered under one roof horses and men, crumbled away and mingled with the dust. The vaquero and his bands of Spanish cattle fled to wider ranges. The plow turned the sod where the brilliant wild flowers had bloomed for ages undisturbed, and silken corn and golden wheat ripened in the little valley. Year by year more acres of the fertile land were laid under cultivation. The canvas tent was followed by a tiny, unpainted redwood cabin with a dirt floor, and that in turn by more pretentious homes. It was years before the title of the land was established, and we were kept in continual commotion through the persistent efforts of squatters to obtain possession. The surveys of the Spanish owners were very imperfect and caused a world of trouble and annoyance to their successors. The usual mode of measurement in early days, before surveyors and surveying instruments were in the country, was for a vaquero to take a fresh mustang and gallop an hour in any direction. The distance thus traversed was called ten miles. Smaller distances were subdivisions of the hour's ride; and, as the speed of the horse was variable you may easily see that the survey thus made would be a very irregular one and would be likely, as it did, to give rise to many complications in later transfers of the land.

The valley was settled principally by emigrants from Missouri and Arkansas, and they brought with them the shiftless ways of farming and housekeeping prevalent in the West and South, which have, in a measure, prevented the improvement and advancement that might have been expected from so fertile and productive a country. I remember as an illustration of the principles of early housekeeping, being called to help take care of a neighbor who was very ill. I sat up all night by the sick woman in company with another neighbor, a volunteer nurse. Growing hungry toward morning we concluded to get breakfast, so I sent the daughter of the house, a girl of seventeen years, to bring me some cream to make biscuits. She was gone a long time, and I waited with my hands in the flour for her to come back. Finally she made her appearance with the cream, and when I asked the cause of the delay, she answered, "Well, old Bob was in the cream, and I had to stop and scrape him off."

To emphasize the statement, "old Bob", the cat, came in wet from his involuntary cream bath. I made the bread with water that I pumped myself. The out-door management of the men was as badly conducted as the indoor system of their wives. A general air of dilapidation seemed to pervade and cling to the houses and barns of the farmer from the West. He sat cross-legged on the fence and smoked a clay pipe in company with the "old woman", while the pigs and chickens rooted and scratched unmolested in his front garden. The Western farmers still, in some few instances, hold possession, and from the highway as you pass you may detect the unmistakable signs of their early training, but by far the greater part of the pioneer population has been succeeded by economical, industrious, energetic, thrifty families from the North and Canada, and they have converted the little valley into a cultivated and blooming garden. The redwood shanty has given way to large and well-built pleasant homes, furnished with comforts and often luxuries. Instead of the barefooted, rag-covered urchins of early times, who ran wild with the pigs and calves, all along the roads one may see troops of rosy, well-clad children on their way to school. The old-time Sabbath amusements of riding bucking mustangs into the saloons, drinking all day at the various bars, running footraces, playing poker, and finishing the day with a free fight are things of the past. The sobering influence of civilization has removed all such exciting but dangerous pastimes as playing scientific games of billiards by firing at the balls with a pistol, taking off the heads of the decanters, behind the counter with a quick shot, and making the bar-keeper shiver for his well-curled hair.

MARY BALLOU, *"Hogs in my Kitchen"* (1852)

Mary Ballou (1809–1894) and her husband arrived in California from New Hampshire in 1852 and ran a boarding house. Ballou's letter to her son combines poignancy ("I wept for a while then I commenced singing") with upbeat good humor. Although unpolished and filled with spelling errors, she conveys the novelty of experience in a strange and unpredictable mining community. Her account provides a vivid depiction of the hardship of cooking for a crowd of miners in a home that lacked even the basic separation between the outdoors and the interior. She notes how hogs and mules drift in and out of her kitchen and yet she manages to cope and use the rough environment of the mining frontier to her economic advantage. What particular experiences provided Ballou with the greatest satisfaction?*

California Negrobar October 30 1852

My Dear Selden

we are about as usual in health. well I suppose you would like to know what I am doing in this gold region. well I will try to tell you what my work is here in this muddy Place. All the kitchen that I have is four posts stuck down into the ground and covered over the top with factory cloth no floor but the ground. this is a Boarding House kitchen. there is a floor in the dining room and my sleeping room coverd with nothing but cloth. we are at work in a Boarding House.

Oct 27 this morning I awoke and it rained in torrents. well I got up and I thought of my House. I went and looket into my kitchen, the mud and water was over my Shoes I could not go into the kitchen to do any work to day but kept perfectly dry in the Dining so I got along verry well. your Father put on his Boots and done the work in the kitchen. I felt badly to think that I was de[s]tined to be in such a place. I wept for a while and then I commenced singing and made up a song as I went along. my song was this: to California I did come and thought I under the bed I shall have to run to shelter me from the piercing storm.

now I will try to tell you what my work is in this Boarding House. well somtimes I am washing and Ironing somtimes I am making mince pie and Apple pie and squash pies. Somtimes frying mince turnovers and Donuts. I make Buiscuit and now and then Indian jonny cake and then again I am making minute puding filled with rasons and Indian Bake pudings and then again a nice Plum Puding and then again I am Stuffing a Ham of pork that cost

* Yale University Press.

forty cents a pound. Somtimes I am making gruel for the sick now and then cooking oisters sometimes making coffee for the French people strong enough for any man to walk on that has Faith as Peter had. three times a day I set my Table which is about thirty feet in length and do all the little fixings about it such as filling pepper boxes and vinegar cruits and mustard pots and Butter cups. somtimes I am feeding my chickens and then again I am scareing the Hogs out of my kitchen and Driving the mules out of my Dining room. you can see by the descrption of that I have given you of my kitchen that anything can walk into the kitchen that choeses to walk in and there being no door to shut from the kitchen into the Dining room you see that anything can walk into the kitchen and then from kitchen into the Dining room so you see the Hogs and mules can walk in any time day or night if they choose to do so. somtimes I am up all times a night scaring the Hogs and mules out of the House. last night there a large rat came down pounce down onto our bed in the night. sometimes I take my fan and try to fan myself but I work so hard that my Arms pain me so severely that I kneed some one to fan me so I do not find much comfort anywhere. I made a Bluberry puding to day for Dinner. Somtimes I am making soups and cramberry tarts and Baking chicken that cost four Dollars a head and cooking Eggs at three Dollars a Dozen. Somtimes boiling cabbage and Turnips and frying fritters and Broiling stake and cooking codfish and potatoes. I often cook nice Salmon trout that weigh from ten to twenty pound apiece. somtimes I am taking care of Babies and nursing at the rate of Fifty Dollars a week but I would not advise any Lady to come out here and suffer the toil and fatigue that I have suffered for the sake of a little gold neither do I advise any one to come. Clarks Simmon wife says if she was safe in the States she would not care if she had not one cent. She came in here last night and said, "Oh dear I am so homesick that I must die," and then again my other associate came in with tears in her eyes and said

that she had cried all day. she said if she had as good a home as I had got she would not stay twenty five minutes in California. I told her that she could not pick up her duds in that time. she said she would not stop for duds nor anything else but my own heart was two sad to cheer them much.

now I will tell you a little more about my cooking. somtimes I am cooking rabbits and Birds that are called quails here and I cook squrrels. occasionly I run in and have a chat with Jane and Mrs Durphy and I often have a hearty cry. no one but my maker knows my feelings. and then I run into my little cellar which is about four feet square as I have no other place to run that is cool.

October 21 well I have been to church to hear a methodist sermon. his Text was let us lay aside every weight and the sin that doth so easely beset us. I was the only Lady that was present and about forty gentleman. So you see that I go to church when I can.

November 2 well it has been Lexion day here to day. I have heard of strugling and tite pulling but never saw such a day as I have witnessed to day the Ballot Box was so near to me that I could hear every word that was spoken. the wind Blows verry hard here to day. I have three lights Burning and the wind blows so hard that it almost puts my lights out while I am trying to write. if you could but step in and see the inconvience that I have for writing you would not wonder that I cannot write any better you would wonder that I could write at all. notwithstanding all the dificuty in writing I improve every leishure moment. it is quite cool here my fingers are so cold that I can hardly hold my pen. well it is ten o clock at night while I am writing. the people have been Declareing the votes. I hear them say Hura for the Whigs and sing whigs songs. now I hear them say that Morman Island has gone whig and now another time a cheering. now I hear them say Beals Bar has gone whig now another time cheering. well it is getting late and I must retire soon there is so much noise I do not expect to sleep much to night. there has been a little fighting here to day and one chalenge given but the chalenge given but the chalenge was not accepted they got together and setted their trouble.

I will tell tell you a little of my bad feelings, on the 9 of September there was a little fight took place in the store. I saw them strike each other through the window in the store. one went and got a pistol and started towards the other man. I never go into the store but your mothers tender heart could not stand that so I ran into the store and Beged and plead with him not to kill him for eight or ten minutes not to take his Life for the sake of his wife and three little children to spare his life and then I ran through the Dining room into my sleeping room and Buried my Face in my bed so as not to hear the sound of the pistol and wept Biterly. Oh I thought if I had wings how quick I would fly to the States. that night at the supper table he told the Boarders if it had not been for what that Lady said to him Scheles would have been a dead man. after he got his pashion over he said that he was glad that he did not kill him so you see that your mother has saved one Human beings Life, you see that I am trying to relieve all the suffering and trying to do all the good that I can.

there I hear the Hogs in my kichen turning the Pots and kettles upside down so I must drop my pen and run and drive them out. so you this is the way that I have to write—jump up every five minutes for somthing and then again I washed out about a Dollars worth of gold dust the fourth of July in the cradle so you see that I am doing a little mining in this gold region but I think it harder to rock the cradle to wash out gold than it is to rock the cradle for the Babies in the States.

October 11 I washed in the forenoon and made a Democrat Flag in the afternoon sewed twenty yards of splendid worsted fringe around it and I made whig Flag. they are both swinging acrost the road but the Whig Flag is the richest. I had twelve Dollars for making them so you see that I am making Flags with all rest of the various kinds of work that I am doing and then again I am scouring candle sticks and washing the floor and making soft soap. the People tell me that it is the first Soft Soap they knew made in California. Somtimes I am making mattresses and sheets. I have no windows in my room. all the light that I have shines through canvas that covers the House and my eyes are so dim that I can hardly see to make a mark so I think you will excuse me for not writing any better. I have three Lights burning now but I am so tired and Blind that I can scearcely see and here I am among the French and Duch and Scoth and Jews and Italions and Sweeds and Chineese and Indians and all manner of tongus and nations but I am treated with due respect by them all.

I immagine you will say what a long yarn this is from California. if you can read it at all I must close soon for I am so tired and almost sick. Oh my Dear Selden I am so Home sick I will say to you once more to see that Augustus has every thing that he kneeds to make him comfortable and by all means have him Dressed warm this cold winter. I worry a great deal about my Dear children. it seems as though my heart would break when I realise how far I am from my Dear Loved ones this from your affectionate mother

Mary B Ballou

BRIDGET (BIDDY) MASON, *Court Trial, Mason v. Smith* (1856)

Although California entered the Union as a free state, Biddy Mason's owner, Robert Marion Smith, brought his slaves with him when he arrived in San Bernardino to join the Mormon community in1851. He had brought Mason, her three children, and his other slaves from Mississippi to Utah and then to California. After four years living as a slave, Mason thwarted Smith's plan to take his slaves with him to

Texas. As the following document demonstrates, Mason sued for her freedom and the California court ruled in her favor in 1856.

Employed as a midwife and a nurse, she managed over a period of years to save enough money to buy some property in downtown Los Angeles. This investment and subsequent real estate transactions made her a wealthy woman, as well as one whose charitable gift giving across the color line made her a legend even during her own lifetime.

How would you describe Mason's use of agency, exercised despite her owner's efforts to keep her enslaved?*

STATE OF CALIFORNIA

COUNTY OF LOS ANGELES.

Before the Hon. Benjamin Hayes,
Judge of the District Court of the
First Judicial District State of California,
County of Los Angeles.

In the matter of Hannah and her children Ann (and Mary, child of Ann), Lawrence, Nathaniel, Jane, Charles, Marion, Martha, and an infant boy two weeks old; and of Biddy and her children, Ellen, Ann and Harriet, on petition for habeas corpus. Now on this nineteenth day of January, in the year of Our Lord, one thousand, eight hundred and fifty-six, the said persons above named are brought before me in the custody of the Sheriff of said County, all except the said Hannah and infant boy two weeks old (who are satisfactorily shown to be too infirm to be brought before me), and except Lawrence, (who is necessarily occupied in waiting on his said mother Hannah) and Charles (who is absent in San Bernardino County, but within said Judicial District) and Robert Smith, claimant, also appears with his Attorney; Alonzo Thomas, Esq. And after hearing, and duly considering the petition for habeas corpus and the return of claimant thereto, and all the proofs and allegations of the said parties and all the proceedings previously had herein, it appearing satisfactory to the judge here that all the said persons so suing in this case to-wit: Hannah and her children, and Biddy, and her said children are

persons of color, and that Charles, aged now six years, was born in the Territory of Utah, of the United States, and Marion (aged four years), Martha (aged two years), Mary, daughter of the said Ann, and aged two years, and the said infant boy aged two weeks, were born in the State of California, and that the said Hannah, Ann, Lawrence, Nathaniel, Jane, and Charles as well as the said Biddy, Ellen, Ann, and Harriet have resided with the said Robert Smith for more than four years, and since some time in the year of our Lord one thousand, eight hundred and fifty-one in the State of California; and it further appearing that the said Robert Smith left and removed from the State of Mississippi more than eight years ago with the intention of not returning thereto, but of establishing himself as a resident in Utah Territory, and more than four years ago left and removed from said Utah Territory with the intention of residing and establishing himself in the State of California, and has so resided in said last mentioned State, since some time in the year of our Lord one thousand eight hundred and fifty-one. And it further appearing by satisfactory proof to the judge here, that all of the said persons of color are entitled to their freedom, and are free and cannot be held in slavery or involuntary servitude, it is therefore argued that they are entitled to their freedom and are free forever. And it further appearing to the satisfaction of the judge here that the said Robert Smith intended to and is about to remove from the State of California where slavery does not exist, to the State of Texas, where slavery of Negroes and persons of color does exist, and is established by the municipal laws, and intends to remove the said before-mentioned persons of color, to his own use without the free will and consent of all or any of the said persons of color, whereby their liberty will be greatly jeopardized, and there is good reason to apprehend and believe that they may be sold into slavery or involuntary servitude and the said Robert Smith is persuading and enticing and seducing said persons of color to go out of the State of California, and it further appearing that none of the said persons of color can read and write, and are almost entirely ignorant of the laws of the state of California as well as those of the State of Texas, and of their rights and that the said Robert Smith, from his past relations to them as members of his family does possess and exercise over them an undue influence in respect to the matter of their said removal insofar that they have been in duress and not in possession and exercise of their free will so as to give a binding consent to any engagement or arrangement with him.

LABOR CONTRACT FOR CHINESE PROSTITUTES (1886)

The conditions of this contract for Chinese prostitutes make absolutely clear the terms of compulsory servitude. Many young women died or became seriously ill before completing their contracts. Although some Chinese women chose prostitution, most were victims of transactions over which they had little or no control. Once in America, they encountered virtual enslavement. Ultimately the sale of Chinese women in the United States ended, but the remedy was not based on humanitarianism but on racial hostility and resulted in a series of restrictive Chinese immigration acts.

In what ways does this contract relate to the current debate over whether prostitution should be considered freely chosen sex work or coercive trafficking?*

The contractee Xin Jin became indebted to her master/mistress for food and passage to San Francisco. Since she is without funds, she will voluntarily work as a prostitute at Tan Fu's place for four and one-half years for an advance of 1,205 yuan (U.S. $524) to pay this debt. There shall be no interest on the money and Xin Jin shall receive no wages. At the expiration of the contract, Xin Jin shall be free to do as she pleases. Until then, she shall first secure the master/mistress's permission if a customer asks to take her out. If she has the four loathsome diseases she shall be returned within 100 days; beyond that time the procurer has no responsibility. Menstruation disorder is limited to one month's rest only. If Xin Jin becomes sick at any time for more than 15 days, she shall work one month extra; if she becomes pregnant, she shall work one year extra. Should Xin Jin run away before her term is out, she shall pay whatever expense is incurred in finding and returning her to the brothel. This is a contract to be retained by the master/mistress as evidence of the agreement. Receipt of 1205 yuan by Ah Yo. Thumb print of Xin Jin in the contractee. Eighth month 11th day of the 12th year of Guang-zu (1886).

---

* Carol Berkin and Mary Beth Norton, *Women of America* (Boston, 1979), 243–44.

CHAPTER 9

The Civil War, Reconstruction:
Gender and Racial Issues

Hardship and the labor scarcity during the Civil War cast women in untraditional roles, and the construction of female gender norms was modified to meet wartime needs. Throughout the divided nation, women assumed the management of farms and plantations. Eager to do more than support the war effort from the home front, on both sides of the Civil War, a number of women disguised as men with assumed names entered the army. Rose O'Neal Greenhow, a passionate defender of the Confederacy, became a spy, as did other women for both the Union and the Confederacy, providing valuable information about enemy operations. The role of spy placed women at risk as they crossed geographic lines into enemy territory. Precisely because the idea of a women spy presented such a contradiction to feminine gender norms of delicacy and docility, women engaging in espionage created less suspicion than a man would.

The Civil War also propelled thousands of women into service as hospital and battlefield nurses and providers of medical supplies. Women in both the North and the South responded to the need for provisions and nursing care, and women's participation was lifesaving. In the North, they played a central role in the work of the U.S. Sanitary Commission. Nursing the wounded soldiers was very different from a woman's household role of caring for sick family members. Some battlefield nurses, such as Clara Barton, struggled to overcome nagging doubts about the "impropriety" of woman nursing wounded men and witnessing the carnage of battle. Women who entered the hospitals confronted the hostility of male doctors, who found them annoying and intrusive; however, like Phoebe Yates Levy Pember, they persevered. Nursing subsequently gained recognition as an appropriate female occupation. Yet until the Civil War, it was considered "unladylike" for women to nurse wounded men.

Even so, male doctors continued to exclude women from the medical profession. In 1873, Dr. Edward H. Clarke, a Harvard Medical School trustee, wrote a scathing report allegedly based on case studies providing multiple examples of how the inadequacies of the female brain and reproductive system made women unsuitable to pursue higher education. Until 1945, Harvard refused to grant women admission to its medical school. Similar gender barriers shaped the legal profession. In the Bradwell decision of 1873, the U.S. Supreme Court upheld the right of the state of Illinois to deny Myra Bradwell admission to the legal profession, despite the fact that she met the qualifications, because the Court claimed that the practice of law and the qualities of womanhood were incompatible. Despite continuation of professional barriers, during the Civil War, the labor scarcity opened the field of clerical work to women, and growing numbers of women were employed as clerks after peace was restored. The expanding field of teaching also offered women occupational opportunities. During Reconstruction, educated African Americans such as Charlotte Forten as well as white women left their homes in the North and moved to the South to meet the educational needs of newly freed slaves.

Although gender roles proved elastic in response to wartime needs, little had changed with reference to underlying structural inequality and a wife's legal nonexistence and subordination to her husband's authority. The case of Elizabeth Packard made clear that continued defiance of a husband's beliefs, in this particular case the husband was a Protestant minister, could result in a declaration of insanity and confinement in a mental institution.

During the Civil War, women suffragists, many of whom were also abolitionists, set aside the fight for women's rights to devote their full attention to campaigning for the emancipation of slaves. With the passage of the Thirteenth Amendment and emancipation achieved, women's rights leaders resumed their struggle for the ballot. Their suffragist crusade was far removed from the experiences of newly freed black women, who joined their husbands in the subsistence life of sharecroppers. Many took in laundry or worked as domestics to supplement their husbands' marginal wages. For the vast majority of married African American women, the norm of the sole male breadwinner was a myth. Work—combined with family care—remained the focus of their lives.

The passage of the Fifteenth Amendments gave African American men the right to vote. To Elizabeth Cady Stanton and Susan B. Anthony, the exclusion of women from the amendment was an inexcusable betrayal on the part of male abolitionists who formerly had linked women's rights to emancipation. Abolitionist men now urged women to be patient as it was the "negro's" hour. Dismissing patience, Stanton and Anthony severed ties with their former comrades. Embittered and defiant, they opposed the Fifteenth Amendment and in 1869 organized the National Woman's Suffrage Association (NWSA), open only to female members. Through their radical publication, *The Revolution,* Stanton and Anthony promoted a wide range of economic and social reforms for women, as well as the right to vote. To enable women to leave abusive marriages, Stanton advocated liberalized divorce laws.

Stanton and Anthony conducted massive petition drives and repeatedly and unsuccessfully sought congressional approval for women's suffrage. In 1872, Anthony tested the right of women as citizens to vote—she was arrested and brought to trial for unlawful voting. In *Minor v. Happersett,* in 1875, the U.S. Supreme Court rejected the suffragist argument that women, as U.S. citizens, had a constitutional right to vote. The Court alleged that only individual states could grant suffrage.

Women less radical than Stanton and Anthony followed Lucy Stone and Julia Ward Howe and joined the American Woman's Suffrage Association (AWSA). Organized in 1869 in opposition to the Stanton-Anthony NWSA, the AWSA included abolitionist men and recognized the Fifteenth Amendment. African American female abolitionists such as Frances Watkins Harper joined the AWSA. In a speech to the Women's Rights Convention in 1866, Watkins had emphasized the need for a biracial coalition of women to move ahead on the dual issues of civil rights and women's rights.

A more moderate organization, the AWSA also enjoyed greater support than the NWSA. Focusing its efforts completely on the right to vote, the AWSA campaigned for women's suffrage on the state level. For more than twenty years, the rival associations pursued their separate objectives and strategies. However, deeply rooted gender assumptions, similar to those of Catharine Beecher and Harriet Beecher Stowe as well as Amelia Barr, about women's special feminine traits making them unfit for public roles, made it difficult for women's rights leaders of either faction to secure a constituency for the vote. Both organizations proved ineffectual in building a mass base of support. Reunited in 1890 as the National American Woman's Suffrage Association (NAWSA), suffragists continued to lack significant public support until the 1900s. Only in the West, in Wyoming, Idaho, Utah, and Colorado, had women gained the right to vote.

Alternative approaches to suffrage also emerged. The Women's Christian Temperance Union (WCTU) supported suffrage as the means to achieving a broad-based agenda of social purity concerns that focused on temperance and privileged women's alleged moral authority. Increasingly over time, suffragists not explicitly concerned with Christian values also emphasized women's moral and maternal qualities, their allegedly unique qualities, rather than women's equality as citizens in their justification of voting rights.

ROSE O'NEAL GREENHOW, *Letter to the Hon. William H. Seward* (Nov. 1, 1861)

Women spies were employed by both the Union and the Confederacy. Women's roles expanded and gender restrictions were temporarily suspended in response to wartime needs. Many women sought to do more than home-based wartime service roles. Most dramatic was the role of female spies. Rose O'Neal Greenhow (1817–1864) was a member of the plantation elite, well known in Washington society and one of the Confederacy's most successful spies. Imprisoned twice by the Union, she was exiled to the South and resumed her wartime work with an official visit to Britain and France to secure support for the Confederate cause. Unfortunately, on her return, her ship, a blockade-runner supplied by the British, ran aground near the North Carolina coast, and she was not able to reach shore. How would you describe the tone of this letter of appeal?*

To the Hon. Wm. H. Seward,

Secretary of State:

Sir—For nearly three months I have been confined, a close prisoner, shut out from air and exercise, and denied all communication with family and friends.

"Patience is said to be a great virtue," and I have practised it to my utmost capacity of endurance. . . .

I therefore most respectfully submit, that on Friday, August 23d, without warrant or other show of authority, I was arrested by the Detective Police, and my house taken in charge by them; that all my private letters, and my papers of a life time, were read and examined by them; that every law of decency was violated in the search of my house and person, and the surveilance over me.

---

* In the public domain.

We read in history, that the poor Maria Antoinette had a paper torn from her bosom by lawless hands, and that even a change of linen had to be effected in sight of her brutal captors. It is my sad *experience* to record even more revolting outrages than that, for during the first days of my imprisonment, whatever *necessity* forced me to seek my chamber, a detective stood sentinel at the open door. And thus for a period of seven days, I, with my little child, was placed absolutely at the mercy of men without character or responsibility; that during the first evening, a portion of these men became brutally drunk, and boasted in my hearing of the *"nice times"* they expected to have with the female prisoners; and that rude violence was used towards a colored servant girl during that evening, the extent of which I have not been able to learn. For any show of decorum afterwards was practiced toward me, I was indebted to the detective called Capt. Dennis. . . .

You have held me, sir, to man's accountability, and I therefore claim the right to speak on subjects usually considered beyond a woman's ken, and which you may class as "errors of opinion." I offer no excuse for this long digression, as a three months' imprisonment, without formula of law, gives me authority for occupying even the precious moments of a Secretary of State.

My object is to call your attention to the fact: that during this long imprisonment, I am yet ignorant of the causes of my arrest; that my house has been seized and converted into a prison by the Government; that the valuable furniture it contained has been abused and destroyed; that during some periods of my imprisonment I have suffered greatly for want of proper and sufficient food. Also, I have to complain that, more recently, a woman of bad character, recognized as having been seen on the streets of Chicago as such, by several of the guard, calling herself Mrs. Onderdonk, was placed here in my house, in a room adjoining mine.

In making this exposition, I have no object of appeal to your sympathies, if the justice of my complaint, and a decent regard for the world's opinion, do not move you, I should but waste your time to claim your attention on any other score.

I may, however, recall to your mind, that but a little while since you were quite as much proscribed by public sentiment here, for the opinions and principles you held, as I am now for mine.

I could easily have escaped arrest, having had timely warning. I thought it impossible that your statesmanship might present such a proclamation of weakness to the world, as even the fragment of a once great Government turning its arms against the breasts of women and children. You have the power, sir, and may still further abuse it. You may prostrate the physical strength, by confinement in close rooms and insufficient food—you may subject me to harsher, ruder treatment than I have already received, but you cannot imprison the soul. Every cause worthy of success has had its martyrs. . . . My sufferings will afford a significant lesson to

Rosie O'Neal Greenhow and her Daughter
(Library of Congress)

the women of the South, that sex or condition is no bulwark against the surging billows of the "irrepressible conflict."

The "iron heel of power" may keep down, but it cannot crush out, the spirit of resistance in a people armed for the defence of their rights; and I tell you now, sir, that you are standing over a crater, whose smothered fires in a moment may burst forth.

It is your boast, that thirty-three bristling fortifications now surround Washington. The fortifications of Paris did not protect Louis Phillippe when his hour had come.

In conclusion, I respectfully ask your attention to this protest, and have the honor to be, &c, (Signed)

Rose O. N. Greenhow

JULIA WARD HOWE, *Battle Hymn of the Republic*

Overshadowed by the more dynamic Stanton and Anthony, in her own lifetime Julia Ward Howe (1819-1910) was celebrated as the author of the lyrics for *The Battle Hymn of the Republic,* the defining Civil War song that memorialized the righteousness of the Union cause. Howe wrote the lyrics in 1861 and the song was published a year later. The song still resonates in the present era. The chorus was not part of the song as first published. Although a contemporary of Stanton and Anthony, Howe did not join the suffrage struggle until after the Civil War. With her colleagues Lucy Stone and Thomas Wentworth Higginson in 1869 she helped organize the American Woman's Suffrage Association, (AWSA) the cautious rival of the Stanton and Anthony, National Woman's Suffrage Association (NWSA) founded earlier in the same year. For many years Howe served as one of the editors of the organization's *Woman's Journal.* Abolitionist men such as Higginson and Frederick Douglas played key roles in the AWSA, promoted African American male voting rights and also supported their female associates in the campaign for women's suffrage.

Howe advocated other reforms including pacifism and a mother's day celebration that would link women across national borders in the cause of universal peace. She also played a key role in the repudiation of Dr. Edward H. Clarke's medical misinformation that served to frighten women from attending college. The lyrics of her famous hymn appear below. In what ways did Howe fuse religion with the Union cause?*

Mine eyes have seen the glory
Of the coming of the Lord;
He is trampling out the vintage
Where the grapes of wrath are stored;
He hath loosed the fateful lightning
Of His terrible swift sword;
His truth is marching on.

Chorus
Glory! Glory! Hallelujah!
Glory! Glory! Hallelujah!
Glory! Glory! Hallelujah!
His truth is marching on.

I have seen Him in the watchfires
Of a hundred circling camps
They have builded Him an altar
In the evening dews and damps;

I can read His righteous sentence
By the dim and flaring lamps;
His day is marching on.

Chorus
Glory! Glory! Hallelujah!
Glory! Glory! Hallelujah!
Glory! Glory! Hallelujah!
His truth is marching on.

I have read a fiery gospel writ
In burnished rows of steel:
"As ye deal with My contemners,
So with you My grace shall deal":
Let the Hero born of woman
Crush the serpent with His heel,
Since God is marching on.

---

* *The Battle Hymn of the Republic,* lyrics originally published *The Atlantic Monthly,* 1862, did not include the chorus.

Chorus
Glory! Glory! Hallelujah!
Glory! Glory! Hallelujah!
Glory! Glory! Hallelujah!
His truth is marching on.

He has sounded forth the trumpet
That shall never call retreat;
He is sifting out the hearts of men
Before His judgement seat;
Oh, be swift, my soul, to answer Him;
Be jubilant, my feet;
Our God is marching on.

Chorus
Glory! Glory! Hallelujah!
Glory! Glory! Hallelujah!

Glory! Glory! Hallelujah!
His truth is marching on.

In the beauty of the lilies
Christ was born across the sea,
With a glory in His bosom
That transfigures you and me;
As He died to make men holy,
Let us die to make men free;
While God is marching on.

Chorus
Glory! Glory! Hallelujah!
Glory! Glory! Hallelujah!
Glory! Glory! Hallelujah!
His truth is marching on.

CLARA BARTON, *Nursing on the Firing Line* (c. 1870)

In this document, Clara Barton (1821–1912) described the ordeals she faced as a battlefield nurse caring for wounded Union soldiers. Although she won national acclaim for her nursing, her contribution also involved fund-raising and collecting and distributing medical supplies. Like other Civil War women nurses, Barton had to overcome enormous resistance. How did Barton deal with the argument that nursing wounded soldiers was inappropriate and "unseemly for a woman"?*

I was strong and thought I might go to the rescue of the men who fell. The first regiment of troops, the old 6th Mass. that fought its way through Baltimore, brought my playmates and neighbors, the partakers of my childhood; the brigades of New Jersey brought scores of my brave boys, the same solid phalanx; and the strongest legions from old Herkimer brought the associates of my seminary days. They formed and crowded around me. What could I do but go with them, or work for them and my country? The patriot blood of my father was warm in my veins. The country which he had fought for, I might at least work for, and I had offered my service to the government in the capacity of a double clerkship at twice $1400 a year, upon discharge of two disloyal clerks from its employ—the salary never to be given to me, but to be turned back into the U.S. Treasury then poor to beggary, with no currency, no credit. But there was no law for this, and it could not be done, and I would not draw salary from our government in such peril, so I resigned and went into direct service of the sick and wounded troops wherever found.

But I struggled long and hard with my sense of propriety—with the appalling fact that I was only a woman whispering in one ear, and thundering in the other the groans of suffering men dying like dogs—unfed and

---

* From Perry Epler, *Life of Clara Barton* (New York: Macmillan, 1915), 31–32, 35–43, 45, 59, 96–98.

unsheltered, for the life of every institution which had protected and educated me!

I said that I struggled with my sense of propriety and I say it with humiliation and shame. I am ashamed that I thought of such a thing.

When our armies fought on Cedar Mountain, I broke the shackles and went to the field. . . .

Five days and nights with three hours sleep—a narrow escape from capture—and some days of getting the wounded into hospitals at Washington, brought Saturday, August 30. And if you chance to feel, that the positions I occupied were rough and unseemly for a *woman*—I can only reply that they were rough and unseemly for *men*. But under all, lay the life of the nation. I had inherited the rich blessing of health and strength of constitution—such as are seldom given to woman—and I felt that some return was due from me and that I ought to be there. . . .

You generous thoughtful mothers and wives have not forgotten the tons of preserves and fruits with which you filled our hands. Huge boxes of these stood beside that railway track. Every can, jar, bucket, bowl, cup or tumbler, when emptied, that instant became a vehicle of mercy to convey some preparation of mingled bread and wine, or soup or coffee to some helpless famishing sufferer who partook of it with the tears rolling down his bronzed cheeks, and divide his blessings between the hands that fed him and his God. I never realized until that day how little a human being could be grateful for, and that day's experience also taught me the utter worthlessness of that which could not be made to contribute directly to our necessities. The bit of bread which would rest on the surface of a gold eagle was worth more than the coin itself.

But the most fearful scene was reserved for the night. I have said that the ground was littered with dry hay and that we had only two lanterns, but there were plenty of candles. The wounded were laid so close that it was impossible to move about in the dark. The slightest misstep brought a torrent of groans from some poor mangled fellow in your path.

Consequently here were seen persons of all grades, from the careful man of God who walked with a prayer upon his lips, to the careless driver hunting for his lost whip—each wandering about among this hay with an open flaming candle in his hands.

The slightest accident, the mere dropping of a light could have enveloped in flames this whole mass of helpless men.

How we watched and pleaded and cautioned as we worked and wept that night! How we put socks and slippers upon the cold, damp feet, wrapped your blankets and quilts about them, and when we had no longer these to give, how we covered them in the hay and left them to their rest!

Clara Barton (Matthew Brady/National Archives and Records Administration)

PHOEBE YATES LEVY PEMBER, *A Southern Woman's Story* (1879)

Phoebe Yates Levy Pember (1823–1913) was a member of an elite Southern Jewish family. In 1862, she was appointed to the position of matron of the Confederate Chimborazo Hospital in Richmond, Virginia. In the following excerpt, Pember recounts the activism of Southern women on behalf of the Confederacy. Her story serves as a reminder that men governed hospital nursing. The presence of women in hospitals was bitterly resented although desperately needed. What information does Pember's account supply about male resentment? What role did southern women play?*

The women of the South had been openly and violently rebellious from the moment they thought their states' rights touched. They incited the men to struggle in support of their views, and whether right or wrong, sustained them nobly to the end. They were the first to rebel—the last to succumb. Taking an active part in all that came within their sphere, and often compelled to go beyond this when the field demanded as many soldiers as could be raised; feeling a passion of interest in every man in the gray uniform of the Confederate service; they were doubly anxious to give comfort and assistance to the sick and wounded. In the course of a long and harassing war, with port blockaded and harvests burnt, rail tracks constantly torn up, so that supplies of food were cut off, and sold always at exorbitant prices, no appeal was ever made to the women of the South, individually or collectively, that did not meet with a ready response. There was no parade of generosity; no published lists of donations, inspected by public eyes. What was contributed was given unostentatiously, whether a barrel of coffee or the only half bottle of wine in the giver's possession.

About this time one of these large hospitals was to be opened, and the wife of George W. Randolph, Secretary of War, offered me the superindendence—rather a startling proposition to a woman used to all the comforts of luxurious life. Foremost among the Virginia women, she had given her resources of mind and means to the sick, and her graphic and earnest representations of the benefit a good and determined woman's rule could effect in such a position, settled the result in my mind. The natural idea that such a life would be injurious to the delicacy and refinement of a lady—that her nature would become deteriorated and her sensibilities blunted, was rather appalling. But the first step only costs, and that was soon taken.

A preliminary interview with the surgeon-in-chief gave necessary confidence. He was energetic—capable—skillful. A man with ready oil to pour upon troubled waters. Difficulties melted away beneath the warmth of his ready interest, and mountains sank into mole-hills when his quick comprehension had surmounted and leveled them. However troublesome daily increasing annoyances became, if they could not be removed, his few and ready words sent applicants and grumblers home satisfied to do the best they could. Wisely he decided to have an educated and efficient woman at the head of his hospital, and having succeeded, never allowed himself to forget that fact.

The day after my decision was made found me at "headquarters," the only two-story building on hospital ground, then occupied by the chief surgeon and his clerks. He had not yet made his appearance that morning, and while awaiting him, many of his

---

* From Phoebe Yates Pember, *A Southern Woman's Story: Life in Confederate Richmond,* Bell Irwin Wiley, ed. (Jackson, TN: McCowat-Mercer, 1959). Reprinted by permission of Broadfoot Publishing Company.

corps, who had expected in horror the advent of female supervision, walked in and out, evidently inspecting me. There was at the time a general ignorance on all sides, except among the hospital officials, of the decided objection on the part of the latter to the carrying out of a law which they prognosticated would entail "petticoat government"; but there was no mistaking the stage-whisper which reached my ears from the open door of the office that morning, as the little contract surgeon passed out and informed a friend he met, in a tone of ill-concealed disgust, that *"one of them had come."*

CHARLOTTE FORTEN, *Letter to William Lloyd Garrison* (1862)

A member of one of the nation's most prominent free African American families, Charlotte Forten (1837–1914) joined other women who served as teachers to contraband slaves under the protection of the Union army. In what ways did Forten find in her teaching experience "great happiness" but also that it was "more fatiguing than at the North"?*

St. Helena's Island, South Carolina

November 20, 1862

My Dear Friend:

St. Helena's Island, on which I am, is about six miles from the mainland of Beaufort. I must tell you that we were rowed hither from Beaufort by a crew of negro boatmen, and that they sang for us several of their own beautiful songs. There is a peculiar wildness and solemnity about them which cannot be described, and the people accompany the singing with a singular swaying motion of the body which seems to make it more effective.

As far as I have been able to observe, the negroes here rejoice in their new-found freedom. It does me good to see how *jubilant* they are over the downfall of their "secesh" masters. I do not believe that there is a man, woman, or even a child that would submit to be made a slave again. They are a truly religious people. They speak to God with a loving familiarity. Another trait that I have noticed is their natural courtesy of manner. There is nothing cringing about it, but it seems inborn, and one might almost say elegant. It marks their behavior toward each other as well as to the white people.

My school is about a mile from here, in the little Baptist church, which is in a grove of white oaks. These trees are beautiful—evergreen—and every branch heavily draped with long, bearded moss, which gives them a strange, mournful look. There are two ladies in the school besides myself—Miss T and Miss M—both of whom are most enthusiastic teachers. At present, our school is small—many of the children being ill with whooping cough—but in general it averages eighty or ninety. It is a great happiness to teach them. I wish some of those persons at the North who say the race is hopelessly and naturally inferior could see the readiness with which these children, so long oppressed and deprived of every privilege, learn and understand.

I have some grown pupils—people on our own plantation—who take lessons in the evenings. It will amuse you to know that one of them,—our man-of-all-work—is name *Cupid*. (Venuses and Cupids are very

---

* From Charlotte Forten, "Letter to William Lloyd Garrison." Reprinted in *We Are Your Sisters: Black Women in the Nineteenth Century,* edited by Dorothy Sterling, copyright © 1984 by Dorothy Sterling. Used by permission of W. W. Norton & Company, Inc.

common here.) He told me he was "feared" he was almost too old to learn, but I assured him that that was not the case, and now he is working diligently at the alphabet. One of my people—Harry—is a scholar to be proud of. He makes most wonderful improvement. I never saw anyone so determined to learn. . . .

These people have really a great deal of musical talent. It is impossible to give you any idea of their songs and hymns. They are so wild, so strange, and yet so invariably harmonious and sweet. There is one of their hymns—"Roll Jordan Roll"—that I never listen to without seeming to hear, almost to feel, the rolling of waters. There is a great rolling wave of sound through it all. . . .

After the lessons, we talk freely to the children, often giving them slight sketches of some of the great and good men. Before teaching them the "John Brown" song, which they learned to sing with great spirit, Miss T. told them the story of the brave old man who had died for them. I told them about Toussaint, thinking it well they should know what one of their own color had done. They listened attentively and seemed to understand. We found it rather hard to keep their attention in school. It is not strange, as they have been so entirely unused to intellectual concentration. It is necessary to interest them every moment, in order to keep their thoughts from wandering. Teaching here is consequently far more fatiguing than at the North.

ELIZABETH PACKARD, Excerpt from *The Prisoner's Hidden Life or Insane Asylums Unveiled* (1868)

Elizabeth Packard (1816–1897) had the audacity to question her minister husband's religious beliefs privately as well as in a Bible study group. When she refused to submit to her husband's pressure to repudiate her views, he declared her insane and had her committed to an asylum where she remained imprisoned for three years. At the time of her commitment, she had six children and had been married more than twenty years. Her youngest child was only eighteen months old. Her husband alleged that her religious beliefs endangered her children and demonstrated her insanity.

This was the Civil War era and little had changed in the husband's legal right to control his wife. Elizabeth Packard's defiance was a smaller-scale reenactment of resistance to orthodoxy and male authority and subsequent punishment that Anne Hutchinson had endured two hundred years earlier. Fortunately for Packard, her ordeal had a happier resolution. A courtroom trial in 1864 led to a verdict in her favor. The trial focused on whether her husband, after her release from three years in the asylum, had the legal right to imprison her in a room. This was carrying even a husband's power too far. Her personal freedom secured, Packard spent the rest of her life engaged in a struggle to rally support for laws that would limit a husband's power to have his wife committed to an insane asylum. What significance does Packard give to the loss of a married woman's identity? How did this loss of identity relate to Packard's personal ordeal?*

XII Introduction

It is to delineate these spiritual wrongs of woman, that I have given my narrative to the public, hoping that my more tangible experiences may draw the attention of the philanthropic public to a more just consideration of married woman's legal disabilities; for since the emancipation of the negro, there is no class of American citizens, who so much need legal protection, and who receive so little, as this class.

As their representative, I do not make complaint of physical abuses, but it is the usurpation of our natural rights of which we complain; and it is our legal position of

---

* In the public domain.

nonentity, which renders us so liable and exposed to suffering and persecution from this source.

In the following narrative of my experiences, the reader will therefore find the interior of woman's life delineated through the exterior surroundings of her bitter experiences. I state facts through which the reader may look in to woman's soul, as through a mirror, that her realm of suffering may be thus portrayed.

I therefore commence my narrative where my persecution commenced, with the marital usurpation of my rights of opinion and conscience, and as I progress, will note such incidents as I can best employ to portray my feelings, rather than the recital of the physical abuses I witnessed; since my Coadjutors and the Committee have so graphically described the exterior life of the prisoner, it is unnecessary for me to enlarge on this feature of prison life in Insane Asylums. . . .

I have been Illinois State's Prisoner three years in Jacksonville Insane Asylum, for simply expressing religious opinions in a community who were unprepared to appreciate and understand them. I was incarcerated June 18, 1860, and liberated June 18, 1863. Fortunately for me, all these obnoxious views were presented in writing, and are now in my own possession, although they were, secretly taken from me, at the time of my abduction, and retained for years in the hands of my persecutor, Rev. Theophilus Packard, who was at that time the pastor of the Old School Presbyterian Church at Manteno, Kankakee County, Illinois.

He had been my husband for twenty-one years, and was the father of my six children, five of whom are boys, and one girl. At the time he forced me from my dear little ones, my daughter was ten years old and my babe eighteen months. I was in perfect health and of sound mind, and cheerfully and faithfully performing the duties of wife and mother to the entire satisfaction of my family and society, so far as I know. And, since the only plea Mr. Packard makes in defence of this course is, that my religious views were dangerous to the spiritual interests of his children and the community, I feel called upon to present these views, frankly and candidly, that my readers may judge for themselves whether my imprisonment can be justified on this basis.

As an Introduction therefore to my "Hidden Life" in my prison, I shall present these views just as I presented them to the bible class in Manteno, a few weeks before my incarceration. I became connected with this class at the special request of Deacon Abijah Dole, the teacher of the class, and with the full and free consent of my husband. Mr. Dole gave as his reason for wishing me to join his class, that he found it impossible to awaken any interest, and he fondly hoped that I might bring forward some views which might elicit the attention he desired. I seated myself among his pupils, who then numbered only six men in all, as a sincere seeker after the truth. Mr. Dole allowed his pupils to be regarded as mutual teachers, so that all were allowed to ask questions and offer suggestions. Availing myself of this license, others were encouraged to follow my example, so that our class soon became the place of animating discussions, and as our tolerant teacher allowed both sides of a question to be discussed I found it became to me a great source of pleasure and profit. Indeed, I never can recollect a time when my mind grew into a knowledge of religious truths faster, than under the influence of these free and animated discussions. The effect of these debates was felt throughout the whole community, so that our class of seven soon increased to forty-six, including the most influential members of the community.

About this time a latent suspicion seemed to be aroused, lest the church creed be endangered by this license of free inquiry and fair discussion; and a meeting of some of the leading church-members was called, wherein this bible-class was represented as being a dangerous influence, involving the exposure of the creed to the charge of fallibility.

FRANCES WATKINS HARPER, *"We Are All Bound Up Together," Address to the 11th National Women's Convention, New York* (1866)

Frances Watkins Harper (1825–1911) worked for years as a domestic, despite her literary gifts and education. Almost all doors of employment were closed to freeborn African American women. Harper was an abolitionist, a crusader for civil rights, and as she described in the following address, a supporter of women's rights who joined the cause as the result of her own experiences as a widow. African American women linked racial equality and women's rights because of their experience of interlocking racial and gender oppression. White women addressed the need for gender equality and rights in a universal language that ignored or glossed over the racial discrimination women of color confronted. Supporting the ballot for African American men, Harper rejected Stanton's and Anthony's bitter denunciation of the omission of women from voting rights. In the following speech to the Women's Rights Convention in 1866, Harper tried to alert her mainly white audience to the need to address racial injustice. In her speech, she refers to the hostile environment of racial segregation that African American women, including the iconic Harriet Tubman, confronted in the North as well as the South. In the last paragraph, her reference to "Moses" refers to Tubman, who was known as the Moses of her people, for leading them out of slavery (see Chapter 5). What events in Harper's life awakened her to the need to support women's rights as a gender-based reform? Why does Harper devote a significant part of her speech to woman's "wrongs"? What does her title "We Are All Bound Up Together" mean?*

I feel I am something of a novice upon this platform. Born of a race whose inheritance has been outrage and wrong, most of my life had been spent in battling against those wrongs. But I did not feel as keenly as others, that I had these rights, in common with other women, which are now demanded. About two years ago, I stood within the shadows of my home. A great sorrow had fallen upon my life. My husband had died suddenly, leaving me a widow, with four children, one my own, and the others stepchildren. I tried to keep my children together. But my husband died in debt; and before he had been in his grave three months, the administrator had swept the very milk crocks and wash tubs from my hands. I was a farmer's wife and made butter for the Columbus market; but what could I do, when they had swept all away? They left me one thing and that was a looking glass! Had I died instead of my husband, how different would have been the result! By this time he would have had another wife, it is likely; and no administrator would have gone into his house, broken up his home, and sold his bed, and taken away his means of support. I took my children in my arms, and went out to seek my living. While I was gone; a neighbor to whom I had once lent five dollars, went before a magistrate and swore that he believed I was a non resident, and laid an attachment on my very bed. And I went back to Ohio with my orphan children in my arms, without a single feather bed in this wide world, that was not in the custody of the law. I say, then, that justice is not fulfilled so long as woman is unequal before the law.

We are all bound up together in one great bundle of humanity, and society cannot trample on the weakest and feeblest of its members without receiving the curse in its own soul. You tried that in the case of the negro. You pressed him down for two centuries; and in so doing you crippled the moral strength and paralyzed the spiritual

---

* Frances Ellen Watkins Harper, *We Are All Bound Up Together: Proceedings of the Eleventh Women's Rights Convention* (New York: Robert J. Johnston, 1866), pp. 45–48.

energies of the white men of the country. When the hands of the black were fettered, white men were deprived of the liberty of speech and the freedom of the press. Society cannot afford to neglect the enlightenment of any class of its members. At the South, the legislation of the country was in behalf of the rich slaveholders, while the poor white man was neglected. What is the consequence to day? From that very class of neglected poor white men, comes the man who stands to day, with his hand upon the helm of the nation. He fails to catch the watchword of the hour, and throws himself, the incarnation of meanness, across the pathway of the nation. . . .

This grand and glorious revolution which has commenced, will fail to reach its climax of success, until throughout the length and brea[d]th of the American Republic, the nation shall be so color-blind, as to know no man by the color of his skin or the curl of his hair. It will then have no privileged class, trampling upon outraging the unprivileged classes, but will be then one great privileged nation, whose privilege will be to produce the loftiest manhood and womanhood that humanity can attain.

I do not believe that giving the woman the ballot is immediately going to cure all the ills of life. I do not believer that white women are dew-drops just exhaled from the skies. I think that like men they may be divided into three classes, the good, the bad, and the indifferent. The good would vote according to their convictions and principles; the bad, as dictated by preju[d]ice or malice; and the indifferent will vote on the strongest side of the question, with the winning party. You white women speak here of rights. I speak of wrongs. I, as a colored woman, have had in this country an education which has made me feel as if I were in the situation of Ishmael, my hand against every man, and every man's hand against me. Let me go to-morrow morning and take my seat in one of your street cars—I do not know that they will do it in New York, but they will in Philadelphia—and the conductor will put up his hand and stop the car rather than let me ride.

A Lady—They will not do that here.

Mrs. Harper—They do in Philadelphia. Going from Washington to Baltimore this Spring, they put me in the smoking car. (Loud Voices—"Shame.") Aye, in the capital of the nation, where the black man consecrated himself to the nation's defence, faithful when the white man was faithless, they put me in the smoking car! They did it once; but the next time they tried it, they failed; for I would not go in. I felt the fight in me; but I don't want to have to fight all the time. To-day I am puzzled where to make my home. I would like to make it in Philadelphia, near my own friends and relations. But if I want to ride in the streets of Philadelphia, they send me to ride on the platform with the driver. (Cries of "Shame.") Have women nothing to do with this? Not long since, a colored woman took her seat in an Eleventh Street car in Philadelphia, and the conductor stopped the car, and told the rest of the passengers to get out, and left the car with her in it alone, when they took it back to the station. One day I took my seat in a car, and the conductor came to me and told me to take another seat. I just screamed "murder." The man said if I was black I ought to behave myself. I knew that if he was white he was not behaving himself. Are there no wrongs to be righted? . . .

We have a woman in our country who has received the name of "Moses," not by lying about it, but by acting out (applause)—a woman who has gone down into the Egypt of slavery and brought out hundreds of our people into liberty. The last time I saw that woman, her hands were swollen. That woman who had led one of Montgomery's most successful expeditions, who was brave enough and secretive enough to act as a scout for the American army, had her hands all swollen from a conflict with a brutal conductor, who undertook to eject her from her place. That woman, whose courage and bravery won a recognition from our army and from every black man in the land, is excluded from every thoroughfare of travel. Talk of giving women the ballot-box? Go on. It is a normal school, and the white women of this country need it. While there exists this brutal element in society which tramples upon the feeble and treads down the weak, I tell you that if there is any class of people who need to be lifted out of their airy nothings and selfishness, it is the white women of America. (Applause.)

CATHARINE BEECHER AND HARRIET BEECHER STOWE, *Why Women Should Not Seek the Vote* (1869)

Suffragists combated women's acceptance of their submissive roles and their resistance to identifying with the need to vote. In the following document, two of the nation's best-known women—Catharine Beecher (1800–1878), the advocate of teaching as a woman's profession, and Harriet Beecher Stowe (1811–1896), the author of the enormously successful abolitionist novel, *Uncle Tom's Cabin*—expressed their views on women's suffrage. The sisters' personal achievements testified to the expansion of women's roles, yet both rejected voting rights for women. Which specific aspects of their argument support women's subordinate roles? Why did they believe that the entire suffrage effort was doomed to failure?*

Many intelligent and benevolent persons imagine that the grand remedy for the heavy evils that oppress our sex is to introduce woman to political power and office, to make her a party in primary political meetings, in political caucuses, and in the scramble and fight for political offices; thus bringing into this dangerous *melée* the distinctive tempting power of her sex. Who can look at this new danger without dismay? . . .

Let us suppose that our friends have gained the ballot and the powers of office: are there any real beneficent measures for our sex, which they would enforce by law and penalties, that fathers, brothers, and husbands would not grant to a united petition of our sex, or even to a majority of the wise and good? Would these not confer what the wives, mothers, and sisters deemed best for themselves and the children they are to train, very much sooner than they would give power and office to our sex to enforce these advantages by law? Would it not be a wiser thing to *ask* for what we need, before trying so circuitous and dangerous a method? God has given to man the physical power, so that all that woman may gain, either by petitions or by ballot, will be the gift of love or of duty; and the ballot never will be accorded till benevolent and conscientious men are the majority—a millennial point far beyond our present ken.

---

* From Catharine Beecher and Harriet Beecher Stowe, "Why Women Should Not Seek the Vote," 1869. Reprinted in *Major Problems in American Women's History*, 2d ed., Mary Beth Norton and Ruth M. Alexander, eds., copyright © 1996 by Houghton Mifflin Company.

ELIZABETH CADY STANTON, *On Marriage and Divorce* (c1870)

Elizabeth Cady Stanton (1815–1902) the mother of seven children, combined motherhood with a life-long commitment to a wide range of women's rights reforms. The author of the Declaration of Sentiments, (Chapter 7) her half-century friendship and collaboration with Susan B. Anthony added to the momentum of women's rights reforms. In an era when it was difficult for a women to obtain a divorce, Stanton advocated liberal divorce laws. She addressed the New York State Senate Judiciary on the subject of divorce reform in 1861 and returned to the issue on different occasions, including the Women's Rights Convention in 1870 that contains the following excerpt. Divorce reform was a radical idea at a time when marriage was regarded as a life-time arrangement and for many a religious sacrament. Stanton argued that marriage was a civil contract that for a variety of reasons could be dissolved. Her views on marriage and divorce alienated more cautious women reformers. How did Stanton link the power of men to the abuse of women? On what grounds did she advocate divorce?*

All this talk about the indissoluble tie and the sacredness of marriage, irrespective of the character and habits of the husband, is for its effect on woman. She never could have been held the pliant tool she is today but for the subjugation of her religious nature to the idea that in whatever condition she found herself as man's subject, that condition was ordained of Heaven; whether burning on the funeral pile of her husband in India, or suffering the slower torture of bearing children every year in America to drunkards, diseased, licentious men, at the expense of her own life and health, and the enfeebling of both the mind and body of her progeny. Women would not live as they now do in this enlightened age in violation of every law of their being, giving the very hey-day of their existence to the exercise of one an-imal function, if subordination to man had not been made through the ages the cardinal point of their religious faith and daily life. It requires but little thought to see that . . . the indissolu-ble tie was found to be necessary in order to establish man's authority over woman. The argument runs thus:

Men all admit that if two cannot be agreed they must part. This may apply to partners in business, pastor and people, physi-cian and patient, master and servant, and many other relations in life; but in the case of parent and child, husband and wife, as their relations cannot be dissolved, there must be some alternate authority to decide all matters on which they cannot agree, hence man's headship. These cases should be distin-guished, however; the child is free to act on his own opinions, by law, at a certain age, and the tie is practically dissolved between him and the parent so soon as he earns his own bread. The child is under the parent's control only during its minority; but the wife's condi-tion is perpetual minority, lifelong subjection to authority, with no appeal, no hope on the indissoluble tie theory. The practical effect of this is to make tyrants of men and fools of women. There never was a human being yet on this footstool godlike enough to be trusted with the absolute control of any living thing. Men abuse each other. Look in your prisons, jails, asylums, battle-fields and camps, they abuse their horses, dogs, cats. . . . They abuse their own children, and of course they will abuse their wives, taught by law and gospel that they own them as property, especially as a wife can vex and thwart a man, as no other living thing can . . .

---

*From Elizabeth Cady Stanton, "On Marriage and Divorce," reprinted in Paulina Wright Davis, *History of the National Woman's Rights Movement for Twenty Years . . . From 1850 to 1870* (New York: Journeymen Printers' Cooperative Association, 1871), 62–83.

SUSAN B. ANTHONY, *Proceedings of the Trial* (1873)

No woman in American history did more for the suffrage cause than Susan B. Anthony (1820–1906). Her decision to vote in the 1872 presidential election put into action suffragists' hope that women already possessed the right to vote under the Fourteenth Amendment. This strategy failed. Women, including Virginia Minor, were turned away at the polls. Anthony managed to cast a ballot but was subsequently arrested by a U.S. marshal and brought to trial.

The following excerpt from the trial documents Anthony's defiant outrage. How does her speech illuminate feminist demands for equal rights? In what ways does her defense echo the rationale for equality found in the Declaration of Sentiments (see Chapter 7). Ultimately the U.S. Supreme Court resolved the issue of whether the Fourteenth Amendment gave women the right to vote. The negative decision was expressed in *Minor v. Happersett* (1875). Women possessed citizenship but only the individual states could determine suffrage eligibility. For women, the Reconstruction-era promise of suffrage ended with this Supreme Court decision.*

JUDGE HUNT [*Ordering the defendant to stand up*]: Has the prisoner anything to say why sentence shall not be pronounced?

MISS ANTHONY: Yes, your honor, I have many things to say; for in your ordered verdict of guilty, you have trampled under foot every vital principle of our government. My natural rights, my civil rights, my political rights, my judicial rights, are all alike ignored. Robbed of the fundamental privilege of citizenship, I am degraded from the status of a citizen to that of a subject; and not only myself individually, but all of my sex, are, by your honor's verdict, doomed to political subjection under this, so-called, form of government.

JUDGE HUNT: The Court cannot listen to a rehearsal of arguments the prisoner's counsel has already consumed three hours in presenting.

MISS ANTHONY: May it please your honor, I am not arguing the question, but simply stating the reasons why sentence cannot, in justice, be pronounced against me. Your denial of my citizen's right to vote, is the denial of my right of consent as one of the governed, the denial of my right of representation as one of the taxed, the denial of my right to a trial by a jury of my peers as an offender against law, therefore, the denial of my sacred rights to life, liberty, property and—

JUDGE HUNT: The Court cannot allow the prisoner to go on.

MISS ANTHONY: But your honor will not deny me this one and only poor privilege of protest against this high-handed outrage upon my citizen's rights. May it please the Court to remember that since the day of my arrest last November, this is the first time that either myself or any person of my disfranchised class has been allowed a word of defense before judge or jury—

JUDGE HUNT: The prisoner must sit down— the Court cannot allow it.

MISS ANTHONY: All of my prosecutors, from the 8th ward corner grocery politician, who entered the compliant, to the United States Marshal, Commissioner, District Attorney, District Judge, your honor on the bench, not one is my peer, but each and all are my political sovereigns; and had your honor submitted my case to the jury, as was clearly your duty, even then I should have had just cause of protest, for

---

*From An Account of the Proceedings of the Trial of Susan B. Anthony, on the Charge of Illegal Voting, at the Presidential Election in Nov., 1872, and on the Trial of Beverly W. Jones, Edwin T. Marsh and William B. Hall, The Inspectors of Election by whom her Vote was Received (Rochester, NY: 1874).

not one of those men was my peer; but, native or foreign born, white or black, rich or poor, educated or ignorant, awake or asleep, sober or drunk, each and every man of them was my political superior; hence, in no sense, my peer. Even, under such circumstances, a commoner of England, tried before a jury of Lords, would have far less cause to complain than should I, a woman, tried before a jury of men. Even my counsel, the Hon. Henry R. Selden, who has argued my cause so ably, so earnestly, so unanswerably before your honor, is my political sovereign. Precisely as no disfranchised person is entitled to sit upon a jury, and no woman is entitled to the franchise, so, none but a regularly admitted lawyer is allowed to practice in the courts, and no woman can gain admission to the bar—hence, jury, judge, counsel, must all be of the superior class.

JUDGE HUNT: The Court must insist—the prisoner has been tried according to the established forms of law.

MISS ANTHONY: Yes, your honor, but by forms of law all made by men, interpreted by men, administered by men, in favor of men, and against women; and hence, your honor's ordered verdict of guilty; against a United States citizen for the exercise of *"that citizen's right to vote,"* simply because that citizen was a woman and not a man. But, yesterday, the same man made forms of law, declared it a crime punishable with $1,000 fine and six months imprisonment, for you, or me, or you of us, to give a cup of cold water, a crust of bread, or a night's shelter to a panting fugitive as he was tracking his way to Canada. And every man or woman in whose veins coursed a drop of human sympathy violated that wicked law, reckless of consequences, and was justified in so doing. As then, the slaves who got their freedom must take it over, or under, or through the unjust forms of law, precisely so, now, must women,

to get their right to a voice in this government, take it; and I have taken mine, and mean to take it at every possible opportunity.

JUDGE HUNT: The Court orders the prisoner to sit down. It will not allow another word.

MISS ANTHONY: When I was brought before your honor for trial, I hoped for a broad and liberal interpretation of the Constitution and its recent amendments, that should declare all United States citizens under its protecting gis—that should declare equality of rights the national guarantee to all persons born or naturalized in the United States. But failing to get this justice—failing, even, to get a trial by a jury *not* of my peers—I ask not leniency at your hands— but rather the full rigors of the law."

JUDGE HUNT: The Court must insist—

[*Here the prisoner sat down.*]

JUDGE HUNT: The prisoner will stand up.

[*Here Miss Anthony arose again.*]

The sentence of the Court is that you pay a fine of one hundred dollars and the costs of the prosecution.

MISS ANTHONY: May it please your honor, I shall never pay a dollar of your unjust penalty. All the stock in trade I possess is a $10,000 debt, incurred by publishing my paper—*The Revolution*—four years ago, the sole object of which was to educate all women to do precisely as I have done, rebel against your manmade, unjust, unconstitutional forms of law, that tax, fine, imprison and hang women, while they deny them the right of representation in the government; and I shall work on with might and main to pay every dollar of that honest debt, but not a penny shall go to this unjust claim. And I shall earnestly and persistently continue to urge all women to the practical recognition of the old revolutionary maxim, that "Resistance to tyranny is obedience to God."

Excerpt from *MINOR V. HAPPERSETT*, (1875)

The *Minor v. Happersett* Supreme Court decision from the perspective of women's history was an infamous obstruction that erased all hope of women as citizens gaining the right to vote under the terms of the Fourteenth Amendment. Virginia Minor (1824–1894), in a manner similar to that of Susan B. Anthony, also attempted to vote in the election of 1872. Unlike Anthony who actually managed to vote, Minor's attempt to register to vote was thwarted by the registrar. With the support of her husband, she filed a lawsuit against Happersett, the St. Louis, Missouri, voting official who refused to allow her to register. Her lawsuit expressed the hope of many suffragists that the Fourteenth Amendment could be interpreted to include women's right to vote. The case ultimately resulted in a hearing before the Supreme Court. In a unanimous decision the Court ruled against the claim that women as citizens possessed a constitutional right to vote.

Although Virginia Minor's name is linked to this Supreme Court decision, she also was a leading advocate for suffrage in her home state of Missouri and helped to organize and to serve as president of the Missouri Woman's Suffrage Association. She remained a suffrage activist until her death. On what grounds did the Supreme Court rule against the right of women to vote? The following document is an excerpt from the Supreme Court decision.*

ERROR to the Supreme Court of Missouri; the case being thus:

The fourteenth amendment to the Constitution of the United States, in its first section, thus ordains;

"All persons born or naturalized in the United States, and subject to the jurisdiction thereof, are citizens of the United States, and of the State wherein they reside. No State shall make or enforce any law, which shall abridge the privileges or immunities of citizens of the United States. Nor shall any State deprive any person of life, liberty, or property, without due process of law; nor deny to any person within its jurisdiction, the equal protection of the laws."

And the constitution of the State of Missouri thus ordains:

"Every male citizen of the United States shall be entitled to vote."

Under a statute of the State all persons wishing to vote at any election, must previously have been registered in the manner pointed out by the statute, this being a condition precedent to the exercise of the elective franchise.

In this state of things, on the 15th of October, 1872 (one of the days fixed by law for the registration of voters), Mrs. Virginia Minor, a native born, free, white citizen of the United States, and of the State of Missouri, over the age

of twenty-one years, wishing to vote for electors for President and Vice-President of the United States, and for a representative in Congress, and for other officers, at the general election held in November, 1872, applied to one Happersett, the registrar of voters, to register her as a lawful voter, which he refused to do, assigning for cause that she was not a "male citizen of the United States," but a woman. She thereupon sued him in one of the inferior State courts of Missouri, for wilfully refusing to place her name upon the list of registered voters, by which refusal she was deprived of her right to vote.

The registrar demurred, and the court in which the suit was brought sustained the demurrer, and gave judgment in his favor; a judgment which the Supreme Court affirmed. Mrs. Minor now brought the case here on error.

CHIEF JUSTICE WAITE delivered the opinion of the court.

The question is presented in this case, whether, since the adoption of the fourteenth amendment, a woman, who is a citizen of the United States and of the State of Missouri, is a voter in that State, notwithstanding the provision of the constitution and laws of the State, which confine the right of suffrage to men alone. We might, perhaps, decide the case

---

* *Minor v. Happersett*, Supreme Court of the United States, 1875, 21 Wall (88 U.S.) 162.

upon other grounds, but this question is fairly made. From the opinion we find that it was the only one decided in the court below, and it is the only one which has been argued here. The case was undoubtedly brought to this court for the sole purpose of having that question decided by us, and in view of the evident propriety there is of having it settled, so far as it can be by such a decision, we have concluded to waive all other considerations and proceed at once to its determination . . .

In this condition of the law in respect to suffrage in the several States it cannot for a moment be doubted that if it had been intended to make all citizens of the United States voters, the framers of the Constitution would not have left it to implication. So important a change in the condition of citizenship as it actually existed, if intended, would have been expressly declared.

But if further proof is necessary to show that no such change was intended, it can easily be found both in and out of the Constitution. By Article 4, section 2, it is provided that "the citizens of each State shall be entitled to all the privileges and immunities of citizens in the several States." If suffrage is necessarily a part of citizenship, then the citizens of each State must be entitled to vote in the several States precisely as their citizens are. This is more than asserting that they may change their residence and become citizens of the State and thus be voters. It goes to the extent of insisting that while retaining their original citizenship they may vote in any State. This, we think, has never been claimed. And again, by the very terms of the amendment we have been considering (the fourteenth), "Representatives shall be apportioned among the several States according to their respective numbers, counting the whole number of persons in each State, excluding Indians not taxed. But when the right to vote at any election for the choice of electors for President and Vice-President of the United States, representatives in Congress, the executive and judicial officers of a State, or the members of the legislature thereof, is denied to any of the male inhabitants of such State, being twenty-one years of age and citizens of the United States, or in any way abridged, except for participation in the rebellion, or other crimes, the basis of representation therein shall be reduced in the proportion which the number of such male citizens shall bear to the whole number of male citizens twenty-one years of age in such State." Why this, if it was not in the power of the legislature to deny the right of suffrage to some male inhabitants? And if suffrage was necessarily one of the absolute rights of citizenship, why confine the operation of the limitation to male inhabitants? Women and children are, as we have seen, "persons." They are counted in the enumeration upon which the apportionment is to be made, but if they were necessarily voters because of their citizenship unless clearly excluded, why inflict the penalty for the exclusion of males alone? Clearly, no such form of words would have been selected to express the idea here indicated if suffrage was the absolute right of all citizens.

And still again, after the adoption of the fourteenth amendment, it was deemed necessary to adopt a fifteenth, as follows: "The right of citizens of the United States to vote shall not be denied or abridged by the United States, or by any State, on account of race, color, or previous condition of servitude." The fourteenth amendment had already provided that no State should make or enforce any law which should abridge the privileges or immunities of citizens of the United States. If suffrage was one of these privileges or immunities, why amend the Constitution to prevent its being denied on account of race, &c.? Nothing is more evident than that the greater must include the less, and if all were already protected why go through with the form of amending the Constitution to protect a part?

It is true that the United States guarantees to every State a republican form of government. It is also true that no State can pass a bill of attainder, and that no person can be deprived of life, liberty, or property without due process of law. All these several provisions of the Constitution must be construed in connection with the other parts of the instrument, and in the light of the surrounding circumstances.

The guaranty is of a republican form of government. No particular government is designated as republican, neither is the exact form to be guaranteed, in any manner especially designated. Here, as in other parts of the instrument, we are compelled to resort elsewhere to ascertain what was intended.

The guaranty necessarily implies a duty on the part of the States themselves to provide such a government. All the States had governments when the Constitution was adopted. In all the people participated to some extent, through their representatives elected in the manner specially provided. These governments the Constitution did not change. They were accepted precisely as they were, and it is, therefore, to be presumed that they were such as it was the duty of the States to provide. Thus we have unmistakable evidence of what was republican in form, within the meaning of that term as employed in the Constitution.

As has been seen, all the citizens of the States were not invested with the right of suffrage. In all, save perhaps New Jersey, this right was only bestowed upon men and not upon all of them. Under these circumstances it is certainly now too late to contend that a government is not republican, within the meaning of this guaranty in the Constitution, because women are not made voters.

The same may be said of the other provisions just quoted. Women were excluded from suffrage in nearly all the States by the express provision of their constitutions and laws. If that had been equivalent to a bill of attainder, certainly its abrogation would not have been left to implication. Nothing less than express language would have been employed to effect so radical a change. So also of the amendment which declares that no person shall be deprived of life, liberty, or property without due process of law, adopted as it was as early as 1791. If suffrage was intended to be included within its obligations, language better adapted to express that intent would most certainly have been employed. The right of suffrage, when granted, will be protected. He who has it can only be deprived of it by due process of law, but in order to claim protection he must first show that he has the right.

But we have already sufficiently considered the proof found upon the inside of the Constitution. That upon the outside is equally effective.

The Constitution was submitted to the States for adoption in 1787, and was ratified by nine States in 1788, and finally by the thirteen original States in 1790. Vermont was the first new State admitted to the Union, and it came in under a constitution which conferred the right of suffrage only upon men of the full age of twenty-one years, having resided in the State for the space of one whole year next before the election, and who were of quiet and peaceable behavior. This was in 1791. The next year, 1792, Kentucky followed with a constitution confining the right of suffrage to free male citizens of the age of twenty-one years who had resided in the State two years or in the county in which they offered to vote one year next before the election. Then followed Tennessee, in 1796, with voters of freemen of the age of twenty-one years and upwards, possessing a freehold in the county wherein they may vote, and being inhabitants of the State or freemen being inhabitants of any one county in the State six months immediately preceding the day of election. But we need not particularize further. No new State has ever been admitted to the Union which has conferred the right of suffrage upon women, and this has never been considered a valid objection to her admission. On the contrary, as is claimed in the argument, the right of suffrage was withdrawn from women as early as 1807 in the State of New Jersey, without any attempt to obtain the interference of the United States to prevent it. Since then the governments of the insurgent States have been reorganized under a requirement that before their representatives could be admitted to seats in Congress they must have adopted new constitutions, republican in form. In no one of these constitutions was suffrage conferred upon women, and yet the States have all been restored to their original position as States in the Union.

Besides this, citizenship has not in all cases been made a condition precedent to the enjoyment of the right of suffrage. Thus, in Missouri, persons of foreign birth, who have declared their intention to become citizens of the United States, may under certain circumstances vote. The same provision is to be found in the constitutions of Alabama, Arkansas, Florida, Georgia, Indiana, Kansas, Minnesota, and Texas.

Certainly, if the courts can consider any question settled, this is one. For nearly ninety years the people have acted upon the idea that the Constitution, when it conferred citizenship, did not necessarily confer the right of suffrage. If uniform practice long continued can settle the construction of so important an instrument as the Constitution of the United States confessedly is, most certainly it has been done here. Our province is to decide what the law is, not to declare what it should be.

We have given this case the careful consideration its importance demands. If the law is wrong, it ought to be changed; but the power for that is not with us. The arguments addressed to us bearing upon such a view of the subject may perhaps be sufficient to induce those having the power, to make the alteration, but they ought not to be permitted to influence our judgment in determining the present rights of the parties now litigating before us. No argument as to woman's need of suffrage can be considered. We can only act upon her rights as they exist. It is not for us to look at the hardship of withholding. Our duty is at an end if we find it is within the power of a State to withhold.

Being unanimously of the opinion that the Constitution of the United States does not confer the right of suffrage upon any one, and that the constitutions and laws of the several States which commit that important trust to men alone are not necessarily void, we affirm the judgment.

EDWARD H. CLARKE, *Sex in Education; Or a Fair Chance for the Girls* (1873)

A Harvard Medical School trustee, Dr. Edward H. Clarke argued against higher education for women at a time when increasing numbers of young women were applying to medical schools. At Harvard, Clarke voted against opening admission to women. In Clarke's medical opinion, intellectual effort ruined the mental and reproductive health of college women. Arising out of a combination of medical ignorance and a lengthy tradition of patriarchal control that argued for women's limited intellectual capacity, Clarke's views also expressed the increasing cultural emphasis on the need to safeguard the female reproductive function. What "evidence" did Clarke provide that a college education puts women's "complicated reproductive mechanisms" at risk? What purpose would this fear serve?*

This case needs very little comment: its teachings are obvious. Miss D— went to college in good physical condition. During the four years of her college life, her parents and the college faculty required her to get what is popularly called an education. Nature required her, during the same period, to build and put in working order a large and complicated

reproductive mechanism, a matter that is popularly ignored—shoved out of sight like a disgrace. She naturally obeyed the requirements of the faculty, which she could see, rather than the requirements of the mechanism within her that she could not see. Subjected to the college regimen, she worked four years in getting a liberal education. Her way of work was sustained

---

* From Edward H. Clark, M.D., *Sex in Education, or A Fair Chance for the Girls* (Boston: James R. Osgood and Co., 1873), 78–87.

and continuous, and out of harmony with the rhythmical periodicy of the female organization. The stream of vital and constructive force evolved within her was turned steadily to the brain, and away from the ovaries and their accessories. The result of this sort of education was, that these last-mentioned organs, deprived of sufficient opportunity and nutriment, first began to perform their functions with pain, a warning of error that was unheeded; then, to cease to grow; next, to set up once a month a grumbling torture that made life miserable; and, lastly, the brain and the whole nervous system, disturbed, in obedience to the law, that, if one member suffers, all the members suffer, became neuralgic and hysterical. And so Miss D—— spent the next few years succeeding her graduation in conflict with dysmenorrhea, headache, neuralgia, and hysteria. Her parents marveled at her ill health; and she furnished another text for the often-repeated sermon on the delicacy of American girls.

It may not be unprofitable to give the history of one more case of this sort. Miss E—— had an hereditary right to a good brain and to the best cultivation of it. Her father was one of our ripest and broadest American scholars, and her mother one of our most accomplished American women. They both enjoyed excellent health. Their daughter had a literary training—an intellectual, moral, and aesthetic half of education, such as their supervision would be likely to give, and one that few young men of her age receive. Her health did not seem to suffer at first. She studied, recited, walked, worked, stood, and the like, in the steady and sustained way that is normal to the male organization. She *seemed* to evolve force enough to acquire a number of languages, to become familiar with the natural sciences, to take hold of philosophy and mathematics, and to keep in good physical case while doing all this. At the age of twenty-one she might have been presented to the public, on Commencement Day, by the president of Vassar College or of Antioch College or of Michigan University, as the wished-for result of American liberal female culture. Just at this time, however, the catamenical function began to show signs of failure of power. No severe or even moderate illness overtook her. She was subjected to no unusual strain. She was only following the regimen of continued and sustained work, regardless of Nature's periodical demands for a portion of her time and force, when, without any apparent cause, the failure of power was manifested by moderate dysmenorrhea and diminished excretion. Soon after this the function ceased altogether, and up to this present writing, a period of six or eight years, it has shown no more signs of activity than an amputated arm. In the course of a year or so after the cessation of the function, her head began to trouble her. First there was headache, then a frequent congested condition, which she described as a "rush of blood" to her head; and, by and by, vagaries and foreboding and despondent feelings began to crop out. Coincident with this mental state, her skin became rough and coarse, and an inveterate acne covered her face. She retained her appetite, ability to exercise, and sleep. A careful local examination of the pelvic organs, by an expert, disclosed no lesion or displacement there, no ovarian or other inflammation. Appropriate treatment faithfully persevered in was unsuccessful in recovering the lost function. I was finally obliged to consign her to an asylum.

Excerpt from *Bradwell v. Illinois* (1873)

Law was even more of a male preserve than medicine. In *Bradwell v. Illinois,* the U.S. Supreme Court upheld traditional gender roles. As with other restrictive arguments made in the post–Civil War period, women's feminine nature and reproductive function were used to deny them the right to practice law.

The last lines of the document refer to the fact that the plaintiff was married. Apparently, the Court found married women pursuing careers "repugnant." In what ways did the concept of gender influence the Court's decision?*

In regard to that amendment, counsel for plaintiff in this court truly says that there are certain privileges and immunities which belong to a citizen of the United States as such; otherwise it would be nonsense for the XIV Amendment to prohibit a State from abridging them, and he proceeds to argue that admission to the bar of a State of a person who possesses the requisite learning and character is one of those which a State may not deny.

In this latter proposition we are not able to concur with counsel. We agree with him that there are privileges and immunities belonging to citizens of the United States, in that relation and character, and that it is these, and these alone, which a State is forbidden to abridge. But the right to admission to practice in the courts of a State is not one of them. The right in no sense depends on citizenship of the United States. . . .

[From a Concurring Opinion]

The claim that, under the XIV Amendment of the Constitution, which declares that no State shall make or enforce any law which shall abridge the privileges and immunities of citizens of the United States, the statute law of Illinois, or the common law prevailing in that State, can no longer be set up as a barrier against the right of female to pursue any lawful employment for a livelihood (the practice of law included) assumes that it is one of the privileges and immunities of women as citizens to engage in any and every profession, occupation, or employment in civil life.

It certainly can not be affirmed, as a historical fact, that this has ever been established as one of the fundamental privileges and immunities of the sex. On the contrary, the civil law, as well as nature herself, has always recognized a wide difference in the respective spheres and destinies of man and woman. Man is, or should be, woman's protector and defender. The natural and proper timidity and delicacy which belongs to the female sex evidently unfits it for many of the occupations of civil life. The constitution of the family organization, which is founded in the divine ordinance, as well as in the nature of things, indicates the domestic sphere as that which properly belongs to the domain and functions of womanhood. The harmony, not to say identity, of interests and views which belong, or should belong, to the family institution is repugnant to the idea of a woman adopting a distinct and independent career from that of her husband.

Amelia Barr, *Discontented Women* (1896)

Amelia Barr (1831–1919) was a novelist who wrote romantic stories about love and married life. Before she was forty years old, three of her six children and her husband died from Yellow Fever. Her success as an author provided the family's sole source of income. Although well aware of the many injustices women had to overcome in pursuing a career, she identified with the opponents of women's suffrage. Her argument against suffrage provides an excellent example of how anti-suffragists used gendered assumptions to deny women the ballot. Note how Barr contrasts "virile virtues" with "feminine softness." She claims that men possess reason, but women cannot go beyond their feminine natures, which "substitute sentiment for reason." Anti-suffragists viewed women's desire to vote as unnatural.

---

* *Bradwell v. Illinois,* Supreme Court of the United States, 1873, 83 U.S. (16 Wallace) 130, 141.

Barr linked women's discontent to Eve and believed it was necessary for women to control their own discontent. Her stress on women's "original sin" contradicted the conventional nineteenth-century emphasis on womanly virtue. How would you evaluate this gendered argument against women's suffrage? Discuss whether any part of Barr's argument would have relevance today?*

Discontent is a vice six thousand years old, and it will be eternal; because it is in the race. Every human being has a complaining side, but discontent is bound up in the heart of woman; it is her original sin. For if the first woman had been satisfied with her conditions, if she had not aspired to be "as gods," and hankered after unlawful knowledge, Satan would hardly have thought it worth his while to discuss her rights and wrongs with her. That unhappy controversy has never ceased; and, without reason, woman has been perpetually subject to discontent with her conditions and, according to her nature, has been moved by its influence. Some, it has made peevish, some plaintive, some ambitious, some reckless, while a noble majority have found in its very control that serene composure and cheerfulness which is granted to those who conquer, rather than to those who inherit.

Finally, women cannot get behind or beyond their nature, and their nature is to substitute sentiment for reason—a sweet and not unlovely characteristic in womanly ways and places; yet reason, on the whole, is considered a desirable necessity in politics. . . . Women may cease to be women, but they can never learn to be men and feminine softness and grace can never do the work of the virile virtues of men. Very fortunately this class of discontented women have not yet been able to endanger existing conditions by combinations analogous to trades unions; nor is it likely they ever will; because it is doubtful if women, under any circumstances, could combine at all. Certain qualities are necessary for combination, and these qualities are represented in women by their opposites. . . .

The one unanswerable excuse for woman's entrance into active public life of any kind, is *need* and alas! need is growing daily, as marriage becomes continually rare, and more women are left adrift in the world without helpers and protectors. But this is a subject too large to enter on here, though in the beginning it sprung from discontented women, preferring the work and duties of men to their own work and duties. Have they found the battle of life any more ennobling in masculine professions, than in their old feminine household ways? Is work done in the world for strangers, any less tiresome and monotonous, than work done in the house for father and mother, husband and children? If they answer truly, they will reply "the home duties were the easiest, the safest and the happiest."

Of course all discontented women will be indignant at any criticism of their conduct. They expect every one to consider their feelings without examining their motives. Paddling in the turbid maelstrom of life, and dabbling in politics and the most unsavory social questions, they still think men, at least, ought to regard them as the Sacred Sex. But women are not sacred by grace of sex, if they voluntarily abdicate its limitations and its modesties, and make a public display of unsexed sensibilities, an unabashed familiarity with subjects they have nothing to do with. If men criticize such women with asperity it is not to be wondered at; they have so long idealized women, that they find it hard to speak moderately. They excuse them too much, or else they are too indignant at their follies, and unjust and angry in their denunciation. Women must be criticized by women; then they will hear the bare uncompromising truth, and be the better for it.

---

* From Amelia Barr, "Discontented Women," in *North American Review* 162 (February 1896), 201, 205–7, 209.